Chevato

Chevato

The Story of the
Apache Warrior
Who Captured
Herman Lehmann

William Chebahtah &
Nancy McGown Minor

UNIVERSITY OF NEBRASKA PRESS
LINCOLN & LONDON

Library of Congress Cataloging-in-Publication Data
Chebahtah, William.
Chevato : the story of the Apache warrior who
captured Herman Lehmann / William Chebahtah
and Nancy McGown Minor.
p.   cm. — (American Indian lives)
Includes bibliographical references and index.
ISBN 978-0-8032-1097-4 (cloth : alk. paper)
ISBN 978-0-8032-2786-6 (paper : alk. paper)
1. Chevato, d. 1931. 2. Apache Indians—Biography.
3. Comanche Indians—Biography. 4. Apache Indians
—History. 5. Comanche Indians—History. 6. Lehmann,
Herman, 1859–1932. I. Minor, Nancy McGown. II. Title.
E99.A6C443 2007
976.4004'9725—dc22
2007002532

Contents

Illustrations

Photographs

Maps

Tables

Introduction

NANCY McGOWN MINOR

Monday, May 16, 1870, began innocently enough for the family of Philip Buchmeier, a German settler living with his family in a small cabin located about twenty-five miles northwest of Fredericksburg, Texas. Philip Buchmeier had spent the morning in the fields, returning to the cabin around noon. His wife, Augusta Johanna Lehmann Buchmeier, had spent her morning caring for their seven children—six older children from her marriage to Moritz Lehmann plus one younger child from her marriage to Philip. Six months pregnant with her eighth child, Augusta moved slowly in the early spring heat that hung heavily inside the small cabin, preparing lunch for her husband. The older children would eat after Philip had been served; in an effort to keep them busy, she had sent them outside to scare away the birds from a small patch of wheat growing near the house. Willie and Herman Lehmann flopped down on the ground at the edge of the wheat, while Caroline Lehmann tended to her two-year-old stepsister, Gusta.[1] Inside the cabin, Philip Buchmeier sat down at the table and began to eat his lunch. Suddenly, he heard one child's panicked voice yelling, "Indians!" That single shout turned his lunch into ashes in his stomach.

A group of eight Indians had appeared at the rock fence that surrounded the wheat field and cabin. Jumping over the fence, some of the Indians grabbed the three older children, successfully making off with two of them. The abductors had plaited hair, and some were wearing U.S. Army jackets and coats, even though the weather was warm. Philip Buchmeier sprang up from the table and ran for his gun; as he snatched it up and raced for the cabin door, he could hear several gunshots. Fearing the worst, he burst through the open door only to see his stepdaughter, Caroline, lying on the ground, while the Indians slung his two stepsons, Willie and Herman, onto the backs of their horses. The Indians galloped away with their captives before Buchmeier could fire a shot.

Caroline proved to be unhurt. Willie escaped from his Indian captors several days later and was returned home by local teamsters, but no trace would be found of Herman. When Philip Buchmeier described the missing boy several months later, he stated that "the boy stolen is about 11 years old, slender built, sandy haired, freckles about the nose, blue eyes, rather bashful. His name is Frederick Herman Lehmann."[2]

A raiding party of Mescalero Apaches, on their way home from a raid into Mexico, had kidnapped Herman Lehmann. Carried off to the Mescalero stronghold in New Mexico, Herman was harshly initiated into Apache culture. Yet in spite of his harsh and often brutal treatment, he came to embrace that culture, living with the Mescaleros for five years and only leaving the band after the death of one of his captors. He then joined a band of Comanches and ended up at Ft. Sill, Oklahoma, where he was discovered and, through the influence of Quanah Parker, was returned in 1879 to his family. Herman never quite made the adjustment back to his former life. He had lived as an Indian for nine years—from age eleven to age twenty—and had formed his identity amid Indian culture. He thought of himself as an Indian, and when he was removed from the Comanche Reservation and restored to his family in Texas, he found himself caught between two worlds and not entirely comfortable in either one.

The story of the captivity of Herman Lehmann was first published in 1899. Titled *Indianology*, it contained the reminiscences of Herman and his family. In 1927 his story was again published under the title *Herman Lehmann: Nine Years among the Indians, 1870–1879*, edited by J. Marvin Hunter. Since the 1927 publication, it has been reprinted a number of times and remains one of the most fascinating and well known captivity narratives. Written in a manner sympathetic to the Indians who had captured him and often pointing out the encroachments and attacks perpetrated by Anglos, Herman's story created quite a sensation when it was first published and remains an excellent source of information on Apache and Comanche life. In frank, matter-of-fact language, Herman Lehmann details the facts of his capture, naming the Apaches who had captured him as Carnoviste and Billy Chiwat. As he tells the story of his captivity, the reader can follow his integration into the tribe and his change in status from captive to warrior. Most of the episodes he describes are tales of warfare and raiding, and Herman tells his story much as a warrior would recount his valorous deeds and exploits. When he speaks of his life after being reunited with his family, it is with a resigned tone, and when he recounts visiting again with old Indian friends many years later, he recalls their friendship with warmth.

One Apache given a prominent role in Lehmann's book is Billy Chiwat. He, along with Carnoviste, had kidnapped Herman that May afternoon in 1870, yet Herman called Chiwat his "life long friend" and "a pretty good old Indian."[3] Billy Chiwat was known by several variations on his name—Chiwat, Chebahtah—but he always referred to himself as Chevato (pronounced *she-va-to*). Born in Mexico to a family of Lipan Apaches, orphaned at a young age when Mexican soldiers killed his parents, Chevato joined with the Mescalero Apaches, where his name was spelled in the proper Spanish manner—Chivato. In middle age, however, he left the Mescaleros and became a Comanche through the intervention of Quanah Parker. When his name was translated into the Comanche tongue, it became Chevato, and thus, in this manner, it has passed down to us today.

My coauthor, William Chebahtah, is the grandson of this remarkable man. After serving honorably in the U.S. Marine Corps, Mr. Chebahtah began a civil service career in San Antonio, Texas, where he worked for a number of years with members of my husband's family. When I met him, he recognized my interest in history and began to tell me "Chevato stories." Although well aware of the pitfalls of oral history, I found it amazing that so many facets of Mr. Chebahtah's stories rang true to the historical record. Because of this fact, we both thought that it was important that Chevato's oral history be preserved; the preservation project had additional importance to Mr. Chebahtah, as he was the last of Chevato's grandchildren who retained the complete story, and he wanted to pass it on in its entirety to his relatives.

In the process of recording and transcribing the oral history, a number of questions arose. Mr. Chebahtah has been raised in the traditions of the

Comanche tribe and was not familiar with some of the Apache cultural norms; in addition, he wanted to know if some of the events Chevato described had really occurred. I offered to do some research to help answer some of these questions—the result is this book. The chapters contain Chevato's story in italics, exactly as he passed it down to his son, Thomas David Chebahtah. Thomas David chose his second son, William Chebahtah, to learn and pass on the story of his grandfather. What follows each italicized story is the larger historical picture, the background against which Chevato's life played out.

This is the story of Billy Chiwat; this is the story of Chevato, passed down to his son because Chevato recognized that his children lived in a different world from the one he had known as a boy. How did Chevato come to be standing in the Buchmeier yard that May afternoon, swinging Herman Lehmann onto the back of a horse? How did the lives of this Apache man and Texas-German boy come to be intertwined? How did Herman's captor become his good friend? The answers to these questions are only part of Chevato's strange and fascinating tale.

Introduction

WILLIAM CHEBAHTAH

My name is William Chebahtah, and I was raised as a Comanche Indian. My grandfather, Chevato, was a Lipan Apache who came from Zaragosa, Mexico, so my heritage contains traditions of both the Apache and Comanche. I was told this story by my father.

My tribe has, in past years, had a tradition that one child, a male child, would take the history of each family, and he would be schooled in this train of thought. He would be told the family story over and over so that he would become quite proficient. Then the father would test the one he had selected to carry on the history of the family to make sure that the individual would be able to carry on that story, to make sure he would be most effective and most correct. This is the story of my family, as told to me by my father, who was given the story by his father, Chevato.

Chevato. Courtesy of William Chebatah.

Chevato

Part One

The Lipan Apaches, Zaragosa,
and the Mescalero Apaches

1. The Lipan Apaches

My grandfather came from a little town in Coahuila, Mexico, called Zaragosa. He belonged to the Lipan Apaches that lived in Mexico. In earlier times, the Lipan had moved out of Texas into Coahuila, had taken up residence there and acquired the customs of the people of that time. They had small plots of land, goats, and a few head of horses. They would farm their land and grow their crops as best they could. My grandfather was given the name Guillermo, which means William, and was also given the nickname Chivato, or "little goat."[1] Later, as he lived with English-speaking people, he was known as Billy.

The Lipan Apache were akin to the Mescalero because the Lipan and the Mescalero are both Apaches. The Mescaleros were the type of people who were more nomadic and liked to travel, go across the border, and do what they wanted. In doing this, they became a great thorn in the side of the Mexican government because they raided into Mexico and got cattle and horses, whatever they wanted.

In doing so, they would stop at the Lipans in Zaragosa, since the Lipans were akin to them and sympathetic. The Lipans would give them food and mounts, and then the Mescalero would go on their way. When the Mexican government found this out, they were very upset. First, they were going to get the Lipan to convert to the Catholic Church. They sent priests to talk with them. Since the Lipan had their own tradition of worshipping, they didn't want to convert to Christianity and the Catholic Church. And this upset the Mexican government very much. Then the government, knowing they were also aiding the Mescalero, gave them an ultimatum—embrace the Catholic Church and do not aid the Mescalero. So, the answer came back from the Lipans, saying that this could not be done because they had kinship with the Mescalero. Furthermore, they said that they already had a religion and that they didn't need another one.

The Mexican government's demands were not the only threat the Lipans faced. Sometimes, the Lipans in Mexico would also go on raids. Once, while Chevato and his younger brother Dinero were on a Lipan raid in Mexico, they met up with a hostile band of Kickapoos and had to do battle with them. The Kickapoos were outbattling the Lipan, and the Lipan had to fall into retreat. Dinero was knocked off his horse during the retreat, and, as the rest of the Lipan got away, they forgot about Dinero. When they reached a point of safety, Chevato asked them where Dinero was and was told that he was back at the battle site in a ravine. My grandfather told the Lipan to go on their way, but that he had to go back for his brother and would catch up with them later. They told him it would be almost suicide to go back into the ravine where the Kickapoo still were, but he said, "Nevertheless, I'm going to get my brother." So he went back into the ravine.

Sure enough, he had to sneak by those Kickapoos. Chevato was very quiet sneaking in, and he was crawling in the bushes when he ran into Dinero. He told Dinero that there was a horse a few yards upstream in the dry creek bed; he told Dinero that he should go toward the horse and get it, since there were no Kickapoos near the horse. Dinero should then go back to the rest of the Lipans. So Dinero started up the dry creek bed.

While Chevato was in the ravine, two Kickapoos came up and began shooting at him and Dinero. Dinero made his escape, but in battling the Kickapoos, one of them shot my grandfather in his lower abdomen. Chevato just happened to be looking down when he was hit, and, even though he tried to close his eyes, he could see the spurt of blood when the bullet broke the skin. When Chevato saw his own blood, he knew that he was in grave danger. He was losing strength, and he fell into the bushes and passed out. Before he passed out, he said the short prayer, "If it is at all possible, let my life be spared." But he knew that he was in a dangerous situation and that he must use his knowledge of herbs if he was to have any chance to live. In the pouch around his waist, he always carried a first-aid kit of herbs—herbs that he could use as a compress, herbs to put on a wound to stop the bleeding. After his prayer, he took his kit, took the herbs and put them over his lower abdomen. He bandaged himself with a sash, and then he lost consciousness.

When he realized that he regained consciousness, he was lying on his back in the ravine and looking up. He was lying in such a way that he could see a Kickapoo at the top of the ravine; behind the Kickapoo, he could see the sun. The Kickapoo was turned toward the sun—they were sun worshippers—and he had an old musket with the ramrod out. The Kickapoo was giving thanks to the sun god, and Chevato knew that the Kickapoo would kill him when he had finished his prayer. So, he felt for a weapon around him, but found nothing. But he always kept a derringer tied to a small strip of rawhide around his wrist. That's the only thing he had. He grasped the handle of the derringer and realized that he was not too far out of range. He cocked the hammer and the Kickapoo did not hear it. Then he shot the Kickapoo in the back.

He had just enough strength to crawl, and, by chance, he came across a horse. He climbed on the horse, got out of the ravine, and rejoined the rest of the Lipan. It took a long time for him to heal himself of that wound, but Chevato felt that he had survived because of his prayer and the use of his herbs. This is just one of the many incidents and scrapes that Chevato and his brother Dinero encountered living in the wilds.

§

Lipan Creation Story

Down in the lower world, at the beginning, there was no light; there was only darkness. Down there, at the bottom, were some people. They knew of no other places; they lived there.

They held a council down there. They discussed whether there was another world. They decided to send someone above to find out. They looked at each other and asked who should be sent out.

One said, "How about Wind?" They asked him. Wind agreed to go.

Wind went upward. He was a whirlwind. He came to this earth. Nothing but water covered the earth then. He rolled back the water like a curtain.

After the wind had rolled back the water, land appeared. The water was all to one side. . . . At that time the land was very level. There were no mountains on earth. The ground was just like ashes or like the places where there is white alkali on the earth's surface now. . . .

Then they sent Crow out to look over the dry land. . . . The Crow never came back. The people wondered what had happened to him. They wanted news. So they sent Beaver out. [The Beaver never came back], so they sent Badger out. He was faithful to his fellows in the lower world. He came up and looked around. He saw that it was all dry up there. He went back and told the others. Then they were all happy, for he was the only one who did faithful work.

Then they sent four others after that, four men, to look over this world above. These first four who came up on earth to prepare it were called by the word that means Indians. . . . The four chose one from whom was to be made the things of the earth as we know it now. They selected Mirage. They put up Mirage in the form of a ball. They walked away from Mirage and looked. It looked very pretty. That ball of Mirage became part of the earth.

Now they fixed the world. They were going to make hills and mountains. They made a little lightning. They made little arroyos, and water came running to them. That is the way the earth and the mountains, the hills and the water were made. At first it was all level, but of Mirage they made all the things of the earth.

Now all was ready on the earth. Springs and channels were made. All was prepared for the people of the lower world. Then the people of the lower world prepared to ascend. They came to the upper world. They are here now.

After they came up, they moved around the edge of the earth clockwise. All those people were animals, birds, trees and bushes. The real humans were not here yet. Animals, birds, grass and trees were people at that time and could talk as humans do. They had one language and all understood each other. These were the first people. . . . The different kinds of animals and birds, the different grasses and trees, each represents a different tribe.

Then the real humans came out. When they started from the place of emergence, the first to stop were the western people, the Chiricahua [Apaches], perhaps. As they went along clockwise, different peoples dropped off. As they stopped, they became different tribes and had different languages. "You shall be such and such a people and speak this language," they were told. That is how all these different tribes and languages were made....

At the very end of the journey the Tonkawa dropped off with the Lipan. The Lipan were the very last to stop the journey and find a home.[2]

Ta-á kuho shekaú nete (That is all I will tell).[3]

The Lipan Apaches are one of six southern Athapascan or Apachean-speaking groups who "migrated out of the Canadian Mackenzie Basin, [arriving as] latecomers to today's American Southwest some time between AD 1300 and 1500."[4] A hint of their early origins was preserved in the general tribal name by which the Lipans called themselves—*tcici* or *tcicihi*, meaning "People of the Forest."[5] Anthropologist Morris Opler, who studied the cultures of these southern Athapascan groups and who conducted extensive interviews in 1935 with a Lipan friend from Chevato's childhood named Antonio Apache, theorized that despite obvious late connections between the Lipans and the Mescaleros, the Lipans were actually most similar, both linguistically and culturally, to the Jicarilla Apaches. Opler believed that the Lipans were "an off-shoot of a Lipan-Jicarilla group [who migrated] east to the [Great] Plains."[6] The separation of the Lipans from the Jicarillas must have occurred at an early date, however, because a comparison of the myths of the two groups shows that "Lipan mythology looks like a simplified edition of Jicarilla mythology from which late ceremonial flourishes have been eliminated."[7] The separation of the two groups probably occurred during the time period when both ranged across the southern Great Plains, living in buffalo-hide tepees and using large dogs to transport their camps. After the separation, the Jicarillas moved down into the Four Corners area of New Mexico, Texas, Colorado, and Oklahoma—an area they believed to be the "center of the earth."[8] The Lipans continued on, moving into north-central and western Texas, finding both buffalo and antelope on the plains as well as congenial camps along the river bottoms. They acquired horses from early Spanish settlements, becoming excellent horsemen, and adopted a seminomadic life; they planted maize, pump-kins, beans, and squash in a haphazard manner in rich river-bottom soil and camped nearby only long enough for the seeds to sprout and produce, before moving on in search of game, wild fruit, and cactus tunas.

By 1700 the Lipans in north-central Texas were feeling increased pres-sure, as hostile Comanches launched attacks on many plains Apache bands living on the southern edges of the Great Plains. Sporadic attacks soon turned to war, as Comanches battled Apache bands east of the Pecos River. The ferocity of the Comanche attacks on the Lipans, combined with supe-rior battle tactics, resulted in a series of Lipan defeats.[9] These defeats at the hands of the Comanches were the catalysts that pushed the Lipan bands into central and southwest Texas and northern Mexico, where they displaced smaller groups of Coahuiltecan-speaking people. By 1750 the Lipans lived in from ten to fourteen bands averaging 400 to 500 persons each, ranging from the Pecos River on the west, east to San Antonio and the lower Gulf Coast, south into Mexico, and north to the Colorado River.[10]

Lipan Bands and Territories
Eastern Lipan (Lipan *de arriba*)

1. Tséral tuétahä—"Red Hair" band; this band ranged below the Nueces River in Texas, led in 1739 by Cabellos Colorado (Red Hair). This band was extirpated by 1884.

2. Tche shä—"Sun Otter" band; this band ranged from San Antonio, Texas, south to the Rio Grande; primary camp was known as El Atascoso, south of San Antonio.

3. Kó'l Kahä—"Prairie Men" band; this band ranged in central Texas along the upper Colorado River.

4. Tchó kanä—"Rubbing, Pulverizing" band; this band ranged to the west of Ft. Griffin, Texas, to the west side of the Rio Grande. This band was possibly extirpated by 1884.

5. Kóke metcheskó lähä—"High Beaked Moccasin" band; this band ranged south of San Antonio into Mexico, led in 1790 by Zapato Sas (Shoe Cut on a Bias).

6. Tsél tátlidshä—"Green Mountain" band; this band ranged east of the Rio Grande along the lower Guadalupe and Nueces rivers of Texas.

7. Ndáwe qóhä—"Fire Circle" or "Camp Circle" band; this band ranged southwest of Ft. Griffin, Texas, along the Colorado, San Saba, and Llano rivers.

8. Shä-ä—"North" band; this band lived "on the other side of a big mountain, near the Dapéshte River." This band of about 300 persons was removed to the Washita Agency in Oklahoma by 1884.

9. *Tsés tsëmbai*—"Head of wolf, body of man" band; this band lived toward sundown between the upper Brazos and Colorado rivers.

10. Te'l kóndahä—"Wild Goose" band; this band's name was associated with a type of bird. They were renowned as fighters and ranged west of Ft. Griffin.

Western Lipan (*Lipan de abajo*)

1. Kúne tsá—"Big Water" band; this band originally ranged along the Texas bank of the Rio Grande but had moved into Coahuila, Mexico, by 1750. This was Chevato's band.

2. Tsésh ke shénde—"Painted Wood People"; this band lived at Lavón, Mexico; possibly extirpated by 1884.

3. Tüzhä; Täzhä—"Uplanders"; this band lived along the upper Rio Grande and in southern New Mexico by 1850 and had close contact with the Mescalero Apaches.

4. Tcha shka-ózhäyê—"Little Breech-Clout" band; this band lived on the Pecos River in Texas and was closely tied to a group known to the Spanish as the Natagés; the Natagés were affiliated with the Mescalero Apaches. The later designation of the band as Little Breech-Clout may have been taken from the chief circa 1780, Poca Ropa (Little or Scant Clothes).[11]

Caught between their Comanche enemies to the north and the Spanish to the south, the Lipans sought alliance with Spanish missionaries in Texas and northern Mexico. They were adept at playing the Spanish padres against the Comanches, at times attacking other tribes and leaving behind Comanche articles to fool the Spanish into believing the Comanches had been the attackers. They requested that the Spanish establish missions for them, seeking only the military protection afforded by the presidios attached to such missions, as well as a source of food or other gifts provided by the missionaries. The first Spanish mission designated to minister to the Lipans was San Lorenzo in Coahuila, Mexico, located ten miles west of the newly founded villa of San Fernando de Austria (later known as Zaragosa). By March 1755, at least 52 Lipans had entered the mission, with another 2,000 camped nearby. However, the Lipans soon became disenchanted, stating that they had only entered San Lorenzo in Coahuila because the Spanish had refused to give them missions in Texas; furthermore, the food they received from the missionaries was not as plentiful as promised. The Lipans' first mission experience lasted little more than seven months; on the night of October 4, 1755, they revolted, burning all the mission buildings and riding away into the night.[12]

The failure of the first Lipan mission "was attributed, and justly, no doubt, to the natural inconstancy of the Apaches and their reluctance to live in missions outside of the region which they habitually frequented— that is, north and northwest of San Antonio, in the section traversed by the Pedernales, Llano and San Sabá Rivers."[13] Intending to remedy this shortcoming, the presidio of San Luis de las Amarillas and its accompanying mission were established for the Lipan in 1757 on the San Sabá River, near present-day Menard, Texas. The mission, however, existed for only one year, for on the morning of March 16, 1758, over 2,000 Comanches and their allies surrounded the mission shortly after the priests had finished their morning prayers. "Half carried French guns, which they fired in the air as they circled the stockade. However, they spoke pleasantly to the guards, assuring them that they intended the Spanish no harm; they only sought the Apaches [i.e., Lipans] who had killed some of their people."[14] The Lipans, however, were not at the mission, having vanished into the surrounding countryside upon hearing rumors that the Comanches were about to attack. The Spanish padres, anxious to prove to the Comanches that the Lipans were not there, allowed them to enter the gate to inspect for themselves, thereby placing the mission at the mercy of the intruders. Two priests and eight others were killed, and the mission was sacked and burned.

On January 23, 1762, the Spanish made a final attempt at founding a mission for the Lipans, establishing Mission San Lorenzo de la Santa Cruz along the upper Nueces River in an area known as El Cañon (located today in Uvalde County, Texas). Two weeks later, a second Lipan mission was founded near a spring on the west bank of the Nueces about ten miles south of San Lorenzo. The second mission was named Nuestra Senora de la Candelaria del Cañon.[15] In a 1762 report sent to the viceroy, Fr. Diego Ximenez stated that there were about 3,000 Lipans in the area, with about 400 of them gathered at the two missions along the Nueces. Yet the Comanches in the area remained a constant threat. Fr. Ximenez wrote, "Already the enemy knows of these missions because they have spied upon us; they will come to destroy these pueblos. They will find no resistance because our Lipans only seek to hide themselves in these critical times. The soldiers who accompany us are, in proportion to the enemies, very few and inept. Only God will defend us, if indeed we do not perish."[16] The Comanches and their allies began to harass the Nueces missions within a year of their founding, and by 1766 the Lipans had been driven away from the area.[17]

The Comanche attacks after 1750 had penetrated deep into Lipan hunting and settlement territories, plunging a feathered lance into the Lipan homeland. Major attacks, as well as continuous, harassing actions directed against Lipan bands living in central Texas, forced many bands southward, fleeing the aggressive Comanches. Many Lipan groups faded into the hills near the upper Nueces and Frio rivers, while others dispersed into south Texas or crossed the Rio Grande, seeking shelter in the rugged mountains of northern Mexico. The primary result of over half a century of Comanche harassment was a division of the Lipan tribe into two large groupings. The Lipans *de arriba* (the Lipans above), or Eastern Lipans, were a loose grouping of ten bands whose seasonal wanderings were generally confined to the Texas side of the Rio Grande. These bands ranged from the buffalo-hunting grounds on the San Saba and Llano rivers southeast to the lower Guadalupe near the Gulf Coast and west as far as the upper Nueces and Frio rivers. The presidios and missions at San Antonio, la Bahía (Victoria County, Texas), and Laredo suffered their repeated attacks. The Lipans *de abajo* (the Lipans below), or Western Lipans, were a loose grouping of four bands whose primary territory stretched from the lower Pecos River and Big Bend area of Texas south into northern Coahuila and Nuevo Leon. The Western Lipans were, through most of their history, allies of the Mescalero Apaches of southern New Mexico and were composed of an amalgam of Apachean-speaking groups known to the early Spanish as Natagés and Lipiyans, as well as Lipans who had fled into Mexico to escape the Comanches. Chevato was born into the Kúne tsá band of Western Lipans, a band that had been pushed out of Texas by Comanche aggression and had inhabited northern Coahuila since the first Lipan had entered the mission of San Lorenzo in 1755.

In 1767 "Nicholas de Lafora, an engineer accompanying Rubí's inspection of New Spain's northern frontier, reported that many Lipan Apaches inhabited the mountains of Coahuila."[18] He found them living, along with some Mescalero Apaches, in the Bolsón de Mapimí, "a rugged mountain and desert badlands running southward from the Rio Grande between the Sierra Madre Occidental of Coahuila on the east and the Conchos Valley on the west."[19] Rubí's inspection tour resulted in recommendations for the defense of the northern frontier that reversed all previous Spanish policy. Recognizing the fact that the Apaches (particularly the Lipans) were incapable of honoring treaty commitments, Rubí recommended that the Spanish government ally, instead, with the Comanches and their allies. The Spanish Crown accepted most of Rubí's recommendations, yet paid homage to the long Spanish tradition of attempted peaceful conversion of the Indians. The resulting Regulations of 1772 "proclaimed the prime objectives of the king on the northern frontier to be peace, the welfare and conversion of the pagan tribes, and the tranquility of the northern provinces. Even Apaches were entitled to peaceful coexistence if they sincerely wished it."[20] When the new Indian policy was combined with military actions in the Bolsón de Mapimí, the resulting campaigns drove the Lipans

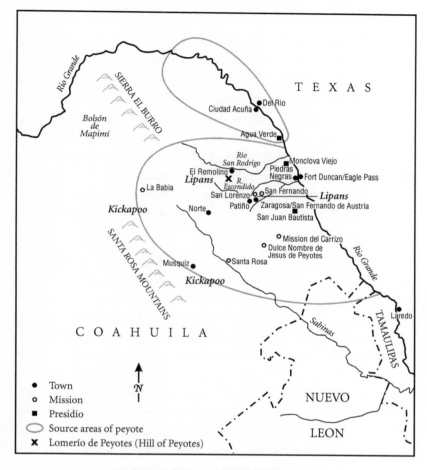

Missions and Towns of Northern Coahuila

and Mescaleros north, forcing them to seek shelter near the Coahuila presidios of San Juan Bautista, Monclova Viejo, and Agua Verde.[21]

The presidio of San Juan Bautista, long the gateway from Coahuila into Texas, was founded in 1701 on the Rio Grande at the site of the present-day city of Guerrero, Coahuila. The presidio of Monclova Viejo (Old Monclova), a fort founded by royal decree in 1772 to defend the citizens of Coahuila from Indian threats, was located on the Rio Grande on the Coahuila side of the river, across from present-day Quemado, Texas. The royal decree of 1772 also mandated the establishment of a fort at Agua Verde, located farther west down the Rio Grande between present-day Piedras Negras/Eagle Pass and Ciudad Acuña/Del Rio.[22] Thus there were three forts or presidios strung out along the Rio Grande that were to act as barriers against Comanche incursions and around which the Lipans were encouraged to settle.

The Western Lipan bands living in Mexico were joined, after 1800, by groups of Texas Lipans fleeing chaotic political developments or epidemics. The story of the Lipan chief Magoosh (1830–1914), as told by Philemon Venego, is illustrative of this migration out of Texas and into Coahuila, as well as into New Mexico.

> As a boy, Magoosh witnessed the fall of the Alamo [1836]. . . . Some years after the Alamo, the Lipans suffered an epidemic of smallpox [1849]. It was in a very virulent form, and few who took it survived. . . . [The Lipans believed they had gotten smallpox] from the Mexicans. When they killed an enemy they used none of the victim's clothing except the ammunition belt (for which they sometimes killed) and the shirt. They suspected that the illness might have been occasioned by their wearing these shirts.
>
> Their Medicine Men could do little or nothing for the victim of smallpox. But they realized that if the groups remained together there probably would be more deaths than if they separated. Magoosh held a council and it was decided that the Lipans should divide into small bands, each to be under the command of a leader or headman and composed of relatives. Venego [father of the storyteller, Philemon Venego] was placed in charge of one family group and told, when and if the sickness ceased, to reassemble at a place to be named by Magoosh.
>
> Venego's band went south to the Rio Grande, crossed it, and settled in the mountains near Zaragosa, a small Mexico village. . . . There they lived on relatively friendly terms with the natives. Though there was not much contact, there was no enmity. The Mexicans hunted in the mountains but lived in small villages near the water. During the years of their stay in Mexico, the Lipans acquired some of the habits and beliefs of their neighbors, especially in the field of witchcraft. All Apaches believed in it,

14

but perhaps not to the same extent as the Mexican[s] among whom the Lipans lived. Many years later, [the Zaragosa group] learned that Magoosh had taken the few remaining members of his band to join the Mescaleros in southern New Mexico.[23]

The best physical description of the early Lipan Apaches comes from the pen of Jean Louis Berlandier, a French botanist who accompanied an official Mexican expedition into Texas. One objective of the expedition was to collect information on the customs, dispositions, and numbers of the Indian tribes of Texas, as well as the flora and fauna of the area. On February 2, 1828, the expedition reached Laredo, Texas, on the northern bank of the Rio Grande. A town of about 2,000 souls, whose houses clustered around a large presidio garrisoned with more than a hundred soldiers, Laredo had suffered from repeated Lipan Apache attacks. The official expedition remained in Laredo for eighteen days, where they were joined by Gen. Anastacio Bustamante, military commander for the Eastern Provinces of Mexico. Berlandier was able to explore the outlying areas and make some drawings and collections of Texas plants. It was also in Laredo that Berlandier saw his first Texas Indians. A large party of Lipans rode into town, led by their chief, Cuelgas de Castro. They had come to Laredo at the invitation of Bustamante, who was negotiating a peace treaty with the Texas Lipans. Berlandier described the Lipans in his diary, using some details that must have been furnished him by Gen. Bustamante, an experienced frontier officer who had many contacts with the Lipans in the course of diplomatic initiatives and military campaigns. Berlandier noted that the Lipan men were

> quite tall, between 5 feet 6 inches in French measurement. They are erect, lithe, well proportioned, graceful in their movements, and by comparison with any I have seen, by far the most agile natives in the country. Their complexion is dark copper, heightened with vermilion paint, but their features, otherwise not at all disagreeable, are disfigured with sundry paintings.... Lipan women are much smaller and less perfectly proportioned than the men. Their average height is about 5 feet. They are lively and quite modest.

Their clothing is generally clean and well made, and their women inspire less disgust than any other native women. They are not so rich as the Comanche because there are no buffalo in their hunting grounds. But extremely well worked deerskin serves to make all their clothing.... Their hair is worn loose or fastened at the nape, sometimes braided and decorated with buckles or plaques of silver, but they never cut it.

The Lipans are a fine group of men, skilled at warfare, excellent horsemen and with great talent for breaking and training wild horses.... Their weapons are the gun, the lance, and the bow, which they handle very skillfully. Their lance is usually tipped with the straight blade of a Spanish saber.... They adorn it with feathers and various gaudy ornaments. But they are not very handy with this weapon since they use both hands to wield it and this means abandoning control of their mounts. They use guns only in special circumstances, but the bow they use continually in hunting and warfare, both offensive and defensive. In their hands, the bow is undoubtedly the most fearfully deadly of weapons....

[T]his is the nation most obedient to its chieftain and least hostile to organized society.... The Lipans are farmers, or at least they have a bent for agriculture. Between their last war with the Spanish, in 1816, and the year 1822—during the period they were at peace with the Comanche—they tended fields of maize, watermelons, etc.... Despite these qualities, the numerous murders they have committed on both sides of the Rio Grande have earned them the hatred of all the inhabitants of the country, who consider them a burden of which they would be heartily glad to be rid.... They are constantly stealing horses, livestock and any herds left unguarded. In a word, they scrape a living by plundering, hunting and begging. Their visits to the garrisons are a distinct annoyance because of their unending demand for gifts.[24]

Indian raiders who crossed the Rio Grande into Coahuila and Nuevo Leon had been a problem since Spanish colonial years, but a combination of peace treaties and military offensives had diffused much of the threat by 1800. After Mexican independence in 1821, however, the raiding intensified; by the 1830s Indian raids had become so intense that local author-

Lipan Apaches in Texas, circa 1828. Gilcrease Museum, Tulsa OK.

ities in the northern Mexican states had begun to complain. The central government, unable to respond, left the problem to local communities to handle in their own way. Bounties were offered for Indian scalps, and traps and ambushes were laid for the raiders, hoping to lure them into the Mexican villages where they could be destroyed, but both policies proved to be complete failures.[25]

The 1840s only saw an intensification of Comanche and Apache raids and terror in northern Mexico. Beginning in the fall of 1840, three major Comanche war parties crossed the Rio Grande, raiding and looting the northeastern Mexican states. The final war party swept into Coahuila in December 1840, piercing south through the state and attacking Zacatecas, located hundreds of miles from the Rio Grande.[26] The Lipans, who had once been forced to seek shelter near the Coahuila presidios, were loosed when Mexico declared its independence. Once Texas was severed from Mexico in 1836, the Coahuilan Lipans were free to raid across the border into Texas. Since the early Texas settlements were located far to the east in the years after 1836, however, the primary Lipan raiding pattern for the years from 1836 to 1850 was from north to south, as Texas Lipan warriors crossed the Rio Grande into Mexico, to be joined by their Coahuila brothers in raids on isolated Mexican ranchos and small villages. Although the following description of a raid into Mexico was given by a Western Apache, a Lipan raid into Mexico must have unfolded in a similar manner:

> When a war party started out, they always left some old man behind to take care of the women. They usually allowed about thirty to forty-five days to be gone, and would tell their people when they expected to be back. A war party figured on carrying just enough food with them to last until they got to Mexico, as when they got there there could be cattle, horses, mules, or burros [to slaughter for food]. When they got down into Mexico, they would make camp on some big, rocky mountain where it was safe. In this camp the boys and older men of the party were left.
>
> The other men went out from here to near some Mexican town. They would go to the town and steal the stock that was in the pastures, as they knew this would be gentle stuff and what they wanted. When they got the stock, they would drive it back to where the others were waiting for them in the mountain camp. This way they were usually away three days.
>
> . . . The times of war or raiding parties used to pick to go to Mexico were in the spring and in August and in the fall. At these times there was lots of water. On a raiding party they usually took from twelve to thirty men, and on a war party about forty men. When they got down into Mexico they used to wait for the moon to get nearly full before they captured the Mexican stock. This was so they could travel at night.[27]

By 1850 Comanche raids into Mexico had ceased to some degree, as U.S. troops began pressuring the Comanches above the Red River to sign treaties limiting their territory and Texas settlers began to expand their settlements to the west. Running the gauntlet through Texas in order to raid into Mexico began to pose too great of a risk for large-scale war or raiding parties. Lipan raids into Mexico had also lessened, as the small Mexican villages became impoverished. The Western Lipans in Coahuila began to fix their sights northward, finding inviting raiding prospects in an expanding Texas population, whose settlers moved ever westward, bringing with them well-fed horses, mules, oxen, and cattle. There were only a few remnants left of the Lipans who had settled in the shadows of the Spanish missions of Coahuila a century earlier. The rest of the Western Lipans had regained their nomadic ways and "made war [on Coahuila] and did not agree upon a peace until the year 1855, after having committed horrible outrages."[28] The Lipan raiders moved back and forth across the Rio Grande, using that river as a shield against pursuing militia, stealing horses and cattle in Texas and driving them south into Mexico.

Around 1850 the landscape of Indian settlement in Coahuila began to change as local communities, beginning with Zaragosa, began to handle their Indian problem, as well as their economic problems, in a unique way. Long considered the one tribe with the best likelihood of being converted to an agricultural way of life, the Lipans were offered a settlement area near the old church of San Fernando de Rosas and near the old presidio of San Fernando de Austria. That area, known by 1850 simply as Zaragosa, was very near the old San Lorenzo mission, site of the first attempted conversion of the Lipans in Coahuila (1755). The location was very familiar to the Lipans, who had inhabited the area sporadically since 1750. It was hoped, by 1850, that this Lipan settlement would be a deterrent to Comanche raiding and serve as a conduit for the horses and cattle stolen by both the Lipans and their allies, the Mescalero Apaches, in Texas. The stolen livestock would be resold from Zaragosa to the state capital of Saltillo, Coahuila, bringing an economic boon to the local economy and protecting local residents from Indian attacks.[29] Thus the Lipans were "adopted" by the town of Zaragosa and settled at an area known as "Hacienda Patiño . . . [in] an attempt to pacify them and teach them agriculture."[30]

Chevato was born into this settlement at Hacienda Patiño in 1852. His family belonged to the Kúne tsá band of Lipans. There were four children in the family: an older brother killed in a battle with the Kickapoos on May 27, 1868;[31] Guillermo (Chevato), born in early 1852;[32] Enriques (Dinero), born in 1860; and a daughter, Pe-chá (later named Ruth), born sometime between 1863 and 1869.

The family had lived in northern Mexico for at least three generations. They could have been among the Western Lipans who were forced out of the Bolsón de Mapimí of Coahuila in 1772 and who settled in the shadow of the presidios strung like a necklace along the Rio Grande. Or they could have migrated west up the Rio Grande from the Gulf Coast area of south Texas or eastern Mexico. One possible clue that might indicate this was the family's migration route can be found in a 1784 report from the governor of the province of Nuevo Santander to the viceroy of Mexico, which tells of the arrival at the small mission of Palmitos (located near present-day Abasolo, Tamualipas) of a captain of the Lipan Indians named Pedro el Chivato (Pedro the Goat). Pedro, described as "old and pernicious," arrived with eighty warriors on horseback and forty warriors on foot armed with bows and arrows, accompanied by women and children.[33] There is evidence among the Lipans of similarities in names over two generations (for example, Josef and his son Josef Chiquito), and there is also evidence of naming similarities over three or four generations (for example, Cabellos Colorado ca. 1730 and Caro Colorado ca. 1850, and Chief White Tooth ca. 1780 and Boneski, or Dry Tooth, ca. 1850). What strengthens the possibility that Chevato's family had migrated from east to west up the Rio Grande over several generations is the statement made by Chevato's brother, Dinero, that their great-grandfather had introduced the use of peyote to the Lipan Apaches.[34] Scholars believe that the Lipans adopted the use of peyote from the Carrizo culture, and the Carrizos could be found in areas south of Laredo, Texas, and east to the Gulf of Mexico.[35] However, there was also a mission in Coahuila (Mission del Carrizo) located close to the Rio Grande near the Dulce Nombre de Jesus de Peyotes mission. Thus a Carrizo influence can be found in Coahuila, located within fifty miles of two of the original Rio Grande missions sheltering the Lipans, as well as near Zaragosa.

The Hacienda Patiño settlement where Chevato was born was planted around 1850, and Lipan bands could soon be found at both Hacienda Patiño and at El Remolino, another Lipan settlement area located northwest of Zaragosa. The bands in both locations were considered to be "on terms of amity and Friendship with the City of Zaragosa."[36] Additional Lipan groups could be found in the mountains southwest of Zaragosa near the small village of Norte.[37]

If the Comanches could be said to have been the Lipans' traditional enemy in the eighteenth century, the Kickapoos would earn that distinction in the nineteenth. The Kickapoo migration to Mexico was of a more recent origin that that of the Lipans. Originally to be found east of the Mississippi River, the Kickapoos had forged a number of alliances with, successively, the Spanish, French, British, and Americans (under Gen. George Rogers Clark). The fortunes of the tribe ebbed and flowed as their alliances proved to be either prescient or unwise. After the War of 1812, however, any political leverage they had once possessed was lost, as they were forced to emigrate, along with many other eastern Indian tribes, west of the Mississippi. In 1819 the Kickapoo band living in Illinois agreed to convey their land to the U.S. government in exchange for annuities and land on a reservation in the southwestern part of Missouri, near the Osage tribe. This arrangement worked well for a time, but conflict with the Osage caused renegade Kickapoo bands to break away. "By 1832, the Kickapoo tribe, numbering about 3,000, had split into a number of bands scattered from Lake Michigan to the Mexican territory [i.e., Texas] . . . [the Texas band] headed by Chief Mosqua, had settled . . . on the Sabine River."[38]

The Kickapoos first entered Mexico in 1839, when a small group presented themselves in Matamoros, asking permission to settle in Mexico and to enlist in the Mexican army. This small group was settled near Morelos, Coahuila. In 1850 a large group of Kickapoos, joined by Seminoles and Mascogos, crossed the border at Eagle Pass. After a short stay near Zaragosa, this second group was settled near Musquiz, Coahuila.[39] Musquiz "adopted" the Kickapoos much in the same way that Zaragosa had adopted the Lipans. The Kickapoos were given water, which allowed them to plant small plots of land, and the town of Musquiz profited from the booty brought back when the Kickapoos raided into Texas. During the 1860s, additional Kickapoos made their way toward the Rio Grande, attempting to escape the Civil War erupting in the United States. Attacked by a party of Texas Confederate troopers out looking for "bushwhackers," or Union men, the Kickapoos fled across the border into Mexico. Their arrival was seized upon by Governor Vidaurri of Nuevo Leon, who concocted a plan to use them as soldiers for the French-led Imperialist troops of Emperor Maximilian against the rebel forces of Benito Juarez. In a quirk of fate, however, the Kickapoos arrived too late. Their chiefs had traveled to Mexico City to meet with Maximilian, who enlisted them in his cause, but by the time the chiefs had returned to the border to gather up their bands, Governor Vidaurri had fled, and Maximilian's cause was doomed.[40] Thus the Kickapoos who had waited in Nuevo Leon to join the Imperialist forces were sent to join the band that had been settled earlier at Musquiz.

By 1868, the year in which the fight with the Kickapoo described by Chevato occurred, six different tribes had found settlement areas in Coahuila. All but one tribe had been "adopted" by Coahuilan towns, alliances had been formed, and antagonisms between both towns and tribes were simmering. The two large Lipan groups living near the town of Zaragosa—one group to the south at Hacienda Patiño and the second group to the northwest at El Remolino—totaled approximately eighty to one hundred persons.[41] Three other much smaller Lipan family groups could still be found near the mission areas of Agua Verde, Monclova Viejo, and San Juan Bautista, as well as small groups of "wild" Lipans living in the mountains west of Zaragosa. A small band of Mescalero Apaches, allies of the Lipans, could also be found near Agua Verde (renamed San Carlos by this time); a larger group of Mescaleros could be found in the neighboring Mexican state of Chihuahua.[42] The Mescaleros and Lipans living in Mexico also retained close ties to their "wild" brethren still raiding in Texas and New Mexico, often acting as receivers of stolen property and offering rest and safety to raiding parties.

Several other tribes had small numbers of members living in Coahuila. A few Cherokees, who had originally come to northern Mexico in 1842, could be found near Zaragosa; they allied with no one, but traded with the local population.[43] Farther south, small numbers of Pottawatomies (about 60 to 100 people) and Seminoles (about 225 to 275 people) lived nearby and were allied with the Kickapoos. The main Kickapoo settlement was near the town of Musquiz, which had adopted that tribe and its Seminole and Pottawatomie allies. The estimated number of Kickapoos in Coahuila was from 750 to 850.[44]

After 1860 the Comanches and Mescaleros continued to raid in Texas, with the Mescaleros in particular traveling on into Mexico to sell their stolen horses. The Mexican Lipans, while settled in one agricultural settlement at Zaragosa, felt no compunction about saddling up and going on raids into Texas as the opportunity arose. The Kickapoos also began riding north, crossing the Rio Grande and raiding Texas ranches. The Coahuila towns had bought immunity from Indian raiding through their "adoption" schemes and were more than willing to participate in any division of spoils brought back into Mexico from across the border.

By 1868 Texas merchants and ranchers had reached the limits of their patience. Although the Civil War was over, the U.S. Army still ruled Texas as the Fifth Military District; frontier forts were being reactivated, and there was talk of moving the Indians to reservations. Finally, there was enough of a military presence in Texas for the wherewithal to do something about the problem of Mexican Indians raiding across the border into Texas.

On March 17, 1868, a meeting of the Committee on Indian Affairs was held at the National Bank in San Antonio, Texas. Made up of concerned "citizens of Western Texas," the committee determined to develop a plan for dealing with the Indians raiding out of Mexico. To that end, they appointed Stephen S. Brown and authorized him to travel specifically to Coahuila, meet with the Indian bands, ascertain the state of affairs, and try to persuade the tribes to return to the United States, where they could join other tribal bands on a reservation. The committee had the full support of the general heading the Fifth Military District, Brevet Maj. Gen. J. J. Reynolds, who requested that Brown make a report of his findings to be passed along to the adjutant general's office in Washington DC.[45] Thus began the first attempt by the U.S. Army in Texas to apply Indian policy used within the United States to Mexican Indian border problems.

Brown arrived at the town of Musquiz in July 1868, determined to tackle the largest problem first—the Kickapoos, whose raids into western Texas were bringing a flood of complaints to fort commanders all along the Rio Grande. As soon as he arrived, however, he found his task vastly complicated, because he had arrived in Coahuila one month after a savage attack by the Kickapoos on the Lipans in retaliation for the theft of Kickapoo horses. When Brown arrived at Musquiz, the Kickapoos were willing to talk to him, but the surviving Lipans could not be found—they had "fled to the Apache."

The "Kickapoo Incident" (described thusly by Chevato's descendants) is rather unusual, from a historical point of view, in that five separate accounts exist of the event—two accounts from actual participants (Chevato's account, as told to his son, and Antonio Apache's account, as told to Morris Opler in 1935) and three accounts from governmental entities or representatives reporting on the event (the prefects of both Zaragosa and Musquiz, who reported to the governor of Coahuila, and the Texas envoy, Stephen Brown). Each source agrees on the basic details and provides more information from different perspectives. The Kickapoo Incident was actually three separate encounters between the Kickapoos and the Lipans that began when several Lipans decided to steal some Kickapoo horses. Since this series of encounters was to have such a profound and dramatic long-term consequence for the Lipans in Coahuila, it is necessary to look closely at the sequence of events, using the words of those who told the story:

1. The Theft of Kickapoo Horses by the Lipans, as told by Antonio Apache (Lipan)

Two Lipan (one from the Zaragosa area and the second from the southern New Mexico Lipan band) were out looking for horses. They had been going around many days, when they came to a Kickapoo camp. The Lipan stayed there all day watching. They saw a Kickapoo go off with the horses. He drove them out to good grass, turned them loose and then went back to camp. The Lipan waited for night. They saw that the horses were good ones. When night came, the Lipan took the fine horses, about thirteen or fourteen of them. One said, "Well, this is what we came after. It's plenty for us. What's the use of looking for more of them?" So they started home with the stolen horses.

When the Kickapoo found their horses missing, a big bunch of them started out on the Lipan trail. The Kickapoo were a couple days ride behind when the Apaches reached home. The Apaches had forgotten about the danger. One morning a man went out to hunt and saw the Kickapoo approaching. He went back to camp and told the Lipan chief. The chief told the women to prepare and move out. He then picked seven brave men to hold off the Kickapoo—one was from the "Big Water" band in Coahuila, another was a Mexican captive who had been raised with that band. The other five were Lipan from New Mexico. The brave men charged at the Kickapoo. As the Lipan camp moved away, the brave men went in the opposite direction, drawing the Kickapoo after them. This direction led right to the plains, where there was nothing and the Kickapoos' horses would tire out.

Finally, the Kickapoo began to catch up with the brave men and the chief (whose name means "He Found a Round Bundle") knew they would have to fight. So the chief stopped and made his ceremony over his shield. He said his prayer. Then he lifted his shield four times to the sun and all his men heard the growl of a bear come from his shield. He told four of the men to get off of their horses and face the enemy; the chief and another man stayed on horseback. The Kickapoo came up and began shooting.

As the Kickapoo shot, they were not given a chance to reload because the Lipan on the ground came at them with lances. They drove the Kickapoo back, killing four men and the Kickapoo chief, but, in the process, the Lipan chief was wounded in the hip. He died after the fight.[46]

11. The Kickapoos Raid the Lipan Camps on May 27, 1868, as told by Antonio Apache (Lipan)

Well, trouble started over the Kickapoo chief who was killed. He had a daughter and she cried all the time. All her relatives tried to stop her, but she kept on. Finally, they got tired of it. They were angry. They started out for revenge against the Lipan.

The Lipan were camped by a stream under the pecan trees and were playing a hoop and pole game. The Kickapoo sneaked up through the thicket. One Lipan saw them at the last minute and yelled, "My friends! The Kickapoo are among us. Run for your weapons!" But the Kickapoo rushed up so fast, that only two men were able to grab their weapons—one man grabbed a gun and a young man grabbed his bow and arrows.

The Lipan with the rifle was able to hold off the Kickapoo while the rest of the Lipan men escaped, but he was stabbed by a Kickapoo lance. He lay there with the lance right through him. A second Kickapoo came along and hit him on the head, for he was still moving. A third came along and took his scalp. He was still alive and said, "It hurts, it hurts!" Even after his scalp was taken, he was still alive. He crawled off. He got his senses back. He took the spear out and used the lance for a cane as he crawled toward the rest of his people.

The one who had gotten to his bow and arrows and fought the Kickapoo [Chevato's older brother], was overpowered and killed. He was a young man of fine appearance. His hair came down to his hips. He fought well. When they closed in on him, he grappled with them. But there were too many for him. But they didn't scalp him, for some reason.

Then the Kickapoo came right to the camps where the children were running about. They killed men, women and children—anyone they met. Many were killed right by their homes. The Kickapoo killed many children, but they only took two children captive. Some Lipan men were able to get to the other side of the arroyo and were saved.[47]

The town council of Zaragosa wrote to the council at Musquiz two days later, informing them of the attack:

The 28th of this month [May 1868] the assistant Judge of the Community [of] Remolino informed me as follows:

"The prisoner Andres of the Lipan tribe being examined at 11 o'clock a.m. says that [the] day before yesterday at sunset, they had been surprised by the Kickapoo Indians on the extreme point of the San Diego [River] where the population is located.

"The Kickapoo came from the point Nataje murdering 5 men, 6 women and three children and wounding seven men and carrying away two boys, twenty-five horses and three tents. The leader[s] of the Lipans named Gicore Soli and Costalites, we here having brought their families, inform me they hope you will consult about the matter. I inform you of all this with the object that you may make such dispositions as you consider convenient. I inform you for the guidance of this last raid on the Lipans so that you may take such measures as are required on this frontier, and that if you consider it, you will induce the Kickapoos to return the horses and the two boys as the tribe Lipan is very near to establishing the peace with the Government which has sent me various documents about the matter on file in my office. I should be much obliged if you would inform me of the result."

Independence & Liberty[48]

Also enclosed with the letter from the Zaragosa council was an additional letter from the prefect of the town, Prefecto Adam, addressed to the Coahuila governor's secretary, also dated May 30, 1868. In the second letter, Prefecto Adam explained that he was passing along the information about the attack on the Lipan camps "that I may be without responsibility in the future."[49]

Not to be outdone, the Musquiz council president, Israel Golard, sent his own letter to the governor's office, dated May 29, 1868, giving the Musquiz version of the event:

Today arrived here the captains Mexepoto and Megrica returning from their expedition that they had made with 40 Kickapoo in the wilderness. Their leaders having given notice to have defeated the Lipan Indians and destroying a ranch of Mescalero and Lipan Indians, located between the old Presidio de la Bahia at the Rio Grande, these tribes had 26

Indians killed of both sexes of which they have brought in the scalps. They brought here also two female Indians, 2 carbines, 5 tomahocks [sic], three six shooters, bows and arrows, etc. In the said fight, the Kickapoos had one man wounded. The Indians have been assisted with sixteen dollars in ammunition which was taken from the district funds. . . . We made a voluntary subscription in this village collecting some things for the purpose of assisting the Indians as good as we could, because all the inhabitants are satisfied that the Indians have made a great and important service of the state and have demonstrated besides that they have no connection with the other tribes.[50]

Texas envoy Stephen S. Brown weighed in with his assessment, saying that the cause of the May attack against the Lipans at Remolino "grew out of horse stealing, they [the Lipans] having possession of Kickapoo horses, and charged with stealing them, but which horses, I understand after investigation, it appeared the Lipans got from the Apaches, whom the Lipans are now calling upon to aid them revenge the death of their people."[51] Brown was unable to meet with the Lipan chiefs because no tribe members could be found; they had all "fled to the Apache." In spite of this fact, Brown still gave his assessment of the Lipan band, although he admitted that he had not visited their camps, nor had he spoken with their chiefs:

They . . . have, with the Mescalero, hung as a cloud of destruction upon the Texas frontier. There is no estimating the lives and captives they have taken and the property they have made away with. Why the Texas public have not entered their complaints against that people especially, I cannot imagine unless it is that the Confederate Texans had no skirmish with them as they did with the Kickapoos during the war. These people [the Lipans] have made peace and war with some one of the Mexican towns on the frontier every few months for years past, and every town has at some time in its relations with the Indians shared the booty of their sweeping raids into Texas and even their robberies from other Mexicans at a short distance. They consort with the Apaches and Comanches. The Mexicans are quite right that the Kickapoos had done a good service to the State.[52]

III. The Lipans Fight the Kickapoos in Revenge for Their Attack
on the Lipan Camps, as told by Antonio Apache (Lipan)

I am going to tell you about a fight with the Kickapoo that happened just before I came away from Old Mexico. At that time they had good rifles. This trouble started over the young fellow who seized his bow and arrows and fought off the Kickapoo in that attack on the Lipan camps. His brother was Dinero Boy; his sister was later known as Ruth Hill, and his other brother was Chavato [sic].

Their father still thought a great deal about his oldest son who was killed by the Kickapoo that time. That is what led to the trouble. He was still angry. He planned to get some horses from the Kickapoo. Finally, he went over and took some horses from the Kickapoo. They took the horses a short distance and waited for the Kickapoo to come, but they didn't come at once. The Lipan went on.

One of the owners of these horses, a Kickapoo, thought very much of his horses. He rolled a cigarette and went to a shaman who could tell how this was going to turn out, whether there would be trouble or whether everything would come out all right. The shaman hesitated; he was a little afraid. Then he said, "I tell the truth. You are a middle-aged man and so am I; we are not children. My power tells me that if you go out, you will have a great fight and two men will be killed. Do you understand that? You'd better think it over carefully." But the man who owned the horses decided to get a group together of twelve men and go after his horses; the shaman was in that group.

The Lipan who took the horses had eight men in their group—some of them were Dinero and Chavato, Miguel Zwazwa, Cardinal Rodriguez and Santavi. The leader was the old man [Chevato's father]. They started for the hills with the horses and the old man, the father, went very slowly; he didn't act frightened. The Lipan went on for a number of days. Finally, they stopped at an open place before they reached the mountains. The old man put a little cloth over a bush and made a shade. Cardinal Rodriguez was a young man, about thirty at the time. He told the old man, "Old man, let's go on to the rough country; let's go a little farther toward the mountains. This is no place to stop! You know those people are bad."

The old man said to him, "Hmm, you're always a coward. You always want to live a little longer."

"Well, old man, when you see the enemy coming, you will run the fastest. You just stay behind now for that purpose." The young man was running around; he was very much worried. Then he looked and saw the Kickapoo coming. He said to the old man, "Well, you stay right there and wait for them, for here they are!"

The old man and his two sons [Chevato and Dinero] stood in an open place waiting for the Kickapoo. Two of them came up and got off of their horses. One, the leader, was painted black all over. The two Kickapoo advanced and the shooting began. The old man had a gun, a .44, and he pulled the trigger and the black Kickapoo dropped right there. Soon another Lipan came up to help the old man and his sons and more Kickapoo came up and began fighting. Then all the Lipan scattered; three had been wounded. The old man and his sons had horses nearby and were about to ride off, when they noticed a wounded Lipan in the shelter of some bushes. The old man was wearing medicine on his necklace and gave the wounded man a quick ceremony and some medicine to eat. The Lipan scattered, intending to gather together at one place in the hills.

But Dinero had run off by himself. All the others ran the other way. He was alone and all he had was his six-shooter and a big shield. When the Kickapoo started to chase the others, Dinero fired at them. They whirled around and began to chase him. Dinero ran over some hills, with the Kickapoo chasing him, and then he turned and stood. He curled up behind his shield while they shot at him. Dinero was just a youth, but he fought bravely.

Meanwhile, the other Lipan had gathered. They missed Dinero. His brother, Billy, was trying to fix his gun. A bullet had jammed during the fight. He handed his gun to another man and took this man's gun and some cartridges. He listened. He heard some shooting at the foot of a hill.

He went there and came to a little ridge. Some mountain laurel bushes were there and Billy peered through them. Dinero Boy was out of his head. He had seen something come from the hill and kept saying, "Come this way, come this way." That's all he remembered afterward. Then he saw someone coming, running down, and heard shooting. It was his brother coming to save him.

Billy came down and started shooting at the Kickapoo. He was shooting at them from one side. He didn't see a Kickapoo come from the other side. This Kickapoo shot and Billy went down.

Billy was lying there. The enemy came up with his ramrod and was standing over him ready to hit him. Billy raised his gun and shot. The Kickapoo went over. Billy took a good breath, rolled over for a moment and then leaped up, though he was wounded, and fired among the Kickapoo. Then he ran for the hill. He fell again over there and the Kickapoo thought they had him and came running. But Billy took another deep breath and ran for some thick bushes and a big rock. But just as he already reached the rock, two Kickapoo came over the top. Both fired. One hit him in the leg and he fell again. The first time he had been shot in the chest, and the bullet had passed through, making a hole on either side of his shirt. Then a bullet hit him just above the groin. He fell right there, leaning against the rock with his gun. He saw the bullet hit the rock in front of him after hitting him and he saw blood spurt. He knew he was badly hurt, but somehow he got behind the rock. He didn't stop and went back over the hill.

His brother, Dinero, was on the other side and the two brothers met. Billy was hurt very badly. The darkness was coming to him, which meant the end. He asked Dinero for medicine that he usually wore around his neck attached to his necklace. But Dinero couldn't find it. In the fight, it had been lost. It was the root of a plant. Then Dinero looked in a little pocket of his shield, which he still had. There he found a very little piece of it and gave it to his brother. Billy's senses began to return, his mind began to clear.

They thought the Kickapoo would still come after them, but they didn't. They just went to their man whom Billy had shot. They put him in a blanket and carried his body to where the other Kickapoo lay, the one Dinero had shot. Both Kickapoo died on the way home. That was the last time they had trouble with the Kickapoo.[53]

The final word on the matter belongs to the Kickapoos, who described their relationship with the Lipans in Coahuila in this manner: "*Esa gente no tiene buen corazon y pore so los matamos*" (Those people were not good of heart, so we killed them).[54]

2. The Massacre at Zaragosa

The Mexican government had told the Lipan in Zaragosa to convert to the Catholic Church, and the Lipan refused. Then the government told them to stop aiding the Mescalero Apaches who would raid down in Mexico. This, the Lipan refused to do. Soon, everyone was saying that the Lipan were the cause of many problems, so the government decided to take action.

A march order was issued to the Mexican troops to go in and subdue the Lipan. The leader of the troops was a man named Diaz.

Having a premonition, Chevato's mother sent Chevato, his brother, and sister out every day away from Zaragosa, so if anything were to happen, if the troops came to their village, the children would be safe. Chevato was about sixteen years old when this happened, his brother was eight years old, and their sister was just a young child, maybe five months or maybe five years old. The children were to go a few miles away and stay there until night. They were to take the goats and go out into the hills west of the Lipan settlement. My grandfather was told that if he heard any kind of shooting, like a raid, to not come back to the village until nightfall. So he did this.

During one of the days, the troops did approach Zaragosa and annihilated the Lipan. Only a few people survived and fled. My father told me only thirteen people survived.

When Chevato heard the shooting, he went back to the village, leaving his brother and sister always outside in safety. So he went back to the village alone. As far as he could tell, everybody had been killed, and there were bod-

ies and animals strewn around that had not been buried. Going to his house, he found his father had been shot and killed. Then he found his mother, who was barely alive. She had just enough strength to tell him to get his younger brother and his younger sister, take some supplies, and cross the Rio Grande and go into Texas. And so he did the request of his mother.

He got two horses and got some things to eat. He left and went back to get his brother and sister, and they crossed the river into Texas. After they had traveled about two days, they came upon a lady and a man in a buckboard wagon. The couple stopped my grandfather and asked what they were doing. I guess they were Anglos but, being close to the border, were proficient in Spanish, as my grandfather could talk to them. My grandfather told them what had happened in Zaragosa, and they were sympathetic. They asked if they could keep my grandfather's sister, who was only a baby. My grandfather didn't want to turn her over, but then the lady said that the child would not survive because she was so young, the land was so harsh, and they had hardly any food. So, the lady convinced my grandfather to leave his sister. The couple talked and shared food and told my grandfather where they lived, so that he could come and visit his sister. And then they went on their way.

My grandfather and his brother went on their way, heading northwest. As they traveled, my grandfather told his brother that he did not think the couple had been truthful about where they lived. He felt that they would never see their sister again, but they both agreed that they had done the best they could for her.

§

By the time the dust had settled after the Kickapoo Incident of 1868, assessment of the Indian situation in Coahuila began. Stephen S. Brown, the Texas envoy, had two unproductive meetings in Musquiz with the Kickapoo chiefs and their allies in July 1868. The chiefs refused to commit their bands to removal across the border into the United States, where they would be reunited with other Kickapoos already on reservations. Brown was told privately, however, that the Kickapoos did want to return across the border, but that the Mexican government did not want them to leave, desiring to keep such Indians as the Kickapoos and the Lipans in place to act as buffers against raiders from the United States. Their role as middlemen in receiving stolen horses and cattle, while not acknowledged, was also thought to be an important reason for keeping these tribes on Mexican soil. After receiving a rather arrogant letter from the governor of Coahuila, Victoriano Cepada, who averred that "very few of [the Indians] living in the deserts of the Territory of Mexico . . . have committed acts of hostility in the state of Texas,"[1] Brown had no choice but to return to Texas and write his report. He proposed, as a "proper, efficient and definite solution of the present grave difficulties and well-grounded complaints of our people . . . that the Government of the U.S. immediately propose a treaty stipulation with the Mexican Government." The proposed treaty would permit Mexico to accept no tribal peoples entering its borders from the United States, with a reciprocal arrangement for the United States (that is, that no tribal peoples from Mexico would be admitted across the U.S. border). The treaty, while acting to prevent future incursions across the border, was also to apply specifically to "all tribal peoples formerly pertaining to the U.S. who are now domiciled in the border state of Coahuila, Mexico."[2]

The Mexican assessment of the Indian situation depended on which town was doing the assessing—Musquiz or Zaragosa. The Musquiz view paralleled the view held by Stephen Brown—that the Kickapoos had done a great service to the state of Coahuila in attacking the Lipans. A short history of Kickapoo and Lipan relations, even though it was written five years after the Kickapoo Incident, was typical of the 1868 attitude of many Musquiz citizens toward both groups:

> There have been cases of horse stealing [by the Kickapoos] in said towns [along the Rio Grande], the stolen animals having been taken to their settlement above Santa Rosa. The small value of the property stolen, the distribution which they were compelled to make by the authorities of Santa Rosa and the services rendered by them in the war against the Comanche, Lipan and Mescaleros, together with the occasional assistance

which they gave as agricultural laborers, contributed to cause the faults of those who engaged in thieving to be regarded with leniency, that is, to induce the authorities not to hold the whole tribe responsible for the acts committed by some individuals belonging to it, to the injury of citizens of Mexico. . . . [Regarding Kickapoo thefts in Texas], [it is] unanimous testimony of respectable inhabitants of the frontier [that the Kickapoo thefts are of] trifling importance.

[The Lipans], perfidious as they always are, excited the hatred of the people of the frontier [and] over the last ten years, have carried desolation and death to the frontier towns of Mexico and the United States.[3]

The negative assessment of the Lipans by the Mexican citizenry continued even after the Kickapoos had attacked the Lipan camps and killed their women and children. This attitude seemed to have been held by everyone in Coahuila except the Lipan supporters in Zaragosa. Yet within a year of the Kickapoo Incident, events would occur that would cause the Lipan faction in Zaragosa to be overruled, paving the way for the attack by Mexican troops. Antonio Apache described the events leading up to the troopers' attack on the Lipans near Zaragosa:

My grandfather [named Caro Colorado (Red Face)] used to carry mail from one town to another. He was . . . a Lipan. They tried some Mexican mail carriers, but these men never came back; they were killed. They were supposed to carry mail between Zaragosa and Norte. . . . They decided to send the mail by my grandfather, for he was an Indian. The Mexican soldiers passed through there all the time looking for raiders, but they didn't bother my grandfather for they knew he was the mail carrier. Some of his people [i.e., the Lipans] lived near the towns [of Zaragosa and Norte], but some were out in the hills making trouble.

One day these Lipan in the hills killed the members of the family of a wealthy Mexican. They were going out to his ranch with his relatives. They were with his hired man and the family of the hired man. An epidemic had broken out in town and they were going to the ranch to get away from it. On the way, they were all killed by the Lipan who had not settled down.

There was a Mexican named Diltso who was a great friend of the Indians [Diltso seems to be a nickname for this Hispanic man, in either the Lipan or Mescalero language; the meaning is unclear]. He was living at Zaragosa. He sent his hired man over to another place with some cattle. He wanted to sell the cattle to an army camp. The Indians saw this man, killed him, took his clothes and left him naked. They killed the cattle too.

The wealthy Mexican who lost his family called a meeting. He wanted to go out and fight the Indians. Diltso defended the Indians. It looked as if Diltso would persuade the others.

But the wealthy Mexican said to Diltso, "If they are your friends, these Indians that you always defend, how is it they killed your hired man and took your cattle? They killed him and put him naked in a kneeling position with his buttocks toward the trail. What kind of friends are those Indians to you that treat you this way?"

Diltso had no answer. He lost support at once. Then the prominent Mexican said, "Now we are going to make an agreement. We are going to gather all our men. In two months we are going to start after them. We'll get them if it takes five years. After five years, if we haven't got them, let them go free."

Diltso came back from the meeting. He had some soldiers there, too. He was an important man. He said to his men, "We are going out to some Indian camps." He told his men to stay there and rode alone to the Indians.

The Indians were moving over the hill. He followed them for a ways. He called to them and said, "If so-and-so is there, tell him to come down here. I have news for you."

"He isn't here; he's gone to Sierra Blanca [the Mescalero stronghold in New Mexico]."

"Well, two of you had better come down and I'll give you the news. I have something important to tell you about what they say they are going to do to you."

But they were afraid to come down. He dismounted and talked to them from a distance of about two hundred yards. He told them about the meeting in which it had been agreed to fight the Indians. He told how he had defended them and lost because they had killed his hired man. He told them what had been decided. He told them to go to the north to a place called Rio Bonito [near Ft. Stanton, New Mexico]. There is a settler there who will not be an enemy. It is a good safe place. There will be no trouble there. Go and stay there for five years; then you can come back. All the while he talked, he called them his children. He said, "My children, that is all I come to tell you. I tried to make you come down here, but you are afraid. I left my men far behind. If I had wanted trouble I would have brought my men right here. But you are afraid of me. I would rather talk to you face to face, but you stay up on the hill. Now I am going home." And Diltso went back to his men and went home.[4]

Antonio Apache's grandfather, Caro Colorado, also received a personal warning of impending military action from Diltso, who asked Caro Colorado to bring the mail from Norte to him so that he could open any letters from the military leader at Norte, in order to learn what the soldiers were planning. When Caro Colorado brought the mail to Diltso, he was told the following:

> Diltso said, "Our friend, an officer who is above me, is a friend of the Indians, too. He is willing to help, to bring you Indians into the towns, for it is because your people are out in the hills that you get into trouble. He wants to bring all of your people in and have you live with us always. He is willing to put up money for the purpose and says I should put up some too. But right now I have little money. He tells me to go to Black Rock [Piedras Negras] and borrow the money there. I will write back to him and you can carry the message."
>
> When my grandfather was out this last time, he saw many soldiers, but on the next trip he saw even more.
>
> The other officer said, "I tried to get your friend to give money, but he says he can't get any money. He says he hasn't got it and can't borrow it.

So don't try to come over any more. When you get back you had better stay there, for the trouble will start shortly. Even if he wants to send you with another message, you had better not come."

Caro Colorado, his family, and relatives left Zaragosa on the third night. They left their campfires burning on the outskirts of town and went to the mountains to tell the other Lipan camps of the impending military attack. "Some of the Indians didn't believe it. They said, 'They can't find us. These mountains are rough and they don't know the countryside as we do.'" But Caro Colorado disagreed, telling the Lipans that thousands of soldiers would soon be out searching for them and they could not escape at that point. Caro Colorado then left the Lipan camps and headed for Norte, as he had relatives there.

"Soon the soldiers came. They were searching on the eastern side of Zaragosa. Some Indians were camping there. The Mexicans captured two women and some children. The Mexicans charged early in the morning, just when day was breaking. Some women got away and some were wounded."

After the initial Mexican attack in Zaragosa, many of the Lipans in Norte and in the hills thought that the problem with the troops was over. Most of the Lipans who had lived near Zaragosa had fled prior to the military attack and were hiding in the hills to the west of town, joined by the Lipan groups who lived in the Norte area. But when some tried to buy ammunition to go hunting, no storekeeper in the area would sell them any ammunition. After the Zaragosa attack, the Mexican troops had followed the Lipans to the hills and were hunting them down, group by group.

They saw smoke signals all over the hills. That meant trouble. The Indians had agreed that if there was trouble, they would warn those in town [Norte] so they could get out safely. The Lipan in the camps at the edge of town wanted to go, but they were waiting for two people who had not appeared.

One of these two got drunk. He had a small keg of whiskey. All his people were waiting for him and he was lying somewhere drunk. Poncho Vinegro [Pancho Venego] and his father were among those waiting for him. They were running around camp in an excited state, not knowing what to do. They didn't like to leave their missing members behind, but they were afraid to stay much longer.

When these two came, they started for the mountains. When they got to the edge of the hills, they could see horse tracks of the Indians who had gone before them. In the town their Mexican friends had told them, "You'd better go on. Those soldiers have had trouble with the Indians to the west. They came from there and they are after you. They are not here for fun; they intend to fight you. We Mexicans who live here don't bother you Indians, but these soldiers are from another place. You'd better leave at once." So this last group, as soon as these two crazy fellows arrived, left for the hills, too.

The Lipan band had split into a number of family groups who moved through the hills west of Zaragosa, trying to evade the Mexican soldiers. Antonio Apache's group circled around and eventually returned to the Norte area. The largest group of Lipans had continued to camp there, and Antonio's group did not want to become separated from them.

Two other families went on to Flat Rock. There they found Billy Chavato's [*sic*] group in a pretty place on the top of the mountain.... [There were a total of three Lipan camps around Flat Rock.] ... These camps kept to themselves. The others, the bigger group, stayed together around Norte.

After they had been camping there many days, Billy's father said, "All our people are at Norte. We had better join them. What is the use for us few to run around in these mountains alone? Let's go back to them. If trouble comes to them, we'll be there, too."

Chevato's family and the other groups headed back to Norte, a move that brought all of the scattered family groups back together, but a move that placed the entire band in danger. Mexican troopers were still searching the hills, trying to locate the main Lipan camp. Other Mexican citizens kidnapped three Lipans when they went into Norte, luring them by giving them whiskey and then throwing them into jail. Two were able to escape from the jail, but the third, a Lipan named Shosh (Bear), was turned over to Mexican soldiers. They tied him on a horse and forced him to show them where the main Lipan camp was located, but Shosh vowed never to give up his people to the soldiers, and he finally escaped. The two prisoners who had broken out of the Norte jail made their way back to the Lipan camp, raising the alarm. All the groups prepared to move out. They split up into family groups, with Chevato's family becoming separated from Caro Colorado's group. It is after this point, in Antonio Apache's story, that Chevato's parents were killed, since only Chevato and his siblings crossed the Rio Grande into Texas. Caro Colorado's group traveled "two days and nights and didn't sleep till the middle of the next day." At that point, they were met by several Mescalero Apaches (the two named by Antonio Apache were Concho and Bigmouth), who guided them across the river.

> The Lipan said, "We have had a great deal of trouble. This is all that is left of us in this district [Zaragosa]. The rest are captured. Just a few, Chavato's [*sic*] family, are elsewhere. . . . We are all who are left. All the rest have been captured and we do not know where they have been taken." All [these events occurred] in 1869.[5]

As the Lipan mail carrier Caro Colorado led his group of survivors toward New Mexico, and as Chevato and Dinero left their sister behind and moved toward the northwest, other mail carriers were delivering letters to the adjutant general's office in Washington DC, which would set the stage for a second massacre of the Lipans in Coahuila. The Texas envoy, Stephen Brown, had submitted his report on the Coahuila Indians to Gen. Reynolds, who then forwarded the report, along with his recommendations, to the adjutant general of the army on September 29, 1868. Once the report reached Washington, other voices weighed in on the matter. In a letter dated February 12, 1869, Maj. Gen. E. R. L. Canby, Fifth Military District of Texas, complained:

> The most serious difficulty that is encountered in this District is protecting the inhabitants from Indian depredations occasioned by the Kickapoo

Indians at Santa Rosa, Mexico, a short distance west of the Rio Grande. They usually cross that river in several parties, penetrate the settlements without being discovered, and escape with their plunder into Mexico. Their depredations are generally confined to stealing horses and killing cattle for their own subsistence while in the Country but occasionally a murder is committed or a captive carried away. The band could be easily destroyed if it were not necessary to enter Mexican Territory in order to reach them.[6]

Also forwarded to the adjutant general were letters from the post commander at Ft. Duncan (now Eagle Pass, Texas) and the commander at Ft. Sam Houston, San Antonio, attesting to the Indian depredations by the Kickapoos living at Santa Rosa. Then, on February 25, 1869, Maj. Gen. Canby alerted the adjutant general's office of the following:

Since the date of my letter of February 12, 1869, in relation to the Kickapoo Indians residing in Mexico, I have learned that these Indians are now desirous of returning to their old homes, and that the Mexican authorities will be glad to get rid of them. I have also learned that the Lipans have made overtures to the Toncawas [sic] now living in this State and under the protection of the troops at Ft. Griffin, to unite with them and return to the protection of the United States. The Lipans now live near San Fernando [i.e., Zaragosa] in the State of Coahuila....

If these bands can be brought within our territory and established upon reservations or reunited with the main body of the tribes from which they separated, it will contribute more than any other measure to the relief of the western frontier of this State, and it will remove the cover under which marauding Mexicans cross the Rio Grande and commit depredations upon the property of the people of this State.

The Governor of Coahuila will, I am advised, give any facilities that may be needed in meeting and conferring with these Indians if the policy of re-establishing them in their old homes should be adopted.[7]

In spite of Canby's assurance, the Mexican government stalled, eventually declining to sign a treaty with the United States regarding the Coahuila Indians. Before the final rejection from the Mexican government, however, other letters were forwarded to the adjutant general's office. One letter was written by Col. Ranald S. Mackenzie, commander at Ft. Clark, Texas. On May 29, 1869, his letter to the Fifth Military District headquarters in Austin, Texas, was forwarded to the adjutant general. Mackenzie forwarded three affidavits from local men who described recent Indian depredations in the Ft. Clark area, and he stated that he was willing to meet with the Mexican commanding officer to come to an understanding regarding the Indian problem. He continued:

> The state of affairs is such that our Government would be but morally right in crossing the frontier and compelling respect, and the conduct of the Mexicans so bad that I can hardly believe that the matter can have been strongly urged on those high in authority in Saltillo. . . . I believe that the Lipans might very possibly be delivered up on demand (there are not more than fifty warriors) and am sure in justice they should be. The Kickapoo could then be readily induced to return to their reserve, and as they were greatly wronged by the Texians [sic] in the first instance, kindness if possible should be employed.[8]

Mackenzie's opinion—that the United States would be morally correct to cross the Rio Grande to permanently solve the Indian raiding problem—found sympathetic ears in Washington. On February 5, 1873, Gen. William T. Sherman wrote from army headquarters to Gen. C. C. Augur, commander of the Department of Texas: "The President [Grant] wishes you to give great attention to affairs on the Rio Grande Frontier, especially to prevent the raids of Indians and Mexicans upon the people and property of Southern and Western Texas." Sherman ordered Mackenzie's Fourth Cavalry to be moved back to the Rio Grande from northwest Texas. He continued: "In naming the 4th for the Rio Grande, the President is doubtless influenced by the fact that Col. McKenzie [sic] is young and enterprising, and that he will impart to his regiment his own active character."[9]

By May 1873 Mackenzie had received the go-ahead from Sherman's replacement, Gen. Philip H. Sheridan, secretly authorizing Mackenzie to cross the Rio Grande. Sheridan was fully aware that he was authorizing an extra-legal attack. It was hoped, however, that the raid would eliminate both the bothersome Kickapoos and the Lipans, solving the problem for both the United States and Mexico. And there the matter would end, with satisfaction on each side of the border. At 6 a.m. on the morning of May 17, 1873, six companies of the Fourth Cavalry, accompanied by thirty-four Seminole scouts, swept out of the brush and attacked camps containing Kickapoos and Lipans. "The Command had a sharp skirmish for a few minutes and killed 19 Indians, whose bodies were found—captured 40 women and children and Costiletos the Principal Chief of the Lipans and 65 ponies."[10] By May 27, 1873, Gen. Sheridan informed the secretary of war, "General Augur telegraphs that the Mexicans on the border are well pleased with the punishment given the Kickapoos by Mackenzie. The remainder of the Kickapoos threaten retaliation, but we are ready for them if they come. If Mr. Fish [secretary of state] will only let this question alone, I think we will be able in a short time to settle Indian raids and cattle thieving on the Rio Grande."[11] The captured Indians were sent to reservations, with the Lipans being sent to the Mescalero Reservation in New Mexico.

The remnants of the Texas Lipan bands had been settled at Ft. Belknap, Texas, by 1861. Joined by the Tonkawas, the two groups were moved to Ft. Griffin, Texas, in 1867. Many of the men enlisted as army scouts and fought during the "final stages of Indian warfare on the southern Great Plains. In 1885 they had moved to the Oakland Agency in the northern part of the Cherokee Nation. Most of these Lipan, who numbered fewer than twenty people by 1890, found homes among their Kiowa-Apache kinsmen."[12]

Mexican president Porfirio Diaz accomplished the final destruction of the Coahuila Lipans. In 1881 he ordered an extermination of "the savage tribes" along the border. The Mexican army's Diaz Division, using maps especially prepared by Blas Flores showing the locations of all Indian camps and *rancherías*, launched an expedition. The soldiers were directed to burn the villages and kill all the inhabitants, regardless of age or sex. The Diaz government was retaliating for acts committed by Apache bands and other renegade tribal bands in the Rio Grande region. Diaz also

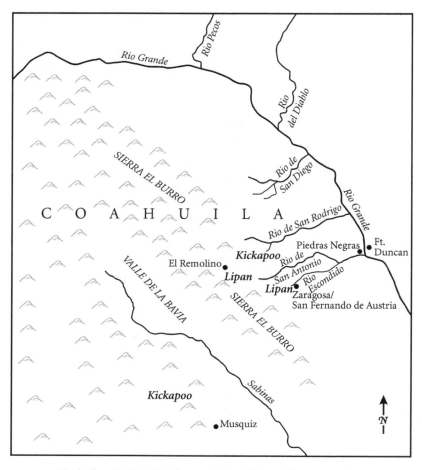

Coahuila, 1860–80. Based on a map used in a military campaign against "savage tribes" of Indians in Coahuila, by Blas Flores, 1881.

suspected all Indian peoples of hiding resistance fighters, who were trying to overthrow the regional governors in the provinces of northern Mexico, and he based his suspicions on false reports from the regional governors and hacienda owners.[13]

By 1903 a mere thirty-seven Mexican Lipans, the pitiful remnant of the Lipan bands who had settled in Mexico more than a century and a half earlier, were found living in northern Mexico. The small number of survivors had fled from Coahuila to the neighboring state of Chihuahua.

When the Catholic priest who served the Mescaleros on their reservation in New Mexico received permission from the governor of Chihuahua for the Lipan remnant to emigrate to the Mescalero Reservation, the Mescalero people and their Lipan kinsmen and women raised the money to reunite the Mexican Lipans with their relatives in New Mexico. The Catholic priest, Father Migeon, arrived in Chihuahua City to find the Lipans housed in a corral on the outskirts of town near the train station. There was little shelter for them and no wood for cooking fires. They were fed with corn that was thrown into the corral and, since they had no wood to make fires, were forced to eat the corn raw. Father Migeon secured their release, and the small band of thirty-seven, the last of the Western Lipans, were loaded onto cattle cars for the train trip to New Mexico.[14]

3. The Mescalero Apaches, Mexican Bandits, and Revenge

My grandfather and his brother continued on their way for about a day and a half until they came to a watering hole. They were watering their horses and getting water for themselves when they noticed some Mescalero Apaches standing over them. The boys were in a depression in the ground where a stream led into a small pond. They felt someone was looking at them and looked up, seeing the Mescaleros above them. Being acquainted with them, they started to talk in their own native tongue. They told the Mescalero leader what had happened in Zaragosa, and the leader said, "If you want, you can go with us." So they went, because they had no supplies left, and their horses were wearing out. The Mescalero gave them new horses and gave them something to eat. They continued on up into what is now Roswell, New Mexico, into what is now called Ruidoso or the Hondo Valley, down through the pass and into the mountains of the Mescalero stronghold. It is now the Mescalero Reservation. And there they began to live with the Mescalero.

My grandfather and his brother stayed at the Mescalero stronghold, and there they told the leaders of the Mescaleros that they really hated the Mexi-

can troops. The leaders assured them that they would have their chance to get their revenge for the murder of their parents. After some time, they were allowed to go on Mescalero raiding parties that went back into Mexico to steal horses from the Mexican troops, bringing the horses back to Mescalero for their own use. They did this numerous times, but it was not satisfying.

My grandfather continued to want his revenge, so on one trip to Mexico, he and his brother stayed behind while the Mescaleros went back to New Mexico. Knowing the language of Mexico and being accustomed to the ways and customs of the people of the area, it was easy for them to blend in. They dressed and acted like Mexican citizens and mingled with the population in a town nearby Zaragosa. They lived like homeless people do today, and in doing so, they met a man who became quite interested in them because of the ideas they had and because of their hatred of the Mexican troops. He liked them very much even though they were young, and he asked them, "Would you like to live as I do?" They asked him what he did for a living, and he said, "Well, we get horses and cattle in the United States and bring them across the river, the Rio Grande, and sell them in Mexico. And then we go and likewise steal stock in Mexico and take them into the United States and sell them across the border in Texas. And along the way, we can kill a few federal troops." This elated my grandfather, and he said that this was just what he was looking for. So they left town with the man and went up into the mountains, the Sierra Madres. There they met up with a large group of men, and they realized that they had fallen into a large group of bandits. The man they had met near Zaragosa protected them until they became well known to the rest of the men. And my grandfather and his brother rode with the Mexican bandits, stealing stock and killing Mexican troops.

This is the way they would steal horses from the Mexican troops. When the troopers would picket their horses on a picket line, my grandfather and the bandits would wait until the middle of the night when the troopers were asleep. Then they would go to the picket line, cut the horses loose, and steal them. Once they had run the horses away, the troopers couldn't get their mounts. Then they would go in and kill the federal troops when they were sleeping.

My grandfather came close to being captured once by a Mexican sentry.

The sentry came upon my grandfather, and the only weapon my grandfather had was a handful of dirt. The sentry asked him what he was doing, and my grandfather answered him in Spanish, saying he was lost. He took a scolding from the sentry, and when the sentry told him to come closer, my grandfather got real close and then threw the dirt in his face. That gained him enough time to get a knife and stab the sentry. This is the way they lived and took revenge on the federal troops in Mexico.

My grandfather and his brother would go on raids with the Mexican bandits getting their revenge, and then they would cross the river, go to the Mescaleros, and stay with them because they wanted the traditions of the Indian way of life. When they were with the bandits, my grandfather was given a nickname. They called him Chivato, which means "little goat," and that is what he called himself ever after.

After the bandit raids, they would split up the money. My grandfather's brother was still young, so when the bandits divided the money, his younger brother always wanted the coins or the change. He thought that the coins were more valuable than the paper money. So the leader of the bandits, who liked my grandfather and his brother, told my grandfather to keep his brother's share of the paper money and just give him the coins. That's how his brother got the nickname Dinero, which means "money" in Spanish.

When Chevato and Dinero were ready to go back and spend some time with the Mescaleros, the bandit leader let them go. He said, "Any time you want to come to Mexico and join us, you know where to find us." Chevato said, "We'll be back. We just want to go and visit with our own people who are living across the river." So Chevato and Dinero went to the Mescaleros.

§

"The Mescalero Apaches of New Mexico had a long record of generosity toward exile bands and tribes of Apaches. Perhaps their looking on the mountain fastness ranging southward from the sacred White Mountain [Sierra Blanca] as a haven from their own seasonal wanderings . . . motivated them to extend fellowship to others."[1] Ranging from the Staked Plains of Texas to the rugged mountains of central New Mexico, the Mes-

47

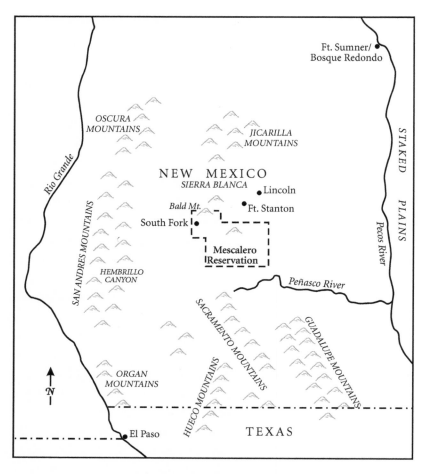

Mescalero Apache Heartland in the 1800s

caleros would always return to their stronghold nestled high in the mountains west of the Pecos River. They would spend winters in the warm country of southern New Mexico; in the spring, they would return to the place they considered their homeland—the headwaters of the Rio Bonito, located on Sierra Blanca.[2] The Mescaleros, however, were of a more nomadic bent than their Lipan cousins, and groups could be found as far north as the panhandle of Texas (the ancestral territory of the group later led by Natzili);[3] as far west as Santa Fe, New Mexico; and as far south as Coahuila and Chihuahua, Mexico. They were equally adept at living in the mountains, in the southern deserts, and on the plains.

Mescalero culture reflected the territory they inhabited. The Mescaleros (the Ndé, or People) saw themselves as existing within a circle of life (*nda-i bijuul siá*) that was anchored in space by four sacred directions. Each direction was associated with sacred colors, planetary or natural phenomena, and animals, each of which had a specific job in support of the existence of the Ndé.[4] Just as the Mescalero nonphysical world was conceived of as a circle, the physical geography of their territory revealed that they were encompassed on four sides by tribes whose influences can be seen in Mescalero culture. To the north of the Mescalero stronghold lay the Pueblo cultures. Even though the Mescaleros and the Navajos had a long history of antagonism, the influence of the entire Pueblo culture of northern New Mexico could be seen in the Mescalero inner world of ceremony and ritual. The masked dancers (*Gą?ha*) who impersonated supernatural beings at the girls' puberty ceremony and the "employment of pollen, turquoise, and abalone in ritual contexts, . . . even the witchcraft cult" can be traced to Pueblo sources.[5] Yet these beliefs were set into a context of shamanism that was understandable and familiar to the Chiricahuas and Western Apache, tribes that inhabited territory to the west of the Mescaleros. Lipan influence in Mescalero culture can be seen in the peyote ceremony and belief in the use of peyote to heal; both aspects were adopted by the Mescalero from the Lipans who lived to the south. Many outer manifestations of Mescalero culture showed a plains Indian influence, reflective of the Comanches, Kiowas, and other plains tribes who lived to the east of the Mescalero. "There was some dependence on the buffalo, but there was no organization or discipline on the buffalo hunt comparable to that of the typical plains tribes. . . . [E]ven the elements reminiscent of plains culture were weakly developed in the Mescalero context."[6] In spite of these influences, however, the Mescaleros were not a plains tribe, nor were they a Pueblo culture or a duplication of the culture of their more remote cousins, the Western Apaches. Rather, Mescalero culture showed influences from all their surrounding neighbors, yet it was a unique amalgam, "a general Apachean pattern, from which they have diverged in interesting and subtle ways in the course of time."[7]

The Mescaleros did not organize themselves into "bands," per se, as did the Lipans. Because of the geography of the primary areas in which they lived (that is, rugged mountains, harsh deserts), where their existence was more of a hunter-gatherer nature, the social organization of the Mescaleros was that of the group. Each local group had a leader and was composed of from ten to twenty families, usually related by blood or marriage. The groups were identified either by the name of the leader or by the name of a "specific place or locality that served as a center or base from which the people moved out, usually in small parties, to forage or hunt."[8] Thus one group might be known as Natzili's camp (after the name of the leader), while a second group of Mescaleros might be known as the Three Rivers Camp (after the location of the camp).[9]

As Opler explains,

> Typical situations which involved a leader included questions of whether to move to another site because of poor . . . hunting, repeated deaths or disease, or the proximity of enemies, whether to sanction a raid or a war party, whether to sponsor an important . . . ritual event to which outsiders might be invited and what to do about charges of witchcraft or gross misbehavior which were disrupting the group. The ability to lead a successful raid and war parties . . . was . . . a great asset for a leader; such expeditions meant booty, and this, in turn, made it possible to distribute favors widely. In a society where generosity was one of the cardinal virtues, such activity built and sustained the good will so important to a leader.[10]

Mescalero leaders after 1800 whose power extended over several groups included Barranquito, Santana, Cadette, Ramón Grande, Peso, San Juan, and Natzili. In addition, the "belligerent chief" Juan Goméz and his followers lived in the Davis Mountains of Texas and harassed travelers on the Santa Fe–San Antonio road.[11]

To the outside world, the Mescaleros were best characterized by the phrase "raiders and traders." Some early contacts with the Spanish, where the Mescaleros were specifically named by that appellation, occurred in the 1772 campaign in Coahuila. The Mescaleros were among the raiders chased out of the Bolsón de Mapimí by Spanish troops, fleeing north with the Lipans to seek shelter in the mountains of the Big Bend area of the Rio Grande.[12] They had settled, in their fashion, in Mexico for a time before 1800 when the padres could entice them into the missions, but they never stayed in one place for very long, always returning to their homeland in the mountains of New Mexico.

Sustained American military contact with the Mescaleros, beginning around 1850, was problematic from the start. American military authorities soon realized that agreements made with one Mescalero leader did not guarantee compliance by other Mescalero chiefs. That problem, however, was not unique to military-Mescalero relations, and the U.S. military had methods of adapting and coping with that situation. The real sticking point, from the army's point of view, was the Mescaleros' propensity for raiding. Although the army, in the years before the Civil War, sought to negotiate with the Mescaleros and even provided rations for them at Ft. Stanton, the national conflict intervened and changed the situation entirely. Once the New Mexico forts were reoccupied by Union troops, a firm hand born of the necessity of the times was extended to the Mescaleros. In September 1862 the military began to pursue the Mescaleros into their homeland. After an attempted attack on Mescalero women and children at Dog Canyon, in which one warrior held off the cavalry troops long enough for the camp to escape, the Mescaleros fled to the safety of Ft. Stanton. There, Cadette, speaking for the tribe, met with the commander, Christopher "Kit" Carson, who told Cadette that his superior, Gen. James H. Carleton, had ordered all Apache males to be killed on sight. If the Mescaleros surrendered, however, they would be spared and sent to a reservation on the Pecos River at Bosque Redondo. There they would be given blankets and food until they could raise crops.[13] In the words of Big Mouth, a Mescalero who was carried in a cradleboard by his widowed mother to Bosque Redondo:

We started north. . . . It was a terrible journey, for the women were attacked by the soldiers, and no officer did anything to prevent it. Mescalero women were chaste and very modest. The men could not look at each other; they could do nothing to protect the women and were ashamed. They wished that they had chosen death . . . but it was too late; they were now captives.

That place at Fort Sumner [i.e., Bosque Redondo] was what is now called a concentration camp. There was nothing there for us except misery and hunger. There were no pines, no streams except the Pecos, and no game. There was no water fit for drinking. We had been accustomed to the clear, cold water from the melting snow of the [Sierra Blanca]. We had to drink the muddy, ill-tasting water from the Pecos. It made us sick; it even made the horses sick. But can one live without water?

They put men and women to work digging ditches and digging up ground with shovels to plant corn. And once a week the soldiers gave us enough food to last perhaps two days. We were not farmers—we were fighters and hunters! Above all, we were free people, and now we were imprisoned within picket lines and made into slaves. The Apache does not mind work, but he does not like slavery.[14]

The Mescaleros endured three years at Bosque Redondo, but on the night of November 3, 1865 (exactly three years from the day of their incarceration), they stole away.[15]

By 1869 the Mescaleros had again become

the great pests of the District [of New Mexico], who infest all the southern portions of the territory and sometimes extend their operations in small parties as far north as Santa Fe. They live almost entirely from the results of their thieving expeditions, are adventurous and cunning and probably exceed all other Indians in cruelty. The small size of their parties and the extremely mountainous and wild nature of the country, render any successful pursuit a matter of great difficulty and frequently of impossibility. . . . The[y] number some 450 men, women and children.[16]

Many of the old Mescalero chiefs who had accompanied their people into confinement at Bosque Redondo had been replaced by 1869. Gone were Ojo Blanco, Viejo, and Schat-hi.[17] Still wielding influence were Ramón Grande, Pablo, Francisco, Santana, La Paz, and Gorgorio (a Mescalero shaman who was gaining political power). The leader of one of the largest Mescalero groups, Cadette, had fled with his people toward the Staked Plains. An 1871 military report from the Department of New Mexico stated, "for the last several years, [Cadette's band of Mescaleros] have been roaming with the Comanches."[18]

The primary connection between the Mescalero Apaches and the Comanches in the years after the Civil War was the trade in stolen cattle and horses facilitated by Hispanic (and some Anglo) traders, or *Comancheros*, who were licensed in New Mexico to trade with the Comanches. The Mescaleros were prolific raiders, but one has to ask a basic question: what did they do with the stolen livestock? They did not accumulate large horse herds, as did the Comanches and Kiowas. They were not a pastoral people, so stolen cattle were not added to already existing Mescalero cattle herds. The harshness and ruggedness of their home territory precluded large-scale cattle raising, and they stole many more cattle than were necessary to feed the tribe. After the cattle and horses brought back from a raid were distributed within the tribe, the excess was sold or traded to the *Comancheros*. In March 1872 a *Comanchero* named Polonio Ortiz was captured by troops from Ft. Concho, Texas. Under interrogation, he admitted that "he and several others from the Pecos valley of New Mexico had left for the Indian country . . . loaded with goods furnished by [New Mexico] traders."[19] The group made its way to Muchoque, a well-known trading location on the edge of the Staked Plains; the site can be found today in Borden County, Texas. "There they found a village of Kwahada Comanches and Mescalero Apaches, numbering '100 lodges, perhaps 200.' . . . As soon as the traders arrived, the Indians sent out a party of 100 men to obtain cattle."[20] The illicit cattle trade that sprang up after the Civil War, as well as the Comanche desire for horses, was the fuel that propelled Mescalero raiding.

The primary Mescalero raiding destination had always been Mexico; by 1850 they had been raiding into Mexico for almost a century. A short, tough people, they would ride down out of the Guadalupe Mountains of New Mexico, cross through the tip of Texas near El Paso, and sweep into Chihuahua. Or they would angle east and cross the Rio Grande near Del Rio or Eagle Pass, riding into Coahuila in their leather war-shirts, fringed on the arms and with a deep fringe in the shape of a V across their chests. With sashes wrapped around their heads like turbans, they would raid the small ranchos and haciendas, stealing horses. Natzili's grandson described one such raid into Mexico:

> Across the river [Rio Grande], the *remudas* [horse herds] of the *haciendas* were very enticing to all the tribes, and they were accustomed to making raids deep into Mexico. The wise *ricos* [rich men] were shrewd enough to understand the Indians' ways and could afford to keep their corrals filled with horses for their raids. They knew that if the Indians met with no resistance and got a good supply of mounts, they would not disturb the *hacienda* or its inhabitants. The Indians preferred to let the cooperative Mexicans live in order to provide them with future supplies of horses.[21]

As the Mescalero raided in Coahuila in the 1860s, they were competing in thievery with groups of Mexican guerrillas as well as with various groups of Mexican bandits who plagued the border areas as a matter of course. The Mexican guerrillas were fighting against the French-led regime of Maximilian and were led by Andres S. Viesca, Francisco Aguirre, Victoriano Cepeda, and Ildefonso Fuentes;[22] the bandits had infested the border region like fleas on a dog since the Treaty of Guadalupe Hidalgo. Although Chevato never named the bandit chief who took the two young Apache boys under his wing after 1869, there is a good probability that he was the famous Mexican bandit and cattle thief known as Areola. To the dismay of the American consul at Piedras Negras, Areola and his gang would steal large numbers of Texas cattle, drive them across the Rio Grande, and sell them in Zaragosa and surrounding towns.[23] The consul, William Schuhardt, described the manner of the thefts:

Chino, Mescalero shaman, 1886. Wearing Mescalero-style turban.
National Anthropological Archives, Smithsonian Institution/#02044600.

The stealing of cattle and horses is carried on continually, unnoticed by the authorities, but they are not ignorant of it. At present, the Mexican thieves do not extend their raids far into the interior of Texas, except when they join the Indians in theirs; they confine their operations to the country adjoining the Rio Grande, but thus they can repeat them continually and expose themselves less. In Resurreccion [*sic*], one of the towns above here a fellow named Areola notorious for being engaged in stealing from Texas and caught at it several times but never punished, and for crimes committed in his own country, carried on with his companions this profitable business publicly to the knowledge of the authorities who dare not interfere with this Mexican patriot, being a man who rendered important services to the cause of General Diaz in his revolution.[24]

When Chevato and his brother, Dinero, were taken in by the Mescaleros, they were age sixteen and a half and age eight, respectively, The nickname Chivato is a good example of the wonderful, humorous flexibility of the Spanish language, where meaning is wrapped around meaning. Already known as Chivato, or "little goat," by other members of the Lipan community near Zaragosa, the bandits attached an additional colloquial meaning to his name. Thus a *chivato* is a "little goat," but the word can also be used to denote a person who is an informer or a "stool pigeon."[25] Chevato and Dinero were young enough to be able to blend into a Mexican village without causing too much scrutiny and were, therefore, the perfect scouts for the bandits, able to assess both targets to rob and possible resistance once the robbery was taking place.

Chevato described the method by which the bandits gave his brother the nickname Dinero, yet there might be a second version of the origin of Dinero's name. This second version was tied to Mescalero Apache custom. If an orphan was reared by nonrelatives, he "was given his father's name, followed by 'Boy.'"[26] In Dinero's case, however, this custom seems to have been modified. The first Mescalero census (1885) lists a forty-six-year-old Lipan widow named Dinero. Since Chevato's brother is consistently named in various documents as Dinero's Boy or Dinero Boy, that would indicate that he was raised by this Lipan widow once he reached the Mescaleros and received her name, rather than the name of his father plus the word "Boy."[27] It also seems very probable that the Lipan widow was also a survivor of the Zaragosa massacre. Dinero was eight years old when he was orphaned and thus needed the care of a foster mother. The next influx of Lipans into the Mescalero groups was after the 1873 raid on El Remolino. By that date, Dinero was sixteen years old and already participating in raids. Thus the name Dinero Boy would also indicate the Lipan widow had joined with the Mescaleros at an earlier date, such as after the 1869 Zaragosa massacre.

4. The Vision Quest

There is a ritual among the Indian people called "finding oneself" or "having a vision" if you so desire and you think you are good enough. Not all times can a person get what they are seeking. That's why Chevato wanted to go back to the Mescaleros. He wanted to find out if he had this gift.

He went back to the Mescaleros and told them that he wanted a vision quest. The Mescalero chief interviewed him, talked to him, and found out that he might be a likely candidate. So the chief told him, "You have to fast. You can only drink water, and you have to go somewhere up high in the mountains." And they were already in the mountains. Chevato had to go up high where it was cold, even in July. So he went with just the water, no food, to the high mountains for his vision quest.

Once he had climbed the mountain, he decided to go down into a little valley where there was a stream. He went into the valley, where he had a premonition that the stream was going to fork. He felt he was supposed to sleep in the fork of the stream. He had a premonition that he was to sleep with his head toward the main stream in the middle of the fork. While he was settling down to do this, he also had a premonition that whatever was to come, whatever he heard, he was not to get up, he was not to run but was to just lie still. If he showed fear, whatever gift that was to be bestowed on him would be taken away.

One night while he was sleeping in the middle of the fork of the stream, he felt the presence of an animal. He thought it was a mountain lion, but he didn't look up. It was moving like a large cat would move, and it came down to where his feet were. He could hear the purr. It walked and straddled his body. It got right up to his face, and it licked his face. Then it backed off and went away.

As soon as the large cat had gone away, Chevato felt something on his chest. He picked it up and found it was a little packet, like someone had made it out of deerskin. It had a leather strip so he could wear it like a medallion around his neck. He also had a premonition that he should never open that little pouch—that was where all his power would come from. It was a gift from the Creator. He would have powers to help people, but he was never to misuse these powers, for the day that he did, he would be destroyed. He would die.

He would also have the power to heal people, even himself. If he was shot, but was unable to see his own blood, then he knew that if he said a prayer, his prayer would activate his power, and he would be able to heal himself. In other words, if at the same time he was shot and at the time he felt the impact of the bullet hitting his body—if at that time he happened to look down at the spot where the bullet had entered his body and saw only the bullet hole, without seeing any blood coming out of the impact point, then his prayer would call up his power and his power would enable him to heal himself and survive. However, if he looked down at the moment of impact and saw blood spurting out of the impact point, then he knew that prayers would be useless, since his power could not be called up; he knew that he must then rely on his knowledge of herbs to survive. And he believed this, and he came back out of the mountains and went to Mescalero a different man, a different person.

He rejoined the Mescaleros and worked his way up to become a leader. He had this gift. Before they were to go off on a raid, he would go off by himself. He told the leaders he didn't even want his brother to go with him. He told my father that when he was alone, he would pray. He would pray for the success of the raid and for the safety of the men.

He would have premonitions about things to come and things that would happen that he could visually see in his mind. On these raids, he might have a feeling that, out of a group of thirty Mescaleros, they would lose about ten on the raid. And then sometimes he would get a premonition that the losses would be fifteen or higher in number. He would tell the chief, and the chief would say, "The stakes are too high in the loss of life, so we won't go in that way." So the raiders would take a different route. They valued his judgment. The times he told the leaders that only one person would die during a raid, that's exactly what happened. That's the way he lived with the Mescaleros, and that's how he gained status in the tribe—by being so accurate with his forecast.

Not only was he accurate with his forecasts, but he had a healing power. He told my father that he could heal people. He could look at a person who had a gunshot wound and could tell right off if that person was going to die or if he had a chance to live. If he had a chance to live, then Chevato could heal him. That's the way it was, and it gave him more respect. It gave Chevato and Dinero more security and safety with the Mescaleros.

§

"The crux of Mescalero religion might be characterized as evangelical or devotional shamanism. It conceived of a universe permeated with supernatural power, which must realize itself through man or not at all. If he were to be long-lived and successful, man had equal need of power. As a result of this dual necessity, power and man met in a mystic experience in which man learned the details of a ceremony and in which power acquired a human representative and advocate."[1] Specific beliefs about power (how to acquire it, how to use it) were held in common by the Chiricahuas, Mescaleros, and Lipan Apaches.[2] Daklugie, son of the Apache chief Juh, described the mystic experience in this way:

> Most Medicine Men acquire Power when they are adolescents. All boys must go alone to the sacred mountains to fast and pray for four days and nights. They can take no food, water or weapon. They have a blanket, but nothing else. Many do not obtain the gift. The few that do attain it in var-

ious ways, usually not until the last night of the ordeal. Then the suppli-
cants may hear a voice, they may see a person, an animal, or even a tree,
plant or stone that is to be their medicine. It talks to them, telling them
what they are to use and how. From that time on, they carry a bit of it in
a small buckskin pouch on a thong around their neck. It is their guide
and their help all their lives.[3]

The ability to receive power through a vision was not limited to young
boys; women could also acquire power in this way. A Lipan story tells of a
woman who had been captured by the Comanches; she escaped and was
trying to get back to her own people when the weather turned wet and
cold. On the trail before her, she saw a hole with a spark of fire coming out.
Looking into the hole, she saw some Prairie-Dog people. She went into the
hole and lived with them for a time, but eventually left to go home to her
own people. "She got back to the camp. She did not tell how she had got
help from the prairie dogs. . . . At first she didn't say anything because she
was hoping that she might get power from Prairie-Dog, that she would
get a vision after she got home. But she never did and so she began to tell
her people what had happened to her."[4]

Power could also be transferred by a shaman to another person without
that person going through a vision process. The key to the transfer was a
thorough knowledge of tribal rituals and traditions. "A person might become a shaman if the owner of a ceremony were willing to teach it to him.
. . . According to Lipan belief, great virtue is attached to the exact duplication of ritual patterns which supernatural helpers [such as Killer-of-Enemies, the Lipan culture hero who taught the first Lipans how to live] have
first established. These have blazed a 'path,' which may be followed with
ease and certain benefit."[5]

The nature of the power being transferred from the supernatural realm
to humankind was of three kinds: "beneficent, neutral, or basically evil. Beneficent power seeks only to cure and protect the Mescalero and searches
for individuals of comparable lofty ideals through whom to operate."[6]
Neutral power could be manipulated by humans for either good or evil.

If manipulated for good, it would then become curative; if manipulated for evil, it would become witchcraft. Supernatural power that was evil was always the power used in witchcraft.

If all things had power and if a person could attain that power through either a vision or through a gift from a shaman, who or what was the ultimate source of all power? All three Apache groups who later found themselves living together on the Mescalero Reservation (the Chiricahuas, Mescaleros, and Lipans) believed in a life-giving creator. The Mescaleros and Chiricahuas called this source Ussen or Yusn; the Lipans called the Creator *yatásetā* or *díatā seta.*[7] The life-giver, however, was a shadowy force, "seldom a source of supernatural power and [rarely] figured in the ordinary ceremonial round."[8]

When Ussen or *yatásetā* is mentioned in Mescalero or Lipan oral histories, it is difficult to know whether the reference is one that has been affected by any late missionary influence. The Lipans had been targets of Catholic missionary efforts in Texas and Mexico since 1750; the Mescaleros in northern Coahuila were exposed to some missionary activity from 1750 to 1800, and the first missionaries to the Mescaleros in New Mexico arrived in 1869. As a general rule, however, in Mescalero or Lipan oral history, when individuals state that they "prayed" during an event, the prayers were, in almost all cases, directed to the personal supernatural power of the individual, rather than to one creating power. It is much more common to find, in Apache oral history, statements and discussions relating to manifestations of power, rather than a human being's relationship with the ultimate power.

The concepts of power, shamanism, and leadership were tightly woven together in Apache thought. The teenage Mescaleros and Lipans who made their way to the top of the mountain, fasting and praying for four days, were seeking to be chosen. Their vision quest lasted four days, because four was the sacred number for both the Mescaleros and Lipans.[9] Those seeking shamanistic power, however, did not climb the mountain as a blank slate, open to an infusion of supernatural power. They had to first have a basic understanding of tribal myths. This knowledge was gained by approaching a shaman, offering a gift of tobacco, and requesting sto-ries of old traditions.[10] Among the Lipans, a man could be selected as chief solely on the basis of his knowledge of tribal myths. "If a man knows the traditions about Killer-of-Enemies and about the eagle, if he knows these two things, he becomes a chief without even being in a fight. . . . Miguel, an old Lipan, told me this."[11]

Once a basic knowledge was gained of tribal myths and traditions (a knowledge that went beyond that gained by all tribal members through regular rituals but a knowledge that was not yet "charged" by an infusion of power), the young man or woman would then be selected to undergo the mountain vision quest. Once on the mountain, the candidate might or might not receive a vision. If a vision was received, as was the case with Chevato, then power was bestowed, giving the young person special "tal-ents" in the area with which the power was associated. Since power was a serious and sacred thing, the individual was to use his or her special "tal-ents" to lead or to benefit the tribe, within his or her special area of ex-pertise. Among the Western Apaches, power manifested itself in the fol-lowing ways:

> Chief Chihuahua had the Power over horses. He could gentle and ride
> the wildest horses. He could heal them of sickness or wounds. I saw him
> cure a horse dying of a rattlesnake bite. . . . And Nana—his Power was
> over ammunition trains and rattlesnakes. Victorio's bravest, such as Kay-
> ennae, might make a raid for bullets and fail. But when Nana, long past
> eighty and crippled, rode all night, he brought back ammunition. . . . Vic-
> torio's sister, Lozen, was famous for her Power. She could locate the en-
> emy and even tell how far away it was.[12]

Among the Mescaleros, one shaman famous for his power was Kahzhan. He had received his power when he was a very young boy; his vision told him that the Mescaleros must return to strict adherence to ancient laws: "They were not to kill one another. They were not to fight other tribes un-less attacked. They were not to get drunk on *tiswin*. And they were to pray to Ussen each day. Especially they were to pray when the sun first broke the darkness."[13] In Kahzhan's case, his power led him to call for a cultural renewal within the tribe.

Sometimes power would manifest itself, but neither the shaman nor the tribe could understand it. The Lipans told a story about this type of misunderstanding:

> The Spotted Wood People [foolish, not-quite human people created before the creation of "real" people] got away from the enemy. They got back to camp. They came together that night. They were making a ceremony. One was working his hands around while he was praying. He had his fingers in a circle. They said, "Friend, what are you doing? It looks as if you are making a hoop with your supernatural power."
>
> Finally, one said, "We'll get up early in the morning and throw him down and then we'll find out what it means."
>
> The one who was making a circle with his hands was being told by his supernatural power that the camp would be encircled during the night. But he couldn't understand what it meant. He was too stupid, so he never found out. The next day the enemy came. The one who said he would throw the shaman down came up last. He threw the shaman down and sat on his breast. He said to the others, "If you had done like this last night, you would have learned what it meant."[14]

Since Chevato's quest was rewarded with a vision, he would have been known as a *gutǫǫl* (the Mescalero term for shaman) or a *téne tés'än* (the Lipan term for shaman).[15] Since Chevato's vision had been of a feline animal, he would have been known as a shaman whose power came through the mountain lion, meaning that he now possessed power in areas associated with a mountain lion, such as agility and the ability to fight in a ferocious manner. "When used against human beings, 'jaguar' or 'mountain lion power' was believed to render them immobile with fright."[16] Chevato would have already known of Lipan myths concerning the mountain lion, such as this tale, which attributes the power of a skillful hunter to the mountain lion:

Mountain-lion had a way of hunting. He came up on a bare hill. He saw some deer at the bottom. He wanted to get them. Finally he came near them. He rolled himself into a ball and rolled down the hill gently. He stopped once and took a rest. Then he started again. He rolled and then rested. He did this three times, all the time keeping the form of a ball. The deer saw that ball come rolling down. They watched it. It looked [strange]. After the third roll, the mountain-lion was only about twenty-five yards from them. Then suddenly Mountain-lion jumped up. In two or three leaps he was among them. Then he got his game.[17]

Once a man or woman received an initial gift of power either from a vision or through instruction, its manifestations could come in many areas. Many became healers, for it was in this role that the person performed his or her primary function within the tribe. Other shamans' power manifested itself in the accuracy of their predictions. The Mescalero shaman Kahzhan always "accompanied Chief Peso on every important raid or hunting trip [because] his predictions never failed."[18] The two areas in which Chevato seems to have been skilled as a shaman were in healing and in forecasting casualties in a raid. He had a wide knowledge of herbal remedies that he tried to pass on to his sons later in his life. Although the Apaches, in general, believed in using blood-letting to alleviate headache, fatigue, or rheumatism,[19] Chevato's beliefs regarding free-flowing blood were specific and different, indicating the possibility that his beliefs had more in common with the Mexican Lipan Apaches than with their Mescalero or Arizona Apache kin. Nineteenth-century folk medicine and modern medicine both recognize the seriousness of free-flowing or spurting arterial blood resulting from a gunshot. Thus Chevato's beliefs regarding blood had a sound foundation in medical fact.

His prowess as a forecaster of war casualties would have been an important asset to the Mescaleros. "Some [shamans] who gained ceremonial knowledge of warfare also gained political influence through this medium."[20] A good example of this fact would be Geronimo; his status within the Chiricahuas was based on his powers as a war shaman, and he only later became a political leader. "A [shaman] for war was taken on a raid whenever possible; he could consult his power on whether to make a certain attack, and where the safest camping places were."[21] Although Herman Lehmann states that Chevato later became a chief in the Mescalero band, this fact is not borne out by Mescalero Agency records.[22] Chevato's powers as a forecaster, while used by the Mescalero chiefs in their decision-making process, never earned him a place in the Mescalero political leadership. However, the powers that Chevato received from his vision quest assured him a place of respect in Mescalero society.

5. The Blackbirds

I was told this story by my father, in order to illustrate the mystic ways of that time. Chevato and Dinero were down in Mexico with a Mescalero raiding party. The raiding party was about fifteen men, and they were camped at a site that had some small rolling hills with a small stream running down in a little valley. They were eating supper and it was just about the time of day when the sun goes down, but they still had a little bit of light. On the other side of the hills, they heard some people talking in their own language. They were carrying on a conversation as if they were in their camp. Chevato and the raiding party were at such a distance that they couldn't make out what the people were saying, but every now and then, they would pick up a name that was being called out.

The raiding party told my grandfather, "Hey, the rest of the camp is just right over the hill. They must have followed us." But Chevato had this uneasy feeling and told them, "No, don't go there. Just forget about it, because it is not what you think." They didn't believe him, and he continued to plead with them, "Don't go over the hill and look." But since they thought that home was right over the hill, they went over the hill to look anyway.

When they got to the crest of the hill, and looked down in the valley where they were supposed to see their families, there was nothing but a big flock of blackbirds sitting on the ground. The birds were just eating and talking their language, their own squabbles. When the raiding party crested the hill, they heard no more of their native tongue and saw only big blackbirds. So, they came back down the hill to where Chevato was and asked him, "Is that why you didn't want us to go up on the hill?" He answered, "Yes, that was the reason. Now, that was an omen. The names of the people that you heard—if you hadn't gone to the hill, it would have been nothing. But now, when we go back home, we have to prepare ourselves, because whatever good or whatever bad is going to happen to these people, you have to understand and grasp it."

So they continued on their way, and after many days, they got back to their village. Sure enough, their village had sustained a raid by another tribe, and these people, about five or six names that had been called by the blackbirds, these people were killed in that raid.

There was a mystic part to living in those days, and there were mystic qualities floating in the air. That's why I was so fascinated to hear the stories of my grandfather and the way they lived back then.

§

For the Mescalero or Lipan shaman, the entire natural world around him was filled with animals and plants imbued with power that could be used to warn or used to assist him. His entire world was a circle oriented in space by four sacred directions and their corresponding sacred colors. The Lipan color/directional pattern associated east with the color black, south with the color blue, west with the color yellow, and north with the color white.[1] Because the shaman respected all aspects of the physical world, it was important that he be aware of animals and birds that possessed evil powers, as well as animals and birds that possessed powers helpful to people. For the Lipan shaman, in particular, this awareness was gained through knowledge of myths.

One animal feared by most Mescaleros was the bear, which, it was believed, could pass bear-sickness to humans through contact. The Western Apaches, Chiricahuas, and Mescaleros did not eat bear meat, avoided their lairs and droppings, and thought that bear odor was offensive.[2] The Lipans, on the other hand, did not fear the bear; they ate bear meat and "did not have a supernatural fear of it."[3] In fact, the Lipans had a myth that turned the Mescalero fear of bear odor on its head; the Lipans' bear story had the bear considering human odor to be offensive:

[This story] happened in recent times and around here [i.e., New Mexico]. It happened among the Northern Lipan [i.e., the Lipans who lived in New Mexico]. A certain woman had been captured by the Mexicans and was a prisoner. She escaped. She came back to her own country. But she could not find the camps of her people. It was getting cold, so she went into a cave. This happened to be a cave used by bears.

She entered the cave. She found two cubs there. She picked up one of them. They were frightened at first, but they saw that they couldn't get away. When she picked up one of them, the other one began to cry. Then she got both of them and held them in her lap. She smoothed down their fur and said, "What soft fur!"

Then the woman asked, "Where is your mother?"

"She's out in the hills somewhere, hunting something to eat. She'll be back when it starts to rain a little."

The mother bear returned. She smelled something she didn't like. She began to growl, "I smell something bad which should not be around here."

The children said, "This woman came in and she likes us and we like her. She rubbed our fur and petted us. We are here with her."

The mother bear said, "I don't want this woman to be around here any longer."

But the children wanted her to stay. So the woman spent about a month there.

Their mother said, "I'll not do anything more till their father comes. Let him settle it as he wishes." She didn't go near her children. She sat with her back to the cubs, who sat with the woman.

The father bear came in then. He said, when he was told about the woman, "Get yucca roots, make a suds, and wash the bodies of these children of ours." The mother bear did what her husband told her to do. The father bear said, "I'll go out and search for the camp of this woman." [The father bear searched and finally found the woman's camp.] Bear gave the woman a water bag. Bear told her to go over certain mesas and to take the whole day for the journey.

She started out. She was afraid the bear would come after her, kill her and eat her. She kept looking back. But it never followed her. She traveled till sundown. She fell asleep under a tree. It happened to be a tree that crows roosted in. She saw the crows come there. They filled the tree. They began to talk . . . telling stories to each other about what they had seen.

One said, "Tomorrow we must go over that gap. Right there is where the people have been butchering those buffalos."

The woman spoke up. She said, "Are all you people telling the truth? I want to follow you. I want you to show me the way home." She got up early the next morning [and followed the crows]. . . . In that way she got back.[4]

While the Lipans did not view the bear in the same manner as the Mescaleros, both tribes had similar fears of certain birds. The owl was considered to be "closely associated with ghosts. Hearing an owl was interpreted to mean that the ghost of a deceased relative—possibly bent upon causing sickness—was close at hand."[5] The Lipans also associated the raven with death, as can be seen in their myth regarding the origin of death:

In the beginning of the world, when the animal people were created, when trees and grass and animals and birds were people, everything was going along well. It went along until the middle of time. There was no death. They began to talk about it. Some said it would be best to have death. Others were against it. . . . Raven was the one who said, "I want death to exist. . . ."

All the birds and animals started to argue. The appointed Raven to be their leader and judge the question. They said, "We want to make a certain rule. If you are willing, it will be this way."

"Well, what is it you want to happen?"

"We desire that, if someone dies, he will come back to life in four days."

Then Raven said, "No. If someone dies, why should he come back in four days? Let him be gone forever. . . ."

A few days later, Raven lost one of his children. He went around and gathered all the people together. He said to them, "Let me tell you something. You people had an argument a few days ago. You wanted to have people come to life four days after death. Now my child has died. I want it the way you said."

"No," the others told him. "You made the rule. Now let your child remain dead." Then Raven cried. He tore off his clothes and stayed half naked. He cut his hair. Now the Lipan do these things.

The owl said to the Raven, "You are the one who made the rule. You are the one who threw away your own child. You look poor now. You are ragged. But it is your own fault. There is no use for you to cry. I'll bury that body and I'll take care of the body after death."[6]

The Mescalero and Lipan association of the owl with death was also extended to the realm of the supernatural, with both tribes believing that some dead persons, "especially dead sorcerers," turned into owls at the moment of their death.[7]

While the Mescaleros and Lipans had similar beliefs regarding death, the afterlife, and ghosts, the Lipans diverged from the Mescaleros in their beliefs regarding the composition of ghosts and the landscape of the afterlife. The Lipan term for ghost, *vakoc*, referred only to the corporeal body of the deceased. They made a distinction between the body of the deceased person and the spirit, or breath, of the deceased (only the spirit of the deceased went to the underworld). The Mescaleros did not make this distinction.[8] To the Lipans, the underworld was divided into two parts—north and south. The spirits of sorcerers inhabited one part of the underworld; the other part was inhabited by the spirits of good people. "Fire and fog harass the wicked, and snakes and lizards are their only food."[9]

Since in Lipan myth the raven had brought death to the world, that bird was associated with evil powers. As can be seen from the Lipan story of the woman and the bears, the crow was also associated with an animal with which contact carried some stigma. Yet the crow did not carry the same association for the Lipans as did the raven. Because of the crow's interest in an animal carcass, the crow was also associated with the hunt, and a hunter would always leave a small portion of the butchered animal for the crows to eat.[10]

Chevato's story, as passed down to his grandson, uses the word "blackbirds." It is unclear whether the birds he was referring to were crows or ravens; the word probably originally referred to birds whose color was black. Since the Mescaleros, however, also believed that "black birds, particularly ravens, [were] considered birds of ill omen by those who [did] not have supernatural power from them,"[11] the rest of the raiding party would have been familiar with Chevato's usage. Chevato's warning called to mind the evil characteristics of the raven and its association with death. The raven association, as well as the accuracy of Chevato's forecast, was borne out by later events, once the raiding party returned home.

6. Chevato and Dinero Leave the Bandits

Chevato and Dinero moved back and forth between the Mescaleros and the bandits for some time. When they were with the bandits, they would steal cattle in the United States and take them into Mexico to sell. One day, they had a lot of cattle, and they had just crossed the Rio Grande into Mexico, headed toward Zaragosa, where they were going to sell them in the market. On the way, they met this fellow who had a small two-room house. Adjacent to the house was a small corral with a few head of cattle, some horses, and a shed for his livestock. This fellow was sitting on the corral fence when the bandits got there. The bandit leader asked the man what the price of the cattle was like in the nearby exchange. The man said, "Not very good." The name of the man sitting on the fence was Mr. Rodriguez.

The bandit leader was a pretty smart fellow in the ways of money, so he asked Rodriguez if he was willing to go as partners and keep the bandits' cattle. When the price had risen, Rodriguez would sell the cattle, and then the bandit leader would come and get his money. Rodriguez said, "What's in it for me?" The leader said, "A percentage," and they agreed on a percentage and struck up a partnership.

In leaving, the leader of the bandits went to Mr. Rodriguez and said in front of everybody, "We entered into a deal, and we shook hands on it. If you ever double cross me, not give me my money, we'll come back and make your life miserable." Mr. Rodriguez said, "No, don't worry about that. We have business. As long as you treat me fair, I'll treat you fair."

So the bandits kept doing things like that with Mr. Rodriguez, and Mr. Rodriguez prospered. He grew into a fairly rich man and became legitimate, like many businesses that started off with illegal activities but ended up legitimate. Mr. Rodriguez also became a lifelong friend of Chevato. Even after Mr. Rodriguez had become a rich man, he never forgot his friendships from the early days. Chevato would, in his later years, go to visit Mr. Rodriguez, and Mr. Rodriguez would always extend the hospitality of his home and treat Chevato as if he were a family member.

One day, Dinero got my grandfather into trouble with the bandits. Impressed with the powers Chevato had received from his vision quest, Dinero had bragged to the bandits that Chevato could do extraordinary things. He said that Chevato could walk on the local molino (a large sheet of metal that was heated), where they baked their bread in the morning. He could walk barefooted on the metal sheet that was red hot, and he would not burn his feet. Dinero had even pledged and taken bets that my grandfather could do this thing.

When Chevato heard what Dinero had done, he had a bad feeling. He knew that he shouldn't use his power in this way. It would be his utter destruction to use his power to show off, while others made bets. But he also had to weigh in his mind the fact that Dinero's life would be in the balance if he were to refuse. Being a religious person, he went to pray. He came to the conclusion that he should admonish Dinero, tell him that he must never tell *others about his powers, but that he should also walk on the molino to save his brother's life. He did admonish Dinero and also told him that he could not take the money he had wagered. This didn't sit well with Dinero, but he soon realized that their lives hung in the balance.*

So Chevato did what Dinero had requested. He took an eagle feather and brushed it underneath each foot, touching the bottom of the foot. He said a prayer and then got on the metal sheet. He walked across the molino, turned around and walked back, and it didn't burn his feet. And Dinero's life was spared.

While Dinero had learned his lesson, word still got out with the bandits that my grandfather had extraordinary powers. One day, the bandits made a wager based on something that Dinero had told them. Dinero had said that if Chevato were ever shot, and did not see his own blood at the moment after the skin was pierced, then all he had to do was say a prayer and nothing would come of it. Chevato wouldn't be wounded, nor would there be any blood, just the hole in his clothes where the bullet went through. Dinero had told the bandits that Chevato was bullet-proof.

When Chevato heard of this second boast of Dinero's, and heard that he had bet money on this, he scorned Dinero. Dinero explained that he had told the bandits about the power to overcome a bullet wound a long time before the molino incident, but my grandfather still refused to help. He refused to help Dinero win the bet, and they left the bandits, crossed the Rio Grande, and headed home to the Mescaleros.

§

The life of Mr. Rodriguez was intertwined with that of Chevato from their first meeting. Rodriguez had an interesting history after his first brush with the bandits. As he gained in wealth, he eventually bought land near Zaragosa that was known as Hacienda Patiño, the site of the Lipan settlement into which Chevato had been born in 1852. The hacienda had been in existence since at least the early 1800s and probably much earlier. The current owner, Epigmenio Rodriguez, states that "in 1842, the hacienda had fifty families. They grew crops, raised cattle and horses and had a commerce going with the United States."[1] A band of Cherokees had, in 1839, fled across the Rio Grande into Mexico, where they had been given amnesty and settled near Zaragosa. In 1842 the Cherokee chief Sequoyah, who had invented a written language for his tribe, arrived in Mexico after fleeing Texas militiamen. The Texans pursued Sequoyah into Mexico, capturing him and taking him back to the border, where he escaped and returned to the Zaragosa area, finding refuge on the Hacienda Patiño. He died there in 1842, and a small remnant of Cherokees continued to live in the area. Epigmenio Rodriguez states that his family "traded corn, beans and sugar for Cherokee horses. They had the best horses in all of the region."[2]

The Hacienda Patiño and much of northern Coahuila were generally congenial areas for Indian settlement since the area saw, at one time or another, settlement by Cherokee, Lipan, Mescalero, Seminole, Pottawatomie, and Kickapoo bands. The Lipans and Mescaleros had been camping and hunting in the area since at least 1750; the other tribes arrived a century later. One reason the Lipans stubbornly chose to stay near Zaragosa was because of a natural feature of the region—the Lomerío de Peyotes. Located west of Zaragosa, the Lomerío was a hilly region where peyote cacti grew in abundance. The Western Lipans had been using peyote in their religious ceremonies since at least the 1780s, and as the Lipans were dispersed out of Coahuila and into New Mexico, they brought with them their special peyote rituals.[3] The Lipan peyote meeting was the one ceremony that they shared with outsiders, and it was the ceremony by which they were most generally known by outsiders.[4] Since peyote can only be found in a limited number of areas within the borders of the United States, the Lomerío and other similar areas in northern Coahuila assumed great importance once the Lipans had been forced out.[5]

Throughout his life Chevato considered Mr. Rodriguez a close friend, taking the train from Oklahoma to visit with him annually in his older years. One reason for the visits would have been to gather peyote; Chevato and other Lipan "peyote singers" had introduced peyote to the Comanches after 1875, and they needed to replenish their supply, since each peyote ceremony could consume up to forty of the small cacti buttons. Yet Chevato always spoke of Hacienda Patiño with the affection one uses when speaking of home. Today, the hacienda is known as Hacienda Patiños-Rodriguez-Salinas and in 2001 was declared an Indigenous People's area by the governor of the state of Coahuila.[6]

7. The Thirty-two Burros

This story happened on one of the tributaries of the Brazos River in Texas. Chevato was with the Mescaleros, and they were on a raid. At that time, game was not plentiful and they didn't have any food. They were on the Brazos River when they spotted a group of Mexicanos, Mexican men, leading thirty-two burros. I remember the number distinctly. The burros had packs on their backs, and the men were walking, leading the burros. At this time, Chevato and the Mescaleros on the raiding party hadn't had anything to eat, and they were very hungry. So they made plans to attack the Mexican transport. They made the attack on them, and they killed all of the Mexican men leading the burros. What they were interested in was the meat of the burros, but when they started looking into the packs, they found gold bars. In each pack were just enough gold bars, placed in the packs so that they wouldn't weigh down the animals. The packs were like large saddlebags and hung on each side of the burro. They had equal numbers of gold bars on each side to balance the weight, but I don't know exactly how many gold bars.

My grandfather said there was a tributary stream going up from the Brazos River. Around the tributary were clustered mesquite trees and caminado, and it was very difficult to see to the bottom of the draw where the tributary ran. That's where they threw the bodies. And then they took the packs off of the thirty-two burros and threw them into the ravine. They killed what they needed and turned the rest of the burros loose.

This is the story my grandfather told my father. Now, the story leaked out one time, when I was about sixteen, and a group of men (some of them distant relatives of my mother) came to our home between Cache and India-

homa, Oklahoma. They had aerial photographs with them of the part of the Brazos River where they thought the tributary was. They pleaded with my father and tried to get more information out of him, but he just told them generally what he had been told. He had no idea where the Brazos River was, where the tributary was, or where his father had thrown the gold bars. It was always a big story around our area of southwest Oklahoma—the story of the gold bars—and I think these men did make a run down to the Brazos to look for the gold. But they never found it.

§

Herman Lehmann also described finding a gold mine in his book, *Nine Years among the Indians*. He stated that Carnoviste, his captor, had decided that the Apache band must find new lands, because their area near Mescalero was being encroached upon by increasing numbers of white settlers. Herman, Esacona (a Mescalero who had been among the raiding party that had kidnapped Herman), and Pinero (Chevato's brother, Dinero, but Herman uses the Comanche form of his name) were sent to find this new territory. After traveling into Mexico, the small group headed north and found what they believed to be the perfect spot high in the mountains of Arizona; at least, Herman believed they were in Arizona. While exploring the area, Herman says that they found outcroppings of gold ore; they each dug out some ore with their knives to take home to their wives or girlfriends. After returning to Mescalero, they told Carnoviste of their find. His reaction, however, was not what they had hoped. Carnoviste told them "that inviting region was not for the Indian, that it would prove a delusion and a snare, and if we went there, it would only increase our troubles, and we gave up all hope of ever finding a land where the white man would not come."[1]

Perhaps Carnoviste's reaction had more to do with the fact that he was an Apache, rather than his view of Indian land issues. Dan Nicholas, a Chiricahua Apache, made the following statement in an oral interview: "One of the most scrupulously observed taboos among Apaches is one regarding gold. Strangely, it seems to have escaped the attention of anthropologists. An Apache may pick up nuggets from the dry bed of a stream but he is forbidden to 'grub in Mother Earth' for it. It is the symbol of the sun and hence sacred to *Ussen*. I have never seen an Apache wear anything made of gold."[2]

Stories of buried or lost gold have always been popular, particularly so in the early part of the twentieth century. Southwestern folklorist J. Frank Dobie's *Apache Gold and Yaqui Silver* is a collection of such tales.[3] In many of these folktales, the search for lost gold becomes a search for an Eden, a lost paradise, or, in Herman Lehmann's case, for a land free of white settlement. Chevato's story is not a metaphor of a search for perfection, but it does pose more questions than it answers. Why would a group of Mexican traders be carrying such a large amount of gold bars?

Before running out the door with a map and a metal detector, pause to consider the following information: the Brazos River has its headwaters in eastern New Mexico and western Texas. It runs almost completely across Texas, with a total course of 1,280 miles, and drains an area of about 45,600 square miles.[4]

8. The Amnesty

My grandfather would have times when he wanted to be alone, away from the Mescaleros, so he would go down to the border at what is now Eagle Pass and Piedras Negras. He would go there and look across the water toward Zaragosa, would look toward home. But he was told that he and his brother were wanted men in Mexico, so he couldn't go home.

Chevato would go to the river, sit there, and look across and get homesick. One day, while he was doing this, he felt little regard for his own life. The urge to go home was stronger than the fear of losing his life, so he got on his horse and he went to Zaragosa.

On getting to Zaragosa, he knew that if he didn't report himself in, they would come looking for him once they found out he was in the area. So he went to the provost marshal, which from my understanding was an army major.

His last name was Ortiz. Chevato turned himself in and told them who he was. They checked and, sure enough, found out that he was a wanted man. Chevato told Ortiz his story about how he had lost his parents, and this officer had some compassion.

In my time in the military, I have met officers that were very cold and callous, where duty came first. But every now and then, you would meet an officer who had compassion. They also cared about duty and getting their job done, but they also had compassion. This Ortiz was such a man. He had compassion on my grandfather; from their talks, he knew my grandfather was not such a bad person. Ortiz went to Mexico City on Chevato's behalf and got an amnesty for him and for Dinero. That allowed them to go back to Zaragosa, and they were quite happy about that. From then on, Chevato never committed any kind of crimes in Mexico. He found out the value of going back to Mexico, his home, so when he went to Mexico, he was an upright citizen.

We talk freely about things that are illegal to do today. Stealing from one person, taking things, which is contrary to my religious belief. But the way my grandfather put it, when talking to his older sons many years later—he said, "I want to tell you how to live in your society. Your ways of life and my way of life are completely different. You have new rules and laws to live by in your life that were not there when I was your age. In my time, as a man, you could have a family, you could have a wife, you could have property. But in my time, you had to be a man to hold onto it.

"If a person came along, or a group of people came along, and decided that they wanted your land, they could take it from you. If they decided they wanted your cattle, they could take them from you. And if they decided they wanted your children, they could take them from you. If they decided they wanted your wife, they could take her and leave you standing by yourself."

Now, that was the rule set forth in the frontier days. So the people back then thought, "Well, I want this," and if you could not protect yourself, then it was your fault. That is largely why, I think, they took from one another, they stole from one another. Because there was no law, the ideology was survival of the fittest. If you weren't strong enough, you didn't survive. So, this is what my grandfather told my father and his brothers when they were about twelve or thirteen years old. And my father and his brothers understood this, and they all lived to be good citizens. But they also knew how their father had lived. At times, he said he wasn't proud of the things he had done, but he had done them to survive.

Chevato always wanted for his children something better. He always wanted something better for his grandchildren. In fact, my grandfather was so much in love with Mexico that, even though he had his family and his children in the United States, he told my father, "Don't you ever forget to tell your children who I am, what I was, and where I came from. And tell them that I loved Mexico and that is a part of their life, even though we now all live in the United States."

Part Two

Herman Lehmann and
Quanah Parker

9. The Capture of Herman Lehmann

Chevato and Dinero were with a Mescalero raiding party coming back out of Mexico and headed home to the Mescalero stronghold in New Mexico. They took the old smugglers' route, crossing the Rio Grande at Eagle Pass, Texas, and heading northeast through Uvalde County, turning north through Bandera County, stealing more horses along the way. They continued north, skirting Fredericksburg. They knew they were being chased by the Texas Cavalry, but they didn't have much fear of them.

The Mescaleros had ways to escape the cavalry troops. They would leave strings of horses at secluded watering holes, pricking the quicks of their hooves just enough to lame them a little so the horses wouldn't wander away from the water. As the horse's hoof healed, it would get used to the water and the grass and stay there, ready for the Mescaleros to come back. As the raiding party moved north, and their horses tired out from the chase, they would find fresh horses hidden at the watering hole, change mounts, and move on, always a step ahead of the cavalry. The Mescaleros feared the Texas Rangers because they were quick and unpredictable, but they never feared the cavalry troops because they were slow.

The captain of Chevato's and Dinero's raiding party was Carnoviste. He was a pretty cruel man. Chevato and Dinero didn't call him Carnoviste—they called him The Wolf. They called him this because he was like a wolf, conniving in many ways. He was all for himself; he was very much a "me" man. Before he captured Herman Lehmann, Carnoviste wasn't hated by the Mescaleros, but people were scared of him, and so that is why he existed.

The raiding party had been successful, and they had stolen many horses. They stopped to rest their mounts on a ridge overlooking a small stream. When they looked down over the ridge, they saw a small cabin on the other side of the stream. The cabin was in a field surrounded by a rock fence, and there were children playing in the field. Carnoviste told the raiding party, "I want one of those children." Chevato and Dinero looked at each other. They saw no need to steal a child because the raiding party was fat as a tick with stolen horses. But Carnoviste was the leader, so they silently rode down from the ridge and crossed the stream. When they grabbed the two boys, the girl tried to get away by crawling through a hole under the rock wall, so they left her behind and rode off with the boys. the boys were Herman Lehmann and his brother, Willie, and Carnoviste took Herman for himself.

Carnoviste (The Wolf) thought to discipline Herman when they got him and they were away from Herman's home; he thought that beating was the best way. He wanted to teach him discipline, but they had no communications, they couldn't understand each other. He beat Herman pretty bad, beat him up, and then tied him to a log on hard ground when they were sleeping. So Chevato told Carnoviste, "Why did you get this young boy? If you're going to treat him that way, he's going to die." There was no sense in capturing him if Carnoviste was going to treat him that way, since he would die. So Carnoviste told Chevato, "If you want to help him, go ahead. I'm not going to help." Chevato then said, "When you tie him up, let's find a better place to lay him. Or at least let's lay him in some sand instead of on the hard ground."

One of the favorite tricks of the Mescaleros, if you were a captive, was to tie your wrists to wrists and ankles to ankles. Then, through the opening of your arms and legs, they would run a long pole. They would then put this pole in the notches of two saplings or young trees and tie it down with rawhide so it was like a lock. Chevato would get some bedding, like leaves or grass, and make Herman a little bed to lie on when he was tied up at night. It wasn't much better, but it was better than the hard ground. When they were near creek beds and Carnoviste would tie Herman to a small tree, Chevato made sure that Herman was lying in sand.

There was also an old way that Chevato knew to make a salve that he used on Herman's body. Carnoviste had stripped Herman Lehmann naked and made him ride a horse. It was spring, and in the Texas sun, it could be almost death for a fair-skinned Anglo. So Chevato did that for Herman Lehmann; he made and put a salve on his blisters.

When they came upon an animal, or when they killed and ate their game, Carnoviste made it seem to Herman that this was what the Mescalero ate every *day. But it was just the hatred Carnoviste had, then he would rub the entrails of the calf or antelope over Herman's face. Chevato, after washing Herman's face off, would give him some regular, good meat to eat. He helped Herman out. And Herman became quite sick when he felt that he would have to eat that kind of diet—raw, bloody meat. But it is the custom with the Indians, if you are sick to your stomach, blood will settle it. That is true. But Carnoviste acted more out of hatred when he did these things to Herman.*

Chevato didn't understand why Carnoviste took Herman in the first place if he was going to treat Herman so badly. Chevato did what he could, without getting himself into trouble. In the hierarchy of the raiding system, the person who organized the raid (Carnoviste) would be in today's terms like a captain. My grandfather would be like a sergeant. You couldn't override the man's seniority or his authority, but you could, if you had a desire to help someone who was a captive, you could go the extra mile. You could act as a go-between to make the captured individual's life a little more bearable. And this is what Chevato did, and this is why Herman Lehmann liked my grandfather—he basically saved Herman's life.

Chevato was not present when Carnoviste was killed, but there has been a lot of controversy that he was killed by some of his own men.

§

For the German and Anglo settlers of central Texas, the years from 1865 to 1871 were punctuated with sudden, terrifying incidents of Indian abductions. During this time, raiding parties of Comanches and Mescalero Apaches were stealing horses with increasing frequency and with relative impunity, but horses could be replaced. It was the random capture of children that brought terror to the Hill Country. In June 1865 the Comanches abducted Rudolph Fischer, son of Gottlieb Fischer of Fredericksburg. In 1866 Lipan Apaches kidnapped eleven-year-old Frank Buckelew from Bandera County; galloping for the Rio Grande, they crossed with their captive into Mexico. In 1867 the Apaches took a young boy named Temple Friend from Llano County; he was traded to the Comanches soon after his abduction. On New Year's Day, 1870, ten-year-old Adolph Korn (or

Kohn) was kidnapped while out tending his family's flock of sheep near San Antonio.[1] The Texas secretary of state, James P. Newcomb, wrote to the commissioner of Indian Affairs that "the father of the Child [Korn] was a loyal citizen throughout the late war and suffered misfortune in consequence and now . . . is bereft of a child by a band of savages."[2] On February 27, 1870, Dorothy Field vanished from Menard County; her family frantically offered a $750 reward payable in gold for her "safe delivery at any point in the United States."[3] One year later, in February 1871, Clinton Smith (age eleven) and his brother Jeff (age nine) were captured near their house on Cibolo Creek, twenty miles north of San Antonio. Their mother watched in horror as a group of about a dozen men, dressed in western attire rather than in Indian garb, rode up to the homestead. Instead of approaching the house, however, the riders began chasing her two sons. The boys, realizing that they were too far away from the house to seek safety from that quarter, sprinted toward the creek bed, the group of strangers in hot pursuit. By the time their mother reached the creek bed, no trace of the boys could be found.

The parents of Clint and Jeff Smith wrote a heartbreaking series of letters to authorities both in Texas and Oklahoma seeking help in finding their sons. Indeed, all of the families of the abducted made every effort possible to enlist the aid of the military and the Indian agencies in recovering their loved ones. The raw pain still cries out from their petitions. Henry M. Smith, in writing to Laurie Tatum, the Indian agent at Ft. Sill, Oklahoma, pleaded, "I beg, aye, pray you, in the name of humanity and the sufferings of my poor children to exert yourself to the utmost of your power and ability, to get them back for me, from these merciless, inhuman creatures."[4] Another letter mentions the most mundane of details in the hopes of aiding in the identification of the boys: "the children had some playthings in their pockets—some old cards and marbles."[5]

Adding to the difficulty in locating the abducted children was the fact that it was impossible, in most instances, to identify to which tribe the abductors belonged because, in all cases where correspondence has survived to describe the events of those terrible days, the abductors were wearing western apparel or military coats, and no items that would indicate tribal affiliation were visible. In addition, the abductions usually happened so quickly that by the time the family had time to gather their senses, the raiding party would be several miles away, carrying a captive who was still in a state of shock. Most families believed that either the Comanches or Kiowas had abducted their loved ones. This was a reasonable assumption, since both tribes had cultural norms that included the capture and integration of children.[6] In the opinion of the Texas Rangers who had tracked the captors of the Smith brothers, the abductors were Comanches or perhaps Kickapoos. In actuality, a raiding party that combined both Lipan Apaches and Comanches had taken the brothers.[7]

There would be one additional abduction in central Texas in 1870, made in the richness of spring at a time when the bluebonnets were just giving way to the Indian paintbrush, a time of the year when yellow coreopsis would blanket the clearings between the oak trees. This time the raiders would try to capture three children.

By the spring of 1870 Indian raids had increased in central and south Texas to such a point that no one who owned a horse felt safe. The following letter to the editor of the *San Antonio Daily Herald* was typical of the frustration felt by many. Dated April 21, 1870, and written from Boerne, Texas (about fifteen miles west of where the Smith brothers would be captured a year later), J. G. O'Grady wrote:

> We had a visit last night from our red brothers. One of my horses ran home this morning with an arrow, very elaborately manufactured, sticking in his jaw. The people are out to ascertain the extent of damages. This is merely an item of news, not a complaint, as the time has passed with us when we were deluded by thinking that there was something to be expected from a tale of our misfortune and losses. So much for our hopes of protection.[8]

The *Daily Herald* editor replied with an editorial dated April 23, 1870, and titled "The Moon and the Indians Again":

On Saturday night last, the Indians made their regular monthly raid into the settlements directly South and West of San Antonio. . . . Were it not for our politically sensitive State and Central Government officials, and the tiptoe balancing condition of our national credit abroad, our citizens, say two hundred and fifty of them, well armed, could match this Mexican Indian murdering and horse stealing game, in about ten days—including nights. Five hundred mounted men, armed with one Remington rifle, two army six-shooters and a Bowie knife each, should proceed across the Rio Grande into Mexico. Let two hundred and fifty bivouac on the west bank, and the same number proceed into the interior, and collect up all the horses in the brands of our citizens, and then return with them. In ten days, 100,000 head could be collected, and no houses or mills burned—Sherman-like—and no sick women and papooses butchered after the order of Sheridan—but all will be done quietly but effectually.

But great Gods, it would never do. The Legislature would stampede and break for Washington. Congress would break up and perhaps secede the South again, and order out an army of 150,000 men this time, and for 120 days. Government bonds in Europe would "drop," and our Government explode. The first telegraphic dispatch to Washington would have it that fifty thousand rebels were in arms in Texas, and marching on Washington, of course. So our people had better hold up a little while longer, and have their wives and children murdered and scalped, and let Mexico have what few remain of our horses. In times like these, it is far better that our good citizens should sacrifice their lives and property for the Government, especially since that Government has of late been so good to them.[9]

The Apaches made a marked distinction between raiding and warfare. In the language of the Western Apaches, the word for raiding ("to search out enemy property") and the word for warfare ("to take death from an enemy") reveal their view of the two separate activities.[10] Warfare was an overt act that had, as its main goal, the avenging of "the death of a kinsman who at some earlier time had lost his life in battle."[11] War parties were composed of up to 200 men from a number of different groups, under the leadership of a single leader and accompanied by a favored shaman. A war party was called together by the relatives of the slain man for the purpose of revenge, and their targets tended to be the town or settlement where the kinsman had been killed. The return of a victorious war party was celebrated with a dance "and, if adult captives had been taken, with their torture and eventual execution by close female relatives of the warrior whose death the party had been sent to avenge."[12]

An Apache raid, on the other hand, was a covert act usually executed by a single local group. Any warrior could step forward to lead a raiding party (status as chief was not required to lead a raid), but the warrior would then have to exhibit the leadership necessary to organize and conduct the raid in such a manner that the group returned with enough booty to meet the needs of the band. After 1860 Mescalero raiders would have sought enough booty (cattle and horses) not only to meet the needs of their group but also to trade for flour, cornmeal, guns, ammunition, and whisky.[13] For Mescalero raiding parties traveling to Coahuila via Texas, the stolen cattle and horses could have been conveniently traded to Hispanic traders or Comanches at Muchoque, a trading spot located north of the Concho River in Texas (the present-day site is near the town of Gail, Borden County, Texas).[14] In addition to Muchoque, Hispanic traders also came directly to the Mescalero camps in New Mexico.[15]

Mescalero raiding parties were made up of from five to fifteen men, since speed and concealment were necessary for success. Once in enemy territory, "the pace quickened, special measures for concealment were taken, and a number of taboos went into effect, including the use of a special 'warpath language.' More than anything else . . . Apache raiders were anxious to avoid armed conflict—not out of fear, but because it would reveal their position and numbers, alert the enemy for miles around, and increase the chances of being intercepted on the way home."[16] They avoided large settlements, preferring to raid in outlying areas. If confronted by army cavalry, Texas Rangers, or groups of settlers, they would race for cover, pushing their stolen horses ahead of them. Then they would split into two groups. One group would circle back to direct sniper fire at the pursuers, while the other group, still herding what horses remained, would seek a safe haven until they could be rejoined by the rest of the raiding party.

A raid into Mexico after 1860, for example, could entail horses or cattle, or both, being stolen along the route and driven either to a trading spot such as Muchoque or driven into Mexico to be sold or traded across the border. On the return trip to Mescalero, the raiding party would also steal livestock. Since speed was often of the essence, the Mescaleros tended to steal horses, since they could be driven more quickly and traded to the Comanches if no Hispanic traders were nearby. Cattle were generally stolen if the site of the theft was near a trading area, since cattle were more difficult to herd in a quick and stealthy manner. The general effect was to leave Texas cattle ranchers along the Staked Plains and north-central Texas at the mercy not only of the Comanche but also the Mescalero raiding parties. Mescalero cattle thefts were sometimes undertaken on a grand scale. At one point Mescalero raiders threatened to steal the entire army beef herd being driven from Texas to New Mexico.[17] The ranchers of south-central Texas, while owning cattle, generally found their horse herds at risk of being stolen in the night by Comanche, Mescalero, Lipan, or Kickapoo raiders.

The general Mescalero philosophy regarding booty stolen during a raid was applied equally, regardless of whether the booty was stolen livestock or stolen children. The grandson of the Mescalero chief Natzili, in speaking of raids into Mexico, expressed the philosophy clearly:

[The Mexicans] knew that if the Indians met with no resistance and got a good supply of mounts, they would not disturb the "hacienda" or its inhabitants. The Indians preferred to let the cooperative Mexicans live in order to provide them with future supplies of horses. If the Mexicans were uncooperative or too poor to cooperate, the Indians stole their women and children. If the boys were young enough, they could make warriors of them. The little girls were also important because Apaches usually spaced their children from four to five years apart and the tribe did not increase rapidly.[18]

88

In other words, the Mescaleros had determined to raid the hacienda, and they were not going to go home empty-handed. What was not mentioned were the many other Mexican children stolen on raids for use as slaves or trade goods. If the raiding party happened to capture a child, woman, or particularly large number of horses or mules either on their way to Mexico or on the return trip to Mescalero, a small detachment of men would be assigned to take the hostages or animals directly to Mescalero, leaving the rest of the raiding party free to continue on.

Led by Carnoviste, the raiding party that abducted Herman Lehmann in May 1870 was composed of eight to twelve men. Chevato and his brother, Dinero, were included in this group, along with two other Mescalero Apaches known as Palle and Esacona.[19] It is unknown what route they took to get to Mexico. It is possible that they followed the same "Mescalero Trail" to Texas that they rode on their return home. This trail ran east from the Mescalero stronghold at Sierra Blanca in New Mexico, crossed the Pecos River, and continued into Texas. Crossing the Staked Plains, they would continue southeast, sneaking past Ft. Concho and continuing on until they reached the San Saba or Llano River. At this point they would turn south and skirt the settlement of Fredericksburg. Still heading south, they would ride down through Bandera County, turning slightly southwest toward Uvalde County. Here the Mescaleros would be about fifty miles west of San Antonio in areas watered by the upper Medina, Frio, and Nueces rivers—the area that comprised the old Lipan heartland. Crossing the Rio Grande near Eagle Pass, they would head into Coahuila to sell their horses to Mexican traders.

In March 1870 several Indian raiding parties were sighted west of San Antonio. The *San Antonio Daily Herald* reported that a party of Indians had passed near Bandera on March 14, heading southeast, where they had lanced three horses near San Jeronimo. The Indians seem to have been in the area for some time previous to their sighting. A second group of Indians, numbering about fifteen, had also been sighted north of Kerrville.[20] It is possible that one of these two groups was Carnoviste's band, headed for Mexico. Generally, a raiding party was away from the main camp for a

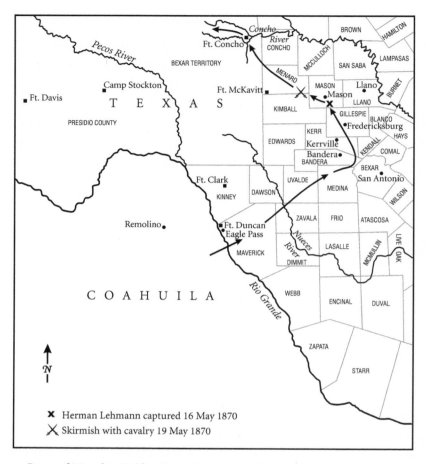

X Herman Lehmann captured 16 May 1870
X Skirmish with cavalry 19 May 1870

Route of Mescalero Raiding Party that Captured Herman Lehmann, May 1870

month or two, so this sighting fits within the time frame of the attack on the Lehmann homestead in May 1870.

In response to these Indian sightings, Company G, Fourth U.S. Cavalry, under the command of W. C. Hemphill, was sent out from Ft. Sam Houston, San Antonio. They left the post on March 5, rode to the San Jeronimo River, then proceeded north to the Medina River. Following the Medina northward, they rode to the headwaters of the Guadalupe River above Kerrville. Company G found no sign of Indians. In the meantime, it seems the Indians had circled back, because they were sighted at Bandera on March 14. On that date Hemphill and the cavalry were about fifty to seventy-five miles north of them. Needless to say, Company G returned to the post without seeing any Indians or finding any sign of them.[21]

By early April 1870 a large raiding party was sighted in Uvalde County, headed north. This party, composed of fifteen to twenty Indians, probably contained Carnoviste's group. Ten horses were stolen from several ranches along the Frio River during the night of April 11. Alfonso Leal, an employee of one of the ranches, was able to save some of the horses from Indian theft. He stated that he had flushed out a group of eight Indians who had begun to whistle at him, Mexican fashion. Since it was a dark night with the moon obscured, the Indians were whistling to see whether Leal was one of their raiding party. Leal responded by shouting, "Hello," to which they replied, "Hello." At this point the group of eight loosed some twenty-five arrows at Leal, who responded with three shots from his six-shooter. No one seems to have been hit. The next morning it was found that the Indians had split into two groups; one group headed north, while the other group with the best horses had circled around. Neither group of Indians was seen in the area again, and the horses were never recovered.[22]

On April 21, 1870, J. G. O'Grady of Boerne found his horse had been shot in the jaw by an Indian arrow. It was obvious that the raiders were working their way north, probably in several small groups.

In the early afternoon of May 16, 1870, Herman and Willie Lehmann were abducted from the field in front of their house. Situated on Squaw Creek, their cabin lay about twenty-five miles northwest of Fredericksburg. On May 30 a report of the abduction appeared in the *San Antonio Daily Herald*:

> The boy of Bachmeier [*sic*; i.e., Willie Lehmann], who escaped from the Indians between San Saba and Kickapoo, came in on Saturday evening and reported as follows:
>
> That he was out with the Indians for four days; that they had some 20 or 25 horses, which they stole since they left Bachmeier's place; that they

had nothing to eat but berries, the Indians being unsuccessful in hunting for deer; that only the elder boy, who is yet missing, was tied with leather ropes at night—in daytime none of them were tied; that they had to watch the Indians' horses. On the 4th day, May 19th, the two boys had been riding with the Indians alongside of a plain wagon road, and concluded to make their escape at the first chance, suddenly the Indians halted off the road; the two boys had to dismount, and were left in charge of one Indian—all the others rode off. About 15 minutes later, the boys heard a sharp firing of guns, and about 5 or 10 minutes after that the Indians came back at full speed—one missing—seized the boys and rode off again at the same gait. They had then only half the number of loose horses left. The oldest boy was with the first Indian, riding behind him. The smaller boy (8 years old) was riding behind the last one to start—When at full speed, this boy fell off the horse, but the Indian either did not find it out immediately, or had no time to stop. As soon as he fell, the boy slipped into some bushes, and slept there all night. Next day, he looked for the road, found it, and happily saw some pieces of bread, which saved him from starving. On the same day, he saw three Indians coming with four horses. Being under the impression that they were perhaps hunting for him, he hid again in the bushes, and slept another night in the prairie. Next day, he continued his journey on the road, and was at last picked up by a Swiss wagoner [sic], fully exhausted, who brought him first up to Flangau, and afterwards delivered him down here [Loyal Valley, Mason County, located near the Bachmeier cabin].

It is certain that the other boy was not killed by the Indians, as reported by the stage driver, because the one that escaped saw his brother yet alive and in the saddle behind the Indian who led the squad in their flight. And it is most probable that the successful attack made by the scout from Ft. McKavitt on the 19th of May, on a lot of Indians on the road from McKavitt to Kickapoo, by which from ten to 15 horses were recovered, was just made on the identical party of Indians who captured the two boys.

No news of Indians, except that an officer from [Ft.] Concho, going through here, reported that six horses were lately stolen by Indians on the Llano River.[23]

Herman Lehmann's account of his capture is a straightforward, simple story made the more terrifying because of the matter-of-fact way in which he tells it. Herman, brother Willie, sister Caroline, and baby stepsister Gusta were in a small wheat field in front of their cabin. They had been sent outside around the noon hour to scare away the birds from the wheat while their mother prepared lunch for the children's stepfather, Philip Buchmeier. The cabin and wheat patch were surrounded by a low (about four-foot high) dry-stack stone wall; these stone walls were a feature of the Texas-German ranches and can still be seen in many places throughout the Texas Hill Country. Suddenly, the children looked up to see themselves surrounded by Indians. Willie was grabbed immediately. Caroline tried to run for the cabin, with the Indians taking several shots at her. She fainted from fright, and the Indians bothered with her no more, thinking she was dead. Herman ran, but was chased down by Carnoviste; Herman fought and had almost succeeded in pulling loose from Carnoviste when Chevato came up. Both Indians grabbed Herman, one holding his head and the other holding his feet, and threw him over the rock wall. His landing stunned him long enough for Carnoviste and Chevato to jump over the wall, grab him, strip him, tie him to a horse, and ride away.[24] The whole abduction probably took no more than fifteen minutes.

The raiding party and their two captives headed north, stealing additional horses from the Mosely ranch. The horse theft was reported in the *San Antonio Daily Herald* on May 21, 1870:

> On Monday, [May] 16th, about 4 o'clock p.m., eight horses were stolen by Indians from Mr. Mosely's ranch near Housemountain, about 5 miles east of this place. One hour afterward, Mr. Ch. Keyser, living 4 miles from here in a northeastern direction, was out hunting for cattle; when crossing a ridge he nearly ran into a lot of Indians who were engaged in catching and saddling a horse belonging to Mr. Keyser for the purpose of driving that horse home. Mr. K. could no do nothing but make a hasty retreat, there being eight or ten Indians in the party. It was afterwards ascertained by Mosely's men, that the Indians had kept a lot of horses herding in the

hills between Mosely's and Keyser's ranches, going backward and forward, adding to the drove. All efforts to follow the drove failed.[25]

Herman states that Carnoviste was left to guard the two boys while the others in the group rode on to steal the horses; he notes that shots were fired, although the newspaper report does not mention this fact. The raiding party continued on, stealing additional horses from the Keyser ranch near the Llano River. They stopped to rest at Willow Creek, near the town of Mason, and afterward the band scattered for a time. One group took Willie, while Herman remained with Carnoviste, Chevato, and Dinero. Willie's group continued on, stealing more horses along the way. Herman's group stopped to catch and slaughter a calf. Carnoviste, who had already beaten and threatened Herman, took the boy's face and plunged it into the entrails of the calf when Herman refused to eat the raw meat.[26]

The entire band then came together again. Herman numbered them a total of twelve men. At this point Herman's story diverges from the published account in the *Herald* on several details. Herman says that the group spied some Rangers dismounted and watering their horses in Lipan Creek, near Ft. McKavitt. In Herman's account, the group makes no contact with the Rangers, but withdraws and leaves their stolen horses behind while riding at top speed to escape, and Willie is thrown off of the horse by his Indian captor. The *Herald* account says that a scouting party out of Ft. McKavitt ran across the Mescalero raiding party holding the two boys. The encounter took place on the road between Ft. McKavitt and the town of Kickapoo, Texas. Herman and Willie had been left by the side of the road while the main body of Indians had ridden off; shots were heard, and the Indians came back, running at top speed. The boys were picked up, but Willie fell off the horse as the group was riding away. About half of the stolen horses were left behind.[27]

The presence of Ft. McKavitt, near present-day Menard, Texas, offered the only real threat to the Mescalero raiding parties using the raiding trail that ran west of San Antonio. First established in 1852 to prevent the Texas Indians from raiding into Mexico, the fort was abandoned in 1859. In 1868 it had been reoccupied,[28] and its commanding officer in 1870 was none other than the nemesis of the Lipans and Kickapoos at El Remolino—Ranald S. Mackenzie. Mackenzie, born in 1840 in New York City and known by the Indians as Bad Hand, had accepted an appointment as colonel of the Forty-first Infantry, a newly formed black regiment. The unit had its first headquarters at Ft. Brown, then at Ft. Clark near the Rio Grande border, and finally at Ft. McKavitt in central Texas.[29]

Mackenzie's scouting party, sent out from Ft. McKavitt on May 19, 1870, was to have an immediate impact on the lives of the Lehmann brothers as well as on the lives of Chevato and Dinero. Willie was able to escape in the turmoil of the contact between the raiding party and the cavalry scouts; the Mescaleros lost most, if not all, of the horses they had stolen. Because of that loss, the raiding party thought that they could not return home without any spoils other than their captive. They decided to stay in Texas and continue to steal horses, while they sent Herman back to Mescalero in the company of Chevato and Dinero.[30] Thus a friendship was born between captors and captured.

10. The Capture of Children

Why did the Indians capture young children? For the Mescaleros, I cannot say because I was not raised there. I was raised with the Comanche. Now, the Comanche had been fighting other Indian tribes for centuries, since pre-Colombian times. And they had very hard fights. Each tribe lost people, and sometimes they lost a lot of people.

With the Comanche, the patriarch of the family is always the father or the grandfather. Let me give you an example using a family with four children—two sons and two daughters—where both sons had been killed in battle. When the father got too old, it would normally be the duty of the sons to take over and support the mother and father. When the daughters get married, they go to their husband's families and are not there to take care of the mother and father. So, when Comanche parents would get to this point, say in their fifties, when they couldn't have any more children and both sons were no more and their daughters were married and off with their husbands, there would be no one to care for them in their old age. So they would tell a raiding party, "I would like a small child. I would like a child I can raise as my own, so when I get old, this child will be old enough to take care of me." This is the whole thinking behind the capture of children. It was not done to be malicious; children were captured because it was a necessity.

These children were treated very well. They were adopted into the tribe, treated as family members, and held in high esteem. The biggest asset of value to a Comanche was his horse herd. It was not surprising for one man to own 1,500 head of horses. This was their wealth. And that child, who was a captive, when he reached maturity and his adopted parents passed away, he might inherit 1,500 head of horses. All the wealth that the family had would be his, and he would carry on the family name.

However, some captives who were a little older and could remember their Anglo or Spanish names decided to keep those names. So today in my tribe, the Comanche tribe, there are some people with Hispanic last names. And that is the reason.

Was capturing children also done to terrorize as well as to replace lost children? Well, you're looking at two different societies here—the Lipan and Mescalero Apaches and the Comanches/Kiowas—when you answer that question. The Comanches and the Kiowas were allied, and their customs were similar (from here on, I'll just say Comanches, although what is said is the same for the Kiowa).

Family was the biggest thing, and children (besides horses) were the most prized possessions. The children were the future. A mother and father loved their children so much that they could not discipline them with corporal punishment. So, punishment for a child (not a beating, but perhaps a small spanking) fell to the mother's cousins. The mother and father loved their children so much that they could not even act harshly to them. So the mother's cousins would do the discipline, because the child's parents knew that every child must have some discipline. So the mother would tell her cousin, "This child has been very bad," and the cousins would come over. It is usually women cous-

ins, not men cousins. The women cousins would chastise the child, sometimes spanking or threatening to spank the child in order to shock the child into behaving. This is the way discipline was handled. Comanche parents, even to my generation, could not even spank their children. So this is one thing that is different with the Comanche, my tribe, as opposed to other tribes.

This method of discipline is really a binding factor. I had a childhood friend who was half Anglo and half Comanche (his mother was a Comanche). We were in high school together, and I would go to visit him, and he likewise would come to see me at my home. Every time I would go to his house, his mother would never call me Bill; she would call me "son." Likewise with my mother. My friend went with my parents and me to visit my sister, who was in a tubercular sanitarium at Shawnee, Oklahoma. We were still in high school, and my father bought me some nice slacks, a shirt, a belt, and some shoes. He didn't ask my friend if he wanted the same, he just bought the same thing. That's the way it was with the Comanche—you treated your friend's children as your own.

That's what made such strong links within the tribe, and that is what bound these captives. Once they were introduced as family members into the tribe, they were thought of as family and that's why they never wanted to leave. That's why it was hard for Herman Lehmann to leave the Comanche culture and come back home. It was hard for Cynthia Ann Parker when the army forced her to go back to her home in Texas. She just pined away, wouldn't eat, and she and her child died. They missed this link.

If the Comanche wanted to capture a child to be raised as a Comanche, they would capture a small child, one that could fit in with the tribe. My people say that Cynthia Ann Parker was five years old. This is what is surprising for me to understand when I first heard about Herman Lehmann. He was a young boy (eleven years old), not a younger child. But that's the way the Apache were. They took children who were older, and they looked at them as servants, not as children to be adopted into the tribe.

If you go back to my home today and look at Comanche society today, especially people in my generation, you will see a lot of Hispanic blood and Anglo blood flows through their veins. Hugh Corwin was an old-time historian and

*authored several books on the Comanche culture. He could speak Comanche.
I was fortunate to be introduced to him when I was in my teens, introduced
by my father. He has since passed away; he was an elderly man when I met
him. He told me that before 1929, you might have been able to find a pure-
blood Comanche, but because of the children who were captives, both Anglo
and Hispanic, he doubted that there were any pure-blood Comanche to be
found after 1929. That's how many children were taken, taken out of Mexico
and Texas and introduced into the Comanche tribe.*

§

A generalization can be made that the Comanche capture of women and
children was a cultural practice propelled by the need to replenish tribal
numbers and care for older, childless members. Yet this practice had far
greater significance for all the plains tribes as well as for the Apaches. Seiz-
ing an enemy's child was not only a blatant affront designed to signify the
weakness of the enemy, but the seizure of women and children also added
to the wealth of the victorious tribe, since they represented wealth that
could be used to replenish the tribe as well as human wealth that could be
used in trade. "The capture of 'enemy' women and children was, therefore,
one extreme expression along a continuum of exchange."[1]

Thus the captive faced a number of possibilities: he or she could be immediately killed or immediately integrated into the tribe through adoption. The captive could be traded to another band or even another tribe; he
or she could be traded to Hispanic traders. The captive might be brought
into the family of the captor as a servant, which established a kinship relationship with the captor. Later, that kinship relationship might be cemented by marriage, which fully integrated the captive into the tribe. Or
the captive could become the slave of the captor, forced to work herding
horses, gathering wood, or tanning hides, and vulnerable to being traded
at any time as a slave.

During the eighteenth century, the plains Apaches developed a lively
trade with the Spanish in New Mexico, and once contact was initiated,
Spanish men, women, and children became fair game for Apache cap-

ture. By 1784 there were 152 captives of both sexes held by the Apaches; the Spanish tried to raise money to redeem them but were unable to fund the redemption of more than a few.[2] After the Spanish abandonment of the Pecos pueblo, one site of Spanish/Apache trading, "the *Natagés* [a group incorporated into the Western Lipans] and Sierra Blancas [Mescaleros] moved south to join their Lipan cousins in developing a raiding economy in the borderlands of Nueva Vizcaya [Mexico]."[3]

As Apache trading contacts with New Mexico waned in the eighteenth century, Comanche trade with the Spanish grew. With increased contact came increased numbers of Spanish captives to be found in the Comanche camps. The period from 1700 to 1750 was one of expansion for the Comanche bands as they developed trade with the Spanish in New Mexico, had limited contact with French traders, pushed the Lipans out of their central Texas homeland, and had contact (sometimes peaceful, sometimes violent) with the Spanish deep into south Texas.[4] The expansion of Comanche territory and trade opportunities brought new Comanche captives from a variety of sources: the Spanish in New Mexico, Texas, and Mexico; the Pueblo cultures; other plains tribes; Texas tribes such as the Caddos; and, of course, their vanquished enemies—the Lipans.

Antonio Apache told a story in 1935 of a Comanche girl whom the Lipan had captured. No mention was made of any facts that would indicate the century in which these events occurred (eighteenth or nineteenth), but the unnamed Comanche girl's story illustrates many facets of the captive's experience:

> What the Comanche wanted were the horses. They were always coming around and they would work up an argument and fight. They would find some excuse, such as bragging about their power, and pretty soon they would get angry and trouble would start.
>
> One time the Comanche had been to the south. They were coming back and they came to a Lipan camp. The Lipan had some horses.... The Comanche drove the Lipan horses off about two miles and stopped. At that place was a lake, and the Comanche watered the horses and began to cook a meal there.

The Lipan started after them and came upon them. The Comanche chief was there and had his horse staked close by. A single Comanche girl was there, too, out on the raid with the Comanche. There was another horse that belonged to this woman. This woman was down at the stream while the men were eating; she had probably gone down to the stream to wash her feet. She saw the Lipan men and called, "Here come the Lipan!" She went back at an easy pace; she didn't run; she wasn't afraid. She thought the Comanche men were going to protect her and didn't hurry. . . .

The girl got on her horse; the chief mounted his horse, too. He told his men to go out and fight. They met the Lipan and had a real fight. Pretty soon the Comanche began to back off. When the woman saw her men weakening, she got off her horse and hit the horse in the face, sending it away. She did this instead of riding to safety because she wanted to do a great war deed. If she were on foot, her men would have to stay and protect her and show their bravery. Among the Comanche, the women had their minds on such things. The Apache were going to give her a chance to escape at first, but she wouldn't take it. Sometimes when Comanche women wanted to fight, they fought. (Lipan women didn't go out and fight with the men like that. They could have done it if they had wanted to, but they didn't want to. The men didn't want them along. They would only get in the way and make it harder. However, if they are in camp, and the camp is attacked, they fight fiercely then, they show their bravery.)

The Comanche girl had gotten off her horse and sent it away. She began to walk toward the Comanche men but she was a big woman and couldn't walk very fast. The Comanche men passed her and she fell behind. . . . One Comanche came back with a rifle to save her, but the Lipan fought furiously. One Lipan ran up, grabbed the Comanche woman, and pulled her aside. The Lipan fought so fiercely that even the Comanche man had to go on, leaving the woman behind.

The Lipan man put the woman aside. He told her in sign language, "You stay here." She sat beside a mesquite bush while the Lipan man ran back to join the fight. She had two pretty blankets in a bag. The Lipan killed all of the Comanche except three, who they allowed to escape because they had known them from before. The man who captured the Comanche woman also captured her horse. He went back to the Comanche woman, told her to follow him, and she did. It looked as if she might try to get away, but she never did. The man took the Comanche woman to his camp. They didn't go straight into camp. They stopped a little way off and made a noise to let those in camp know they were coming. They began to sing and rode into camp, where they had a victory dance.

After a while, this woman could go anywhere she pleased. Someone wanted her to work for them, but her owner said, "No, you people have arms; you can do things for yourselves."

The man who took this woman did not marry her. He took care of her. After she had been there for three years, one young Comanche boy who was there (a boy who had been captured years before and had grown up with the Lipan) married her. So this man who had captured her had a relative-in-law when these two Comanche were married.

Many years passed but the Comanche girl's father had not forgotten her. He went about the Comanche camps, planning a raid against the Lipan to get his daughter back. The Lipan, meanwhile, had forgotten all about it. They were having a good time, moving from place to place without haste. Two Lipan just happened to be out on a little scout and saw a big encampment of Comanche, extending as far as the eye could see. The Comanche were camping for a fight.

When the rest of the Lipan heard the scout's report, the owner of the Comanche girl called her and her Comanche husband in and said to them, "You two have been among us for many years. You may be lonesome for your people. If you want to go back to them, you can. If you want to stay here, you can."

"We wish to go," they said. So, the owner told the Comanche "son-in-law" to get his horse for him. The owner escorted the Comanche couple almost all of the way to the Comanche camp.

When the Comanche girl reached the camp of her people, they asked her who she was. "I am the girl who was captured many years ago." They showed her the camp of her father and when the two met, they embraced and cried for joy. Her father had been just about to lead the Comanche in an attack to get his daughter back and here she was!

The girl's father had a big tipi put up. The head men all came to it. The Comanche couple was brought in and questioned, asking them how the Lipan had treated them as captives.

The girl replied, "The one who captured me is a real man. He took me back. He motioned me to go into his camp. I went in and stayed with them many years. They never treated me roughly nor made a slave of me. But you, my own people, when you take captives, you make them slaves, you work them to death. But the Lipan treated me well. I went out after water myself; they didn't tell me to do it. And in the same way, I gathered wood. I tanned hides and scraped rawhide when I felt like it. I was well treated and was not forced to work hard. The man treated me like a member of his own family."

Then they asked her, "Who is that boy?" She answered, "He is a Comanche, too. Someone must remember when the Lipan and Mexicans captured six Comanche boys. The Mexicans gave them to the Lipan. He was so high." She motioned with her hand to show he was about six years old when he was captured. "He grew up among the Lipan. He doesn't know his own language; he doesn't remember it. All he speaks is Lipan. The other five Comanche boys are still among the Lipan." They questioned the Comanche boy, and he didn't remember anything other than the name by which his Comanche father had called him, Gotsa. Sure enough, when the Comanches went among their camps and questioned their people, his father was found and they were reunited.

The father of the girl said, "I am going over to Lipan country and see what kind of people those Lipan are. They have killed our men many times when we have gone to fight them. Let's visit them this time in a friendly spirit. Let us go and get presents to give to those who had taken such good care of our children."[5]

Looking beyond the obvious Lipan bias in the story, some observations can be made about the experience of captive children from an enemy tribe.

The Comanche girl did not attempt to escape from her Lipan captor, it is inferred, because the male members of her raiding party had not been "man enough" to protect her. This is an obvious instance of Lipan boasting, but is does draw attention to the fact that, at the root of the capture of women and children, were concepts of honor and shame.[6] The honor was heightened for her captor because he also captured the girl's horse. As the girl stressed to her father, she was assigned a role in her captor's family somewhere between that of a servant and that of a family member (that is, she had to perform work, but was not forced to do so). In other words, the Comanche girl had a kinship relation with her captor, but not one of full integration as a family member. When she married the Comanche captive boy, he is referred to as the "son-in-law" of her captor. The Comanche boy's experience is also illustrative. Captured by Lipans and Mexicans, he was given to the Lipans, who raised him as a Lipan (since his age at capture was six—young enough to be easily integrated into the tribe). These facts illustrate the captive trade among the Lipans and the Mexicans, since it seems the Mexicans would hardly just "give" this young boy to the Lipans; there must have been something traded for him. Finally, the story shows that warfare, even among enemies such as the Lipans and the Comanches, could be averted upon the return of captives.

Just as the Lipans captured Comanche children, so Lipan children found themselves captives of the Comanches. One instance is the case of Louis, born in 1863 between the Pecos River and the Rio Grande in Texas. He was born into the Kúne tsá, or Big Water, band of Lipans, one group of which seem to have been moving back and forth across the border in the year of his birth. When Louis was about three years old, Comanches attacked his camp, and Louis was captured by a Comanche named Mawe (Mow-way? the Kotsoteka Comanche chief?). When with the Comanches, the boy was called Louis Kawats. He was traded back to the Lipans about 1872 for four horses and two mules.[7]

The Mescaleros also participated in the capture and trade of children, although no oral history has been recorded relating to the Mescalero perspective on this aspect of their culture. Herman Lehmann does mention seeing several captives among the Mescaleros, both Anglo and Hispanic, a reflection of the population of the Mescalero raiding territory after 1860.[8] A study of early Mescalero census records (circa 1885) reveals only one notation that would indicate a former captive—José Carrillo. Captured from his home in the Mexican state of Chihuahua by the Navajos when he was only a small boy, Carrillo was looked upon as a slave. He was sold to a Mexican hacienda owner and forced to work in the fields. Deciding that his position as a Navajo slave was preferable to that of a hacienda slave, he escaped and made his way back to the Navajos. Some time later, he learned that there were Mexican settlers on the Rio Hondo in New Mexico who spoke Spanish. He decided to escape from the Navajos and join the settlers but in doing so was caught by the Navajos, stoned, and left for dead. He was found by the Mescaleros, who nursed him back to health. He remained with that tribe for the rest of his life, serving as an interpreter for the Indian agent and reservation physician.[9]

The Comanche capture of Anglo children in Texas both terrified and fascinated Texans from the time of the raid on Parker's Fort in 1836 (and continues to fascinate to this day). The terror is understandable, but it must be acknowledged that the fascination arose from the incomprehension most Anglo settlers felt when they discovered that some of the Anglo captives, when located and redeemed from the Comanches, did not want to be returned to their Anglo families. Thus white captives such as Cynthia Ann Parker, Herman Lehmann, and Rudolph Fischer are remembered for their unwillingness to return to Anglo society.

Other Anglo captives, such as the young Smith brothers captured by Comanches and Lipan Apaches in 1871 from near San Antonio, seem to have endured their captivity and, upon release, were reintegrated into Anglo society, although they were viewed by others as being marked by their experience. When the tale of their captivity was later published, it proved to be a rather superficial account, yet it contains hints as to the status assigned to them by their captors. Eleven-year-old Clint Smith was captured by a Comanche named Tasacowadi, a name translated by Clint as Leopard Cat (possibly Spotted Leopard, a Kotsoteka chief?). While treated as a servant,

Clint was allowed to go on raids and was not traded, indicating a kinship relationship. This relationship was also reflected in the terms by which he described his captor's wife; he described the woman as his "foster-mother." Clint's assigned tasks were to herd and water his owner's horses. He also described how he became an accomplished thief, a feat that brought praise from his captor and a skill that must have indicated to his captor Clint's readiness to join the rest of the Comanches on a raid.[10] Although Clint does not name the Comanche band that held him, it was reported that he was being held by Mow-way's band of Kotsotekas.[11] Clint does mention a young Comanche friend named To-ivo-ney; this must have been Too-ah-von-nie, or Looking Child (b. 1859), who later married Che-aun-nee, a daughter of the Kwahada chief Wild Horse.[12] This would indicate that at this date (1871–72), Mow-way's Kotsoteka band also contained elements of Kwahada Comanches, a fact later confirmed after Mackenzie's attack on the Comanche camp at McClellan Creek, Texas, on September 20, 1872, where prisoners from both Mow-way's Kotsoteka and Kwahada bands were taken.[13] Clint also noted in his narrative that there were eighteen other captives being held by Mow-way's band; one might have been Louis, the Lipan who had been captured by the Comanches in 1866 and wasn't traded back to the Lipans until 1872. After a year and a half with the Comanches and the death of his captor, Clint Smith was turned over on October 24, 1872, to Laurie Tatum, the Kiowa agent, and returned to his parents in Texas.

Nine-year-old Jeff Smith became the property of the Lipan members of the raiding party after his capture in 1871. Although Jeff stated that the Lipans sold him to Geronimo, a Chiricahua Apache, historical documents indicate that he remained with the Lipans and was taken by them across the Rio Grande into Mexico. Although the details of Jeff's captivity are sketchy, the two brothers did state that they saw each other once after they were split up, which occurred when the Comanches were on a raid in Texas and were joined by about seventy-five Apaches. Clint was watering Tasacowadi's horses and saw his brother when Jeff came to the stream to get water for his Apache owner. The combined group of Comanches and

Apaches raided in the vicinity of Big Spring, Texas (south of Ft. Concho). Although there is a remote possibility that a band of Chiricahua Apaches could have been raiding with the Comanches sometime between February 1872 and October 1872, no mention of such a combined raid can be found in any military reports. It seems more probable, given the territory of the raid, that it contained a joint force of Comanches and Mescalero/Lipan Apaches. Jeff never mentioned any facts that would indicate any kinship relation with his captor; instead, his limited description of his captivity indicates he was probably looked upon as a slave. Evidence in the dispatches sent to the U.S. State Department from its consul at Piedras Negras, Mexico, gives the details of the ransom of Jeff Smith from the Lipans near Zaragosa. In March 1873 a Mexican named Ramon Perez reported to the U.S. consul that he had seen a white boy among the Lipans camped in the San Rodrigo Canyon near El Remolino, Coahuila. He spoke to the Lipan owner of the boy, who told him that he had purchased the boy from the Comanches while on a raid into Texas. Four months later Jeff Smith was sold to a Mexican trader named Alejo Santos Coy for $150 in gold. Santos Coy then turned Jeff over to the U.S. consul at Piedras Negras, along with a bill for reimbursement for his outlay of $150. The consul, in writing to his superior at the U.S. secretary of state's office, requested that Santos Coy be reimbursed by the U.S. government since "Mr. Smith was unable to pay that sum, being a poor man."[14] Jeff Smith was sent back to his family in Texas when the consul paid the Mexican trader in August 1873.

What seemed to determine whether a young boy would be adopted into an Apache band or sold to Mexican traders seems to have been the amount of moxie or spirit exhibited by the young boy after his capture. From the moment Herman Lehmann reached the Mescalero camp, his future was being determined. "One fat, squabby, heathenish, hellish wench grabbed me, pulled me from the horse, pinched me, slapped me, beat me, threw me down, wallowed me, while the others looked on in great glee."[15] The Mescaleros then burned holes in his ears and in his arms with a hot iron rod. Herman explained, "I fought, kicked and raved, but they beat and burned me until I could stand it no longer and I became exhausted."[16] Exhausted or not, Herman had passed the first test—he had fought back.

The next day they placed raw meat in front of him as well as cooked food (bread, cooked meat, and *piloncío,* or raw sugar). He chose the raw meat, noting, "had I first touched the cooked food . . . the food of civilized man, I would likely have been tortured to death."[17] He was treated as a servant for a time after his capture but was eventually given training as a warrior and began to go on raids with the Mescaleros. He had passed the Apache tests, and, since it seemed that his captor did not want to trade him, he would be considered a Mescalero warrior.

Within two months of Herman's capture, his parents took a series of actions that would ultimately lead to his return nine years later, although when first viewed, their actions seemed to have sealed his fate as a Mescalero. On July 2, 1870, his stepfather, Philip Buchmeier, swore out an affidavit before R. Radeleff, justice of the peace, Precinct 1, Gillespie County, Texas. In the affidavit, he described the sequence of events that led to the abduction of Herman and Willie:

> On the 16th of May 1870, while taking his meal, four children of his playing inside the fence about the house. A party of Indians approached, one child called into the window that the Indians were in the field, upon which he, affiant, jumped after his arms, but before he could make use of them, the Indians had taken three of his children over the fence by his house, of which one escaped again, that, when he jumped out, the Indians decamped and run off, carrying away with them two of his children, boys: that the youngest, Willy, succeeded in his endeavors to escape from the Indians, at about Kickapoo Springs, about 100 miles from his, affiant's, house, that he was brought back by teamsters from Fredericksburg, that the boy stolen is about 11 years old, slender built, sandy haired, freckles about the nose, blue eyes, rather bashful. His name is Frederick Herman Lehmann, and he is stepson to affiant. That affiant is living on Squaw Creek, Mason County, that, according to what the boy Willy, who is about 8 years old, said, the Indians were talking English, that they were dressed, some in U.S. Soldier Jackets, some in U.S. Soldier Over Coats, that they wore their hair plaited, that there were eight Indians, all armed

with Six shooters and bows and arrows, one of them had a lance besides, that the Chief of the tribe was killed, shortly before the boy, Willy, made his escape, by a troop of U.S. Soldiers, a little this side of Kickapoo Spring, that said Willy is a very clever little chap and that he is not in the habit of telling an untruth.[18]

One year passed; Herman did not return home. In May 1871 his mother traveled to the Cold Spring Camp, a nearby cavalry camp. There she told the soldiers the story of Herman's abduction, hoping to get some help from the U.S. Army in finding him. Unfortunately, whether due to Augusta Buchmeier's heavy German accent, lack of English skills, or the obtuseness of the soldier taking down her information, all the information passed along was incorrect. On May 27, 1871, the following letter was sent by Col. J. E. Tourtellotte from the Headquarters, Fifth Military District, Austin, Texas, to Laurie Tatum, Indian agent at Ft. Sill, Indian Territory (the errors are underlined; correct information is enclosed within the parentheses):

Dear Sir:

The General directs me to say that on the 4th Instant a German woman came into our camp near Cold Springs—twenty two miles northwest of Fredericksburg, Texas, and made the following statement—

Her present name is <u>Brockmeyer</u> (Buchmeier) and she lives with her family near said Cold Springs;

About <u>two</u> (one) years since she lived on a ranche [*sic*] six miles west of said Springs;

In the month of <u>June 1869</u> (May 1870)—I may not be correct as to the exact date—a party of Indians—supposed by her to be <u>commanches</u> [*sic*] (Apaches)—approached her house, near which two of their children were playing in a field.

The children were named <u>Lamon</u> (Lehmann) from a former husband and were aged [re]spective eleven and [eig]ht years

The Indians seized the children and placed them on horseback.

After a ride of several miles, and this side of old Ft. Mason, the younger child fell off his horse, crawled into the bushes, and was recovered.

The older boy—now <u>thirteen</u> (twelve) years of age—has not since been heard from, and is supposed to be still in the hands of the <u>Commanches</u> [*sic*] (Apaches).

[Endorsed]

—<u>Lamon</u> (Lehmann) 11 years old captured in <u>1869</u> (1870)
[the Buchmeier affidavit was attached to this letter][19]

When Laurie Tatum received the letter from Col. Tourtellotte, he set in motion events that would have some interesting consequences. He immediately queried the Office of the Superintendent of Indian Affairs in Lawrence, Kansas, as to the government's policy regarding the recovery of captive children. In this instance, by June 1871 he was authorized to employ a scout named Caboone to recover captives.[20] Unfortunately, due to the misinformation contained in the Tourtellotte letter, Caboone was looking for a thirteen-year-old boy named Lamon living as a captive among the Comanche in north Texas or the Indian Territory of Oklahoma; in actual fact, Herman was with the Mescalero Apaches in New Mexico.

In 1872 the U.S. Army began the process of trying to move the Mescaleros to a reservation located at the site of their stronghold on Sierra Blanca in New Mexico and near Ft. Stanton. After their disastrous experience at Bosque Redondo in 1862, the Mescaleros were understandably skittish. Lt. Thomas C. Davis of the District Headquarters in Santa Fe wrote to his superiors in the adjutant general's office at Ft. Leavenworth, Kansas, describing the situation:

Since the acquisition of the Territory, the Mescalero Apache have been known as the most warlike and enterprising tribe in southern New Mexico, and for years the attempts to subjugate them were fruitless. Until three years ago [1872], it was impossible to get them on a Reservation and then they had to be coaxed into coming. In the summer of 1873, when Maj. Price's column marched to the reservation, the Indians defiantly broke for the mountains and it was found utterly impossible to over-take them or drive them back, and they did not again return until they were ready, after probably committing many depredations. . . . [The Mescaleros] are a warlike and turbulent tribe of Indians who for years have not been well-thrashed.[21]

Herman Lehmann was present when some of the Apache groups were coaxed onto the reservation at Mescalero, New Mexico. He described the situation in this way:

> Finally, our chiefs made a treaty with the whites and soldiers in uniform came to our camp. Another white boy and I were kept hidden in the forest. This other boy would not stay, but would slip back to camp when he thought it time for the white inspector to come, so Snapping Turtle carried him away out into a thicket and left him tied to a tree, without food or water, and there he died. The soldiers kept close guard over the Indians for three moons and I had to stay in hiding in the woods but I would slip up to the wigwam of my old chief and get food. We stayed there for some time, when soldiers quit coming around regularly, thinking no doubt that we were pretty well in hand, but some of our boys stole some horses and ran away and we all broke out and followed.... [After a time, Herman's group was followed by soldiers], but we crossed back into New Mexico and were driven back into the reservation, and there we gave up and promised not to run away any more. I always had to "keep hid" or be killed by the red men. I was afraid of the whites anyway.[22]

By 1874 relations between the Mescaleros and settlers living near the Mescalero Reservation had deteriorated. Both groups complained to the military authorities at nearby Ft. Stanton of depredations. To complicate matters, the Indian agent for the Mescalero Reservation refused to cooperate with the military authorities and often warned the Mescaleros of the military's proposed maneuvers. The incident that occurred at William Dowlin's mill in late December 1874 was typical. Dowlin reported to the commander at Ft. Stanton that a group of Mescaleros had killed, wounded, or carried off many of his cattle. In response, the fort's temporary commander, Capt. James H. Stewart, sent orders to a scouting party already in the area, requesting that they bring in the Mescaleros and recover the cattle. The scouting party returned with sixty Mescalero prisoners (only one prisoner was male; the other fifty-nine were women) and about seventy head of cattle. Stewart then used the prisoners as a lure in order to be able to meet with Roman, the Mescalero chief, "with the view, if possible, of having the actual delinquents delivered up and to impress the Indians with a sense of the penalties they incurred by leaving their reservation and committing depredations."[23] Roman appeared for the meeting but "pretended to be highly indignant at the capture and, when the cause was explained to him, maintained a demeanor of high-handed independence and unfriendliness. . . . [After speaking with several more subchiefs, Stewart found] their professions and promises were evasive, vague and unsatisfactory, and although I was led to believe that the Indians who escaped would come in, none have yet appeared."[24] Adding to Stewart's frustration was the fact that the Indian agent, W. D. Crothers, had tried to warn Roman about the scouting party.

About two weeks after the Dowlin's Mill cattle theft, the nearby settlers took matters into their own hands. During the night of December 31, 1874, about thirty citizens attacked the Mescalero camp, driving the Indians out and stealing about sixty horses from the Mescaleros. The Indians fled toward Ft. Stanton; early the next morning Capt. Fechet and about forty men were sent out to pursue the marauders. The new commander at Ft. Stanton, Maj. D. R. Clendennin, noted that "during the last two months [November and December 1874] . . . over two hundred head of stock have been stolen from the Indians located upon the Reservation."[25]

The day after the citizens attacked the Mescalero camp, two ranch hands employed by Steve Stanley were shot by a group of about fifteen Mescaleros. In addition, the wife of one of the ranch hands was taken captive. This prompted Stanley to raise a posse of twenty neighbors, who took out in pursuit of the Mescaleros. The remaining cavalry at Ft. Stanton were then sent out under Capt. James F. Randlett to pursue the pursuers. Maj. Clendennin noted in his report to District Headquarters in Santa Fe on January 5, 1875, that all the Mescalero chiefs and subchiefs were still camped close to the fort; the small group that had retaliated seemed to have been a renegade band.[26]

By January 10, 1875, all the Mescaleros had fled from the reservation and from their camps near Ft. Stanton. They were believed to be hiding in the Guadalupe Mountains. Early in February 1875 a scouting party was sent out, finally locating the main body of Mescaleros under Roman in the Sierra Oscura. The Mescaleros were found to be living in "about 20 large lodges having at the time in them not less than 70 Indians, big and little."[27] When the cavalry attacked the Mescalero camp, the Indians scattered. "No dead or wounded Indians were found, but from the blood on the rocks and the close fire on their camp, they must have sustained some loss."[28] The scouting party recovered tents, about 250 or 300 buffalo robes and various other skins, cooking utensils, clothing, blankets, seventy riding and pack saddles, a large quantity of woolen and cotton cloth, fifty-one horses, three mules, and a two-year-old child found wandering near the camp. All clothing and skins were destroyed, and the horses, mules, and child were turned over to the commanding officer at Ft. Stanton.[29] The military records do not give any hint as to the fate of the captured Mescalero child, and it is unknown whether the child was ever reunited with his or her parents.

11. Herman Lehmann Leaves the Apaches and Becomes a Comanche

Herman Lehmann described in his book how he left the Apache and became a Comanche. He said that a medicine man had killed Carnoviste, and he, in turn, killed the medicine man and thus had to leave the Apache. After wandering alone for many months, he says he saw a Comanche camp and approached them. He told them his story, and they adopted him into the band.

My family has always told a different story. My grandfather, Chevato, told my father that he helped get Herman to the Comanches in Oklahoma.

You have to remember that Lehmann was an Anglo. When you moved from one tribe to another as an Indian, it didn't make that much of a differ-

ence, but Lehmann had to have a bridge to come from the Apache to the Co-manche. It didn't matter if the two tribes were at peace or at war with one another. Lehmann still had to have a bridge. My grandfather Chevato was the bridge. It would have been totally impossible for Lehmann to have quit the Apache way and go to the Comanche way because, for centuries, they had fought each other. Lehmann would have had to have been supported in or-der to move from Apache to Comanche.

Once Herman became a Comanche, however, and was treated the way that the Comanche treated captives, he never wanted to leave. With the Co-manche way of life, you didn't need the bonds of blood. It helped, but you could even be good friends and still claim relationship. As I tell you this, you can see how the whole way of life and loving a family, being part of a family, is very close to a Comanche's heart. When they take you in, you can feel that warmth and you will never be betrayed. You can see why the captives, even though they were captured quite young, were treated quite well. That's why Herman Lehmann could never rest at home. Even though he was only twenty when he was returned to his Anglo family, he missed the friendly, warm re-lationship because, in the tribe, he was no longer just an individual. He was part of that tribe. They didn't look at him by the color of his skin. The Co-manches say, "Oh, is he a taivo? meaning, "Is he white?" Herman Lehmann wasn't a taivo, he was Numa Nu. In the Comanche language, Numa Nu means "The People." And they would answer, "No, he [Lehmann] is Numa Nu," meaning that he was part of the Comanche People. He's the race and that's the way you look at him. So that's why he loved those people and that's why he felt such friendship for Chevato—because Chevato had made it pos-sible for him to enter such a group. Herman became so interwoven into Co-manche society that it was hard for him to adjust back.

§

In Herman Lehmann's account of his life with the Mescaleros and Coman-ches, the event that precipitated his move from one tribe to another was the death of his captor, Carnoviste. A similar set of circumstances can be seen in Clint Smith's captivity, where the death of his captor severed the kinship bond and allowed other members of the tribe to trade him or turn him over to an Indian agent. Lehmann states that the fight in which Carnoviste was killed was among several different groups of Mescaleros and was precipitated by a drunken brawl that occurred when traders brought whiskey to the Mescalero Reservation.[1] This means that Carnoviste's death occurred sometime after 1872 or 1873, when the military began to move the Mescaleros onto a reservation. Chevato's oral history implies that Carnoviste's death might have come at the hands of members of his own group. While that is impossible to prove, it is known that when the first Mescalero census was taken in 1885, Carnoviste's name does not appear, leading to the assumption that he had died before that date.[2]

The death of Carnoviste (which probably occurred sometime between 1873 and 1875) placed Chevato in a problematic and dangerous position. The danger came from events not directly associated with the Mescaleros, but of which the Mescaleros probably soon became very much aware— the arrest of Kiowa leaders Santana, Santank, and Big Tree in May 1871 for murders committed during an attack on a wagon train near Ft. Richardson, Texas. This was the first time that Indian tribal leaders were held accountable for murders committed during raids, and the message was noted by all the tribes. The Kiowa leaders were arrested at the Indian Agency office at Ft. Sill, Oklahoma, when they came in to answer questions put to them by Agent Laurie Tatum. Tatum had been pressuring them to turn in all their captives and had even cut off rations to the Kiowas until all members of the captive Kooser family were turned over.[3] After the arrest of the Kiowa leaders, five Comanche chiefs rode in to Ft. Sill to inquire if any of their people were liable for arrest along with the Kiowas.[4] These five chiefs represented the Comanche bands that had agreed to settle on a reservation near Ft. Sill, but it had to be just a matter of time before the news of the arrests reached the "wild" Comanche bands, such as the Kwahadas, roaming the Staked Plains. This was accomplished by September 1871, when Tatum reported that "about one fourth of the Kiowas have left the reservation and joined the Qua-ha-da band of Comanches."[5]

The Mescaleros would have learned of the arrests of the Kiowa leaders from contacts with those "wild" Comanche bands still not yet on the reservation, possibly during the joint Comanche-Apache raid in the vicinity of Big Spring, Texas, reported in Clint Smith's narrative. The two events (the pressure from the Indian agent to turn over captives and the arrest of the Kiowa leaders for murders committed during a raid), which happened within months of each other in 1871, passed a strong, clear message to both the Comanches and Apaches that the U.S. government was now going to get serious about recovery of captives and murders committed during raids. Leaders could be arrested for murders committed by members of their band, and even individual warriors could be tried for murders committed during raids; food rations could be cut off if the government suspected any captives were being held within the band.

In addition to these developments, the scout Caboone was passing word through the Comanche camps in the summer of 1871 that Agent Tatum was looking for a young German boy named "Lamon" who had been taken from Texas. Caboone, a Mexican captive of the Comanches and an interpreter for the trader William Chisolm, "promised to go among the Indians in search of captives, if paid a compensation of five dollars per day."[6] The Office of Indian Affairs authorized the payment in June 1871, also noting that the Indian agent at Ft. Sill had threatened to withhold annuities in order to force the Comanches to turn over their captives. The Indian Affairs commissioner also stated that "no presents shall be given or promised, as an inducement to the Indians to deliver up any captive. They must be held to their treaty obligations, to bring in captives, without the expectation of a reward or ransom price."[7]

All of these circumstances combined to pose a real dilemma for Chevato. Herman Lehmann stated, "It was the custom of the Indians that when an Indian captured a white child, that child became the property of that particular Indian. Therefore, according to tribal custom, I belonged to Carnoviste and was called his son."[8] Although Chevato had remained friends with Herman, he had no kinship relation and thus no tribal claim on him. Yet the U.S. government might not see it in those terms. Since Chevato was now, after the death of Carnoviste, the only living person to have been directly involved in Herman's abduction, it was very possible that Chevato could have been brought to trial for kidnapping. Adding to the pressure was the fact that, beginning in 1872, the army was coaxing and pushing the Mescaleros onto a reservation. Chevato must have known it would only be a matter of time before someone found Herman or noticed a young boy with blue eyes among the Mescaleros.

When Herman Lehmann's narrative is examined carefully, it becomes apparent that an exact date cannot be fixed for Herman's move from the Mescaleros to the Comanches, based on his version of the event. The chronology in his narrative is so jumbled that the move could have been made at any time from 1872 (when the Mescaleros first came onto their reservation near Ft. Stanton) to 1874 (when the battle of Adobe Walls was fought). In addition, there are elements in this part of his tale that are almost unbelievable. It does seem improbable that he would have lived long enough to tell his story after walking alone, and unannounced, into the Comanche camp at night. In addition, Herman makes no mention of Chevato's participation in his move from one tribe to another.

Which version of this event—Herman's or Chevato's—is more reflective of the historical truth? The Comanches who knew Herman Lehmann always insisted that he was prone to exaggeration,[9] while Chevato's assertion that he was the bridge that brought Herman to the Comanches is supported by an affidavits filed by Quanah Parker and Herman Lehmann in 1901, when Herman was seeking enrollment in the Comanche tribal rolls.

Although the Comanches and the Apaches fought each other fiercely and were not generally allies before 1860, the burgeoning trade in stolen cattle after the Civil War brought elements of the two tribes together in raiding and trading activities. The history of some of the Mescalero groups bears this out. By 1860 one large group of Mescaleros was led by Natzili. They

> claimed a great extent of land about the present site of Amarillo, Texas [i.e., in the heart of Comanche country]. . . . Natzili and his people depended almost entirely on the bison for their livelihood. . . . In addition to using them for their personal needs, Natzili's people also traded hides

with other Indians. . . . The Comanches were especially belligerent and had frequent encounters with the Mescaleros. The people of Natzili's band have a legend of a prolonged conflict, one lasting perhaps ten days, in which they were almost exterminated by Comanches, but they know neither the location nor the date of the encounter.[10]

After this defeat, Natzili and his group took refuge with the Mescaleros on the slopes of Sierra Blanca. By 1871, however, the military authorities in New Mexico were reporting that a large group of Mescaleros, led by Cadette, had been "roaming with the Comanche" for several years.[11] Herman Lehmann, captured in 1870, also reported contact between the Mescaleros and Comanches when he described meeting another Anglo captive, Adolph Korn (or Kohn), when a Comanche band came to visit the Mescaleros.[12] Korn seems to have been held by Mow-way's band of Kotsoteka Comanches, as Clint Smith stated in his narrative that Korn went on raids with him while they were both captives.[13] The encounter between Herman Lehmann and Adolph Korn had to have occurred after May 1870 and before November 14, 1872, since Korn was turned over to Indian agent Laurie Tatum on the latter date.[14]

Among the Comanches, Quanah Parker, in particular, had ties to the Mescalero Apaches after 1860. Parker himself had switched from one band of Comanches to another. Born into the Noconi band of Comanches as the son of Peta Nocona and Cynthia Ann Parker, Parker had left the Noconis and had become affiliated with the Kwahada band after the death of his father and the recapture of his mother. Parker's reason for moving from one band to another seems to have been his unwillingness to follow the Noconis onto the reservation after the 1867 Treaty of Medicine Lodge, preferring to live with a Comanche band that roamed the Staked Plains and continued to raid deep into Texas while other Comanche bands were agreeing to settlement on land around Ft. Sill. Parker, in describing a raid he had made into Mexico with the Kiowa leader Tohausen in 1868, stated, "[F]inally we reached an Apache camp (Mescalero) and remained there for some time. Then we went on the warpath across the Rio Grande."[15]

Quanah Parker, Comanche. Courtesy of National Archives, Select List #116.

The next Kwahada raid was on the Texas settlements near the Red River; this attack prompted the cavalry at Ft. Richardson near Jacksboro, Texas, to pursue the raiding party. During the pursuit, the leader of the raiding party, Bear's Ear, was killed, and Parker assumed leadership. In order to sell the animals stolen in the raid, Parker and several other warriors set off for New Mexico to meet the Mexican traders who made regular visits to the Mescalero Apache camps.[16]

While staying with the Mescaleros, Quanah Parker took his first wife, a Mescalero woman named Ta-ho-yea, said to be the daughter of Old Wolf. After about a year of marriage, however, Ta-ho-yea asked to return to her Mescalero family, citing as her reason her inability to learn the Comanche language. This change of mind was prompted by a visit to the Kwahadas by a group of Mescaleros; seeing old friends and family, Ta-ho-yea decided that she wanted to return home. The yearlong marriage probably took place sometime between 1869 and 1871.[17]

Another strong connection between Quanah Parker and the Mescalero Apaches was the peyote religion, although it must be stressed that this connection did not become fully cemented until after 1874. There have been a number of estimates as to when, exactly, the Comanches in general and Quanah Parker in particular became devotees of the peyote religion. Parker's biographer Bill Neeley cites a Parker descendant who theorized that the Comanches had always used peyote to some degree (that is, in folk or war medicine), but that Parker was the leader who brought the peyote religious rituals to widespread use among the Comanches after 1875.[18] Another Parker biographer, William T. Hagen, theorized that "Quanah's marital connection with the Mescalero [and the Lipans living with the Mescaleros] may account for his introduction to peyote" used in religious rituals.[19] This would place Parker's introduction to ritual peyote use around 1870. However, Parker and the Comanches did not adopt the practice until after June 1874.

In early 1874 "a young Kwahada named Isatai ... announced plans for a ceremony."[20] In May 1874 a number of Comanches, as well as some Cheyennes, Kiowas, Apaches, and Arapahos, met to hear Isatai announce that "he had an interview with the Great Spirit who said that the Caddos, Wichita, and other Indians who were adapting the mode of life of the whites were going down hill fast, in mean [*sic*] and in population, and the Comanche would do the same if they followed the same road." The only way for the Comanches to avert this fate was to "kill off all the white people they could."[21] Acting on Isatai's suggestion, a party of Comanches and Cheyennes attacked a group of buffalo hunters camped at an old trading post whose buildings were made of adobe (the site known as Adobe Walls) on the Canadian River. "Unfortunately, Isatai's *puha* 'power' did not work, and after a loss of six or seven Comanches and an equal number of Cheyennes, the attack was called off."[22] The Comanche defeat at Adobe Walls was a decisive turning point in a number of ways. Many of the outlaw Comanche groups decided to join other Comanche bands already on the reservation near Ft. Sill. Although Quanah Parker and his band of Kwahadas continued their raids for another year, Parker himself seems to have suffered great disillusionment over the failure of Isatai's magic. Parker's interest in the peyote religion was renewed during this period of spiritual disillusionment.

Although the Mescaleros had traditionally used peyote in their religious rituals, calling it *mescal*, it was the Lipan Apaches who created the form of ceremony practiced by the Mescaleros by 1870 and by the Comanches after 1875. The Lipans took the basic peyote ceremony—where peyote "buttons" were consumed as the participants danced around a fire throughout the night—and added their own dimension to the ceremony. Gone was the element of dance; the Lipans introduced special "peyote songs" intended to enhance the spiritual experience. A typical peyote healing ritual was described thusly:

> It is usually performed as an invocation for the recovery of some sick person. It is held in a tipi specially erected for the purpose, and begins usually at night, continuing until the sun is well up in the morning. As many men as can sit comfortably within the tipi may participate, but, as a rule, women do not take part in the ceremony proper, but occupy themselves

with the preparation of the sacred food and of the feast in which all join at the close of the performance. A fire is kept burning in the center of the tipi, enclosed within a crescent-shaped mound, on top of which is placed a sacred peyote. Following an opening prayer by the chief priest, four peyotes are distributed to each participant, who chews and swallows them, after which the sacred songs begin to the accompaniment of the drum and rattle, each man singing four songs in turn, and are kept up all night, varied by the intervals of prayer and other distributions of peyote, with a particular baptismal ceremony at midnight. The number of "buttons" eaten by one individual during the night varies from 10 to 40, and even more, the drug producing a sort of spiritual exaltation differing entirely from that produced by any other known drug, and apparently without any reaction. The effect is heightened by the weird lullaby of the songs, the constant sound of the drum and rattle, and the fitful glare of the fire. At some point during the ceremony the sick person is usually brought in to be prayed for, and is allowed to eat one or more specially consecrated peyotes. At daylight, the Morning Star Song is sung, when women pass in the sacred food, of which each worshipper partakes, and their ceremony concludes with the Meat Song. The rest of the morning is given to friendly gossip followed by a dinner under leafy arbors, after which the various families disperse to their homes.[23]

This is also the ceremonial form of the peyote religion practiced first by Quanah Parker and later by many of the Comanches of all bands, with Lipans playing a central role in the peyote ritual through their function as "peyote singers." Chevato was specifically named as a Lipan peyote singer who had taught the ritual to the Comanches.[24] Chevato's brother, Dinero, elaborated, "I knew about peyote before any of these Indians in Oklahoma country knew about it. I first ate peyote in Mexico. My great-grandfather was the first [Lipan] to make use of it in Mexico, and it was brought among the Indians here [in Oklahoma] years after. It was used as a medicine at first, and no women or young people ate it as they do now. It is called mescal-peyote in Mexico; here in Oklahoma it is called peyote."[25]

After a peyote ceremony, circa 1892. Seated: Quanah Parker (second from left), Chevato (far right). National Anthropological Archives, Smithsonian Institution/#00448100.

Since Chevato and Dinero were instrumental in bringing the peyote rituals to the Comanches through their association with Quanah Parker, and since the Comanches themselves believe that Parker's devotion to the cult was in place by the time he entered the reservation in 1875, it can be assumed that Chevato and Dinero were some of the teachers who, by 1874–75, converted Parker to a new spiritual path. It seems likely that Parker, in an effort to find a new source of *puha*, or medicine power, after the Adobe Walls defeat in 1874, turned or reexamined the peyote religion, finding at last the spiritual solace he was seeking.

Tracing the physical movements of the Comanches and Mescaleros, in order to more closely fix the time in which Herman Lehmann fled to the Comanches, requires a detailed look at events occurring in both tribes. Between Mackenzie's attack on the Comanche camp at McClellan Creek (1872) and the battle of Adobe Walls (1874), outlaw bands of Kwahada and Kotsoteka Comanches roamed free, raiding and stealing horses throughout Texas and New Mexico.

Although the Mescaleros had officially been brought onto their reservation near Ft. Stanton, New Mexico, in 1872, they did not stay there. In the summer of 1873 they fled to the mountains in advance of Maj. William G. Price's column, which was marching toward Mescalero. Once in the mountains, "it was found utterly impossible to overtake or drive them back, and they did not again return until they were ready."[26] Even on the reservation, supervision of the Mescaleros was practically nonexistent, according to the many complaints sent by the military officers at Ft. Stanton. "At the weekly issue of rations," Capt. James Stewart wrote in December 1874, "it is the invariable custom for individual Indians, most usually old squaws, to draw rations for the whole of their respective families, including many warriors, who are at the time of such issue anywhere but at the Indian Agency."[27] The Fechet scouting party, sent out from Ft. Stanton in February 1875, destroyed a Mescalero camp near the Guadalupe Mountains, sending two large Mescalero bands running toward Mexico. These bands, led by Natzili and Pinoli (and including Chevato as part of Natzili's group), did not return to Mescalero until the early spring of 1876.[28]

On June 2, 1875, Quanah Parker and the rest of the Kwahada Comanches entered Ft. Sill. They reported to the commander, Col. Ranald S. Mackenzie, and were placed on the Comanche-Kiowa Reservation nearby under the authority of the Indian Agency. The Indian agent, James M. Haworth, placed Parker in charge of the issuance of rations to his group, thus starting Parker "on the first step up the ladder to leadership of [all] the Comanche."[29]

In the summer of 1877 "Quanah was dispatched by Agent Haworth and Colonel Mackenzie to search for runaways from the reservation. After nearly two months he returned with a party of twenty-one that he had located on the Pecos River."[30] A closer look at the two-month trip that Parker took in 1877 to bring in runaways shows that he traveled to that section of the Pecos River that flows in southern New Mexico and west Texas, well within the radius of the routes taken by the Mescaleros during times they fled their reservation.[31]

Quanah Parker's own version of the events that brought Herman Lehmann to the Comanches places the transfer as occurring in 1877, during his mission to bring in Comanche runaways. Parker's version specifically names Chevato (calling him Che-bah-tah, the Comanche version of his name) as the facilitator:

> [T]he first he [Quanah Parker] knew of Herman Lehmann was when Lehmann was a boy, a captive in the hands of the Apaches, who were encamped on [the] Pecos River in New Mexico. Deponent [Quanah Parker] . . . remembers that General McKinzie [*sic*] was in command at Ft. Sill, Oklahoma, at that time, and that deponent went to the Pecos River at the request of General McKinzie for the purpose of persuading the Comanches who were encamped with the Apaches on the Pecos River to come in to Fort Sill and be at peace with the whites. That among the Comanches who returned to Ft. Sill with deponent there were about six (6) families of Apaches, among said Apaches was Che-bah-tah, an Apache who has since been incorporated with the Comanches. Che-bah-tah brought the boy Herman Lehmann with him. The boy wanted to live with me [Qua-

nah Parker] and I took him to my camp and he was called my boy. He lived with me nearly three years, after which time General McKinzie sent him home to his people.[32]

Herman Lehmann also gave an official account of his transfer from the Apaches to the Comanches in an affidavit filed in April 1901:

> I, Herman Lehmann, being duly sworn depose and say that I was born on Squaw Creek in Mason County, Texas, in the year 1859, and where I lived until the year 1870 when I was captured by a band of Apache Indians who took me away with them. Che-bah-tah [Chevato], who now lives with the Comanche Indians on their Reservation in Oklahoma, was one of the chiefs of the band that captured me. . . . After holding me four years the Apaches turned me over to the Comanches, the Comanches changing my name and adopting me as a Comanche.[33]

If Chevato accompanied Quanah Parker and Herman Lehmann to Ft. Sill, he did not stay there, but returned to the Mescaleros in New Mexico. He certainly had motive to disassociate himself from Herman Lehmann, in view of the fact that two of the Kiowa chiefs tried for the Warren wagon train massacre were sitting in a Texas penitentiary. However, Chevato remembered Parker's help and remembered the fact that he had almost turned himself in to be enrolled as a resident of the Comanche tribe. Twelve years later, Chevato renewed contact with Quanah Parker, requesting that he and his family be allowed to come to Oklahoma, since "my home . . . is at the Camanche [sic] country . . . and we long to come home."[34]

12. Geronimo

One day, Chevato met an army officer who told him that the army was look-ing for Apache scouts. So Chevato rode to Ft. Stanton, New Mexico, to enlist. Once he enlisted, he was assigned as a scout for a group of army surveyors who were surveying the territories of Arizona and New Mexico.

They were somewhere in Arizona when they saw a rider coming up real hard. The rider talked with the officer in charge of the survey group, and the officer sent for Chevato. He asked him, "Do you know an Apache named Geronimo?" The officer explained, "Well, they [the U.S. Army] are having a parley with Geronimo. They want to talk to him, but they don't have an interpreter to speak his language or Spanish. Could you ride back with this man to interpret at the parley?" Chevato agreed, so they got fresh mounts and set off for the parley.

It was about a day's ride away; you don't want to tax a horse or run him to death. Chevato had been told that they needed him to interpret the next day. They rode into the army camp late in the day, since they had gotten a late start. Chevato reported to the commanding officer, the man in charge of the parley with Geronimo. The officer told him, "Well, we've already got an interpreter, but if you want to stay and meet this man, you're welcome to stay."

Chevato said, "I would like to stay, after riding this time." So he was al-lowed to hear the parley. The other interpreter took over, but after the parley was over, Chevato was introduced to Geronimo.

Chevato finished scouting for the surveyors. Geronimo agreed to surren-der and was sent by train to Florida with his tribe. On the way to Florida, they stopped at San Antonio, Texas, and rested in the army quadrangle that still stands at Ft. Sam Houston. They spent two weeks there, Geronimo and his band. After their rest, they boarded the train and were taken to Ft. Mar-ion, Florida. They stayed there for a while, and then they were transferred to Alabama. And there they stayed for a number of years. Finally, they were allowed to come to Oklahoma Territory near Ft. Sill, but they could never *again go back to Arizona. That was part of their treaty. I have heard stories from descendants of these Apaches. On their first day in Oklahoma, when they were starting to get settled in, they could hear the coyotes howling. And the women started to cry. They asked them, "Why are you crying?" And the women said, "It seems like it has been a long time since we've been away from home, but now we hear the sounds of home," meaning the cries of the coyotes. And it was like music to them because it was a part of home, and they had missed their home so very much.*

Geronimo's band stayed at Ft. Sill, and then later on, they were moved about twenty miles north of Ft. Sill. They had their little establishment there; a park was given to them so that it was like a small reservation. In this area, they had a market so that they could buy supplies. They sent traders up there from Ft. Sill to sell them the necessities of life. This little market turned into a town, which still stands today. It is called Apache, Oklahoma, and that is how the town got its name.

Many years after Chevato had been introduced to Geronimo at the parley, he met him again at Ft. Sill. He asked Geronimo, "Do you remember me? I met you at the parley." And Geronimo replied, "Yes, I do remember you." After all, they were kin; they were Apaches.

§

When the Mescaleros were coaxed onto a reservation near Ft. Stanton, New Mexico, in 1872, their movement was in fulfillment of a new "peace policy" instituted by the Bureau of Indian Affairs in Washington DC. As the policy was interpreted in New Mexico and Arizona, the Indians of those territories were to be protected against the "thrashing" desired by such military officers as Lt. Thomas C. Davis of Army Headquarters, Santa Fe, and protected against thefts and attacks by settlers (such as had occurred after the Dowlin's Mill incident in 1874). "The Indians would be settled on their own lands, given protection against Anglos, and encouraged to make a living through agriculture or the raising of livestock."[1] In Arizona, four areas were set aside as Apache reservations: Ft. Apache (Cibecue and northern White Mountain Apaches), Camp Verde (Tonto Apaches and Yavapai),

Camp Grant (San Carlos and southern White Mountain Apaches), and
Ojo Caliente (eastern, or Warm Springs, band of Chiricahuas).[2] The peace
policy had mixed success in New Mexico and Arizona. While some groups
of Mescaleros, for example, found safety and protection on their reservation near Ft. Stanton, other Mescalero groups had no faith in a reservation system where they would be guarded by army troops. The memories
of Bosque Redondo and Gen. James H. Carleton's threat to kill all Apaches
in New Mexico on sight were still fresh. Additional military expeditions,
such as the Fechet scouting trip (1875), caused large groups of Mescaleros to flee to the Guadalupe Mountains or toward Mexico, not returning
until they could be coaxed back onto the reservation. In Arizona, the appointment of Gen. George Crook to head the military department in 1871
did bring peace, for a time, to the Apache bands located on reservations.
After Crook dealt forcefully with the Tonto Apaches in 1872, the other Arizona Apache bands settled down in their assigned areas, but there was
much fear, restlessness, and suspicion.[3] In addition, there were still hostile
Chiricahua factions roaming in Arizona and into Mexico who had never
reported to a reservation.

In 1874 the peace policy of the Bureau of Indian Affairs was changed in
Arizona to a policy of containment, where several bands would be con-
centrated on a single reservation (San Carlos) in order to make them easier to control and to reduce the number of raids.[4] The new policy had disastrous consequences in Arizona.

> There were problems from the start. Many of the groups living at San
> Carlos had never before been associated with one another, and their new
> proximity gave rise to mistrust and suspicion. Then, too, factional dis-
> putes developed within single groups, especially the Chiricahua. Some
> elements, tired of war and constant traveling, seemed to be in favor of
> peace. Others found the conditions at San Carlos intolerable and waited
> for a chance to escape. Among all Apaches there was the feeling that the
> future was uncertain and that . . . anything could happen at any time.[5]

The two large Apache bands that had proved most resistant to the move onto a reservation or to the consolidation at San Carlos—the Warm Springs Apaches led by Victorio and the Chiricahua hostile factions led by Juh and Geronimo—proved to be mercurial and touchy residents once they did agree to come to San Carlos, soon fleeing to the mountains at what they perceived as threats. Victorio's band began a rampage across Arizona that could not be tolerated. By 1879 the army, under the command of Gen. Crook, began to move against the renegade Warm Springs band to return them forcibly to San Carlos. The troopers caught up to Victorio's group at Hembrillo Canyon, New Mexico. Victorio's warriors were accompanied by some 250 Mescalero men, women, and children. The Mescaleros represented a breakaway faction who refused to follow the pleas of the Mescalero leaders, who urged their people to stay on their reservation and not get involved with Victorio. Victorio and his warriors had the upper hand at the beginning of the battle, since they had ambushed the U.S. troops, but when a second company arrived, Victorio and his fighters were overwhelmed and fled with their families to Mexico.[6] Once in Mexico, Mexican troops attacked the Warm Springs Apaches, and Victorio was killed. His Mescalero allies and their families who had survived the battle of Hembrillo Canyon returned to their reservation after the defeat. Thus at the end of 1880 there remained one band of Chiricahua Apaches, led by Juh and Geronimo, that was still at large, raiding through the northern states of Mexico and southern Arizona, leaving death and destruction in their wake.

Many Apache bands complained that they were assigned to a reservation that did not encompass their traditional homeland. This was especially true of the Jicarilla Apaches, whose traditional land lay in the Four Corners area. After being promised land in areas more congenial (and after having those promises broken not once but twice), the Jicarillas were finally moved to the Mescalero Reservation near Ft. Stanton in 1883, a move that was forcefully protested by the Jicarillas.[7]

The Mescaleros, however, could not make this complaint, as their reservation encompassed their traditional area. However, for the Mescaleros, reservation life did prove difficult. Although a small group of Mescaleros did return, starving and afraid, after the Fechet attack on Roman's camp in 1875, two large groups, led by Natzili and Pinoli, had fled to Mexico.[8] Chevato was a member of Natzili's group, and had thus accompanied that leader in the flight across the Rio Grande.[9] It was not until the spring of 1876 that Natzili and his group were coaxed back to the Mescalero Reservation with promises made by a new Indian agent, F. C. Godfoy, of greater protection against thefts and attacks by nearby settlers. The groups returned to Mescalero only to face a smallpox epidemic, which had begun during the winter of 1876. "Those falling ill with a fever were immediately removed from the camps so that their deaths would not make it necessary to move the whole community. Their fevered condition usually led to their tipis being pitched on some eminence where they were exposed to the wind. Here they were provided with a supply of provisions and water and abandoned to their own resources. . . . [Chief] Roman's family was exterminated by the disease." Smallpox also claimed the life of Chief Santana.[10]

By 1879, as Gen. Crook in Arizona prepared to attack Victorio and his renegade group of Warm Springs Apaches, the situation at Mescalero had stabilized to some degree. Natzili had assumed leadership of the largest number of Mescalero groups (including the Lipans) and was praised as "an exemplary Indian and a true friend of the Government,"[11] because he had kept many of the Mescalero warriors on the reservation, refusing to be "seduced by the glitter of Victorio's success."[12]

Other Mescalero leaders from the early reservation period were San Juan, Peso, Jose Mancito, Roman Chiquito (son of Roman), Gorgorio, and Nau-ta-go-lingi (Have You Got Any Tobacco).[13] Yet because a breakaway group of Mescalero had joined Victorio, the military authorities in New Mexico determined that all the Mescaleros must be punished. The Mescaleros were to have their guns and horses confiscated on the theory that without these things, they would have to stay on the reservation.

The disarming of the Mescaleros, accomplished on April 16, 1880, was merely a replay of all the old antagonisms between the military authorities at Ft. Stanton and the Indian agency at Mescalero, antagonisms that had existed since at least 1874. In addition, the disarming of the Mescale-

Mescalero leaders San Juan (left) and Natzili (right). National Anthropological Archives, Smithsonian Institution/#02086600.

ros was only a replay of the government's willful ignorance of the best interest of the Mescaleros in favor of a heavy-handed policy designed to crush all "Apaches" regardless of their demonstrated evidence of cooperation with the Indian agency. The agent, S. A. Russell, believed that the military had assented to his proposition that the agent and the Mescalero chiefs be the ones to disarm the band. Accordingly, Agent Russell and chiefs Natzili, San Juan, Gorgorio, and Roman went out to try to bring the entire tribe onto the reservation. When only sixty-five adult males showed up, Russell and Natzili explained that they must give up their guns and their horses but that all would be returned "after the troubles were over." Not trusting what they heard, many of the men drifted away. The troops, who had stood aside while these events transpired, then overreacted and began shooting. As soon as the first shots were fired, the remaining Mescaleros tried to flee. Fourteen Mescaleros were killed, twenty-five men escaped, and the rest were taken prisoner, along with the women and children who remained.[14] Agent Russell described what happened next:

The Indian camp was about one-third of a mile from the agency. After the occurrence mentioned above, Colonel Hatch ordered all of the Indians to be brought to the Agency, soon as they arrived here they were dismounted, placed under guard, searched for arms and ammunition, and their horses corralled. In this hurried removal, and the search that was made by soldiers, the Indians lost much that was valuable to them and not contraband. The next morning the Indian horses to the number of 200 or more were sent to Ft. Stanton, and the Indians put in the corral, where the old manure was 3 to 5 inches deep. This produced so much sickness among them that they had soon to be removed. This was after Capt. Steelhammer and I had repeatedly assured them that those who remained faithful and did as he requested would be well treated, and their horses put in my hands. In addition to the animals that were sent to Ft. Stanton, a good many were CONFISCATED by the military. I am credibly informed that of the horses sent to Ft. Stanton there are but 42 left, the other having died, been killed, or claimed by citizens.[15]

Those Mescaleros who were not taken prisoner were hunted down and brought back to the reservation.

The troops at Ft. Stanton were ordered back to the reservation in September 1880 to disarm those Mescaleros who still possessed firearms. This time, the disarming occurred without horses being confiscated, although Roman Chiquita, Hosthea, HorseThief, and Maria's Boy were arrested and confined in the Ft. Stanton guardhouse to guarantee the good behavior of the rest of the Mescaleros. Hosthea was a twenty-three-year-old widow, and it is unknown why she was arrested along with the men. The hostages were sent to Ft. Union, New Mexico, in October 1880, but were released soon thereafter.[16]

By 1882 the situation at the Mescalero Reservation had deteriorated even further. Because Congress had neglected to appropriate funds to pay for rations, many Mescaleros were starving, and it was left to the army officers at Ft. Stanton to discover ways to feed them.[17] Probably looking for a way to feed his family, on March 22, 1883, Chevato reported to Ft. Stanton, where he enlisted as an army scout for a term of six months. The enlistment process at Ft. Stanton was similar to that described by an Apache scout who enlisted in Arizona at about the same time. "We lined up to be chosen.... These officers looked me over to see if I was alright. They felt my arms and legs and pounded my chest to see if I would cough. That's the way they did with all the scouts they picked and if you coughed, they would not take you. I was all right, so they took me.... All those scouts who had wives were followed by them to ... [the fort] where they were allowed to draw out five dollars worth of supplies from the commissary for their families."[18]

Chevato was described at the time of his 1883 enlistment as having copper skin and black eyes and measuring five feet ten inches in height. His age was not given in the enlistment record, but he would have been thirty-one. He was assigned to the army camp at South Fork, some miles west of Ft. Stanton, close to the Mescalero Reservation.[19] Chevato was one of four Indian scouts attached to Company D, Fourth U.S. Cavalry, commanded by Capt. John Lee; the other scouts were Eclodenanton, Eyahein, and Sharpo. Two additional scouts enlisted but deserted three months later.[20] Their first assignment was to accompany Lt. George Gale and twenty-five enlisted troops on a scout looking for renegade Indians in the vicinity of Mescalero Springs and out onto the Staked Plains.[21] No renegades were found, but while on the scout, a portion of the company was detached by order of the commander of the New Mexico Military District and ordered to accompany Lt. Thomas Symons, an army engineer, who was tasked with surveying the international boundary between the United States and Mexico.[22]

One of the oddest coincidences in the life of Chevato is the presence, at all junctures, of Col. Ranald S. Mackenzie. The two men never met, and Mackenzie certainly would have had no idea who Chevato was, but Mackenzie's army postings seem to follow Chevato's movements like a shadow. As Chevato and Carnoviste rode away with their captive, Herman Lehmann, they rode near Ft. McKavitt, whose commanding officer in 1870 was Mackenzie. Three years later Mackenzie was transferred to Ft. Duncan (Eagle Pass, Texas) and organized the raid across the border on the Lipans at El Remolino. By 1877 Mackenzie was the commander at Ft. Sill, Oklahoma, where he sent Quanah Parker out to bring in Comanche renegades. Mackenzie's action enabled Chevato to turn over Herman Lehmann to Parker. After a posting to Nebraska and the Black Hills district, Mackenzie received the command of the New Mexico Military District, as well as a promotion to brigadier general.[23]

Mackenzie himself authorized the escort for the surveyor Lt. Symons. Symons arrived in El Paso to begin the survey that would establish an international boundary between Mexico and the U.S. territories of New Mexico and Arizona. As Symons later explained, he applied to Gen. Mackenzie for

> [a]n escort, guides, pack transportation, camp equipage, etc. In my letter I suggested that at least one full troop of Cavalry be furnished and as much more as in his [Mackenzie's] judgment might be necessary, and to enable him to judge of the size of the escort suitable. I informed him that the portion of the line to be examined with this escort was from El Paso westward to where the railroad to Guaymas crosses the boundary. The idea that I wished to convey to Gen. Mackenzie was that it was over this dangerous portion of the line, frequently infested by large bands of hostile Apaches that I wished the strong escort asked for of at least one full troop of cavalry or more, and that beyond the railroad referred to, where danger from hostile Indians ceases, I would not want any longer so large an escort.[24]

Since Chevato's company was already on a scout in the area south of the Mescalero Reservation, a portion of the company that included Chevato and another Indian scout was detached and sent to escort Lt. Symons. They accompanied him along the border of the New Mexico Territory and Mexico, but when they came to the Guaymas railroad crossing, Symons kept his escort instead of sending them back to Ft. Stanton. Chevato's Company D had set out from Ft. Stanton in April 1883, and by the time Symons reached Guaymas, it was mid May. Events were occurring in Arizona that would intervene, providing a detour for Chevato's extended scout.

Geronimo, Juh, and their hostile faction of Chiricahua Apaches had finally entered the reservation at San Carlos, but they had proved to be touchy and suspicious residents. In 1881 they fled in response to rumors of impending arrests of the Apache leadership. Safely hidden in the Sierra Madres of Sonora, Mexico, the Chiricahuas began to raid at will throughout the states of Sonora and Chihuahua as well as crossing the border to raid into Arizona. Determined to destroy the remaining band of "wild" Apaches, Gen. Crook began assembling men and matériel for a major offensive in the spring of 1883. Crook was waiting for two conditions to materialize, conditions "he considered imperative: a sudden reappearance of the Chiricahuas in Arizona to give him the needed 'hot pursuit' excuse, and a guide from the hostile *rancherias* who knew the Sierra Madre."[25] By May 1883 both conditions had been met, and Crook and his troops crossed the U.S.-Mexico border with the acquiescence of the Mexican government. By May 19, 1883, Crook held more than one hundred Chiricahua prisoners. "At a quarter to nine in the morning of May 20, General Crook's scouts suddenly began shrieking and howling as they grabbed their arms and took cover in the trees; when Crook and the other officers demanded to know the cause, the scouts pointed upward. There, on the cliff edge more than a thousand feet above, stood . . . Geronimo and his fighters," seeking a meeting with Crook.[26]

Lt. Symons's escort from Ft. Stanton was composed of both cavalry and infantrymen. The infantry traveled with him as far as the southern end of the Animas Valley, New Mexico, where the harsh terrain forced Symons to send the troopers back along with the wagons that carried their supplies, since the wagon road had become impassable. The cavalry escort, including Chevato, continued on with Symons toward Ft. Huachuca, Arizona, where additional Arizona cavalrymen joined them. Symons explained that he thought it necessary to keep the New Mexico escort because "the men had become conversant with all the varied duties required of them, which they performed intelligently, willingly and cheerfully. I had confidence in them, and they had confidence in me, two things of great importance in a journey to be undertaken across the Sonora and Colorado deserts."[27]

Symons left his escorts at Ft. Huachuca, so the call for a translator for Crook's meeting with Geronimo must have occurred while Chevato and the cavalry escort were between the southern end of the Animas Valley/Guadalupe Canyon and Ft. Huachuca. Crook's line of march crossed directly across their path, since Crook crossed the border at San Bernardino, just west of the southern end of the Animas Valley and Guadalupe Canyon.[28]

When Mackenzie discovered that Lt. Symons had not returned his escort at the Guaymas crossing, he fired off an angry letter to the adjutant general, A. G. Drum. Drum, in turn, fixed the hapless Lt. Symons in his crosshairs and demanded an explanation. Symons provided a meek apology and excuse, citing a misunderstanding on the part of Mackenzie. However, the poor lieutenant seemed to have been terrified to be surveying in an area in which he expected Geronimo to pop out of a bush at any moment, repeatedly citing his fear of "hostile Indians" as the reason for retaining such a large escort.[29]

Crook's meeting with Geronimo near Huachinera, Sonora, resulted in the return of the Chiricahuas to San Carlos. Of course the matter did not end in May 1883. The movements of Geronimo and the Chiricahuas continued to be of concern not only to military officers in Arizona but also in New Mexico. In September 1885 a scouting party was sent out from Ft. Stanton to the Mescalero Agency to see "if any of Geronimo's band of hostile Indians are there or have been there."[30] One of those looking for Geronimo's band at the Mescalero Agency was Chevato. He had enlisted again on September 7, 1885, along with Magoosh, Domingo, HorseThief, and Shosh.[31]

Gen. Nelson A. Miles's campaign against Geronimo in 1886 caused the Military District of New Mexico to adopt some of the same successful strategies used by Crook in 1883, particularly the use of Indian scouts. The call went out at Ft. Stanton, resulting in a large number of Mescaleros enlisting in 1886. In fact, of a total of ninety-two adult male Mescaleros and Lipans, forty-eight had enlisted as Indian scouts by 1886 (see appendix 2).[32] Among those who enlisted in 1886 was Chevato's brother, Dinero.[33] Although none of the Mescalero scouts were used directly in the final cam-

Domingo, Mescalero scout, 1886. Domingo's costume, with the possible exception of the plaid blanket and gun belt, does not represent a Mescalero scout's uniform; the face paint and war club do illustrate Mescalero warfare, while the mountain lion skin shows Domingo had "mountain lion power." National Anthropological Archives, Smithsonian Institution/#02044500.

paign against Geronimo, they patrolled southern New Mexico, closing off any avenues of escape.

Just as the Mescaleros had taken in the Lipans in the nineteenth century, so they were called upon to take in a portion of the Chiricahuas in the twentieth. Three years after Geronimo's surrender in 1886, two Mescalero families were found to be among the Chiricahua prisoners at Ft. Marion, Florida—the family of Ih-tedda (who had married Geronimo and had a daughter, Lenna, by him) and the family of "Alabama Charlie" Smith (a Chiricahua scout who had married a Mescalero woman while serving as a scout at Ft. Stanton). The Mescalero women Ih-tedda and Cumpah (wife of Alabama Charlie) and Cumpah's son had been captured by Geronimo's band just prior to their surrender in 1886. The captives had been swept up with the rest of the Chiricahuas and imprisoned after Geronimo's surrender, where Cumpah and her son were finally reunited with Alabama Charlie Smith. By custom, Smith's marriage to Cumpah also made him a member of the Mescaleros. Both Ih-tedda and the family of Alabama Charlie Smith had been returned to the Mescalero Reservation by 1890.[34] More Chiricahuas arrived at Mescalero in 1913. The new arrivals were composed of survivors of Geronimo's band as well as survivors of the Ft. Apache Chiricahua group who had been imprisoned and then finally released to live near Ft. Sill. They chose to move to the Mescalero Reservation and preserve their status as wards of the government rather than accept land allotted to them in Oklahoma.[35]

13. The Murder Trial

While Chevato and Dinero were with the Mescaleros, each had married a Mescalero woman and had children. Chevato and his wife had three children—two boys and a girl. Dinero had also married, but he allegedly began to carry on an affair with a different woman and was found out by that woman's husband. The husband contacted Dinero, and they became very bitter enemies. Chevato told this story to his children because he wanted to teach them a moral lesson, so this is what happened to Dinero.

After he was found out, Dinero quit seeing the woman, but the damage was already done. It was like a sore that festered up. One day, the irate husband met Dinero, and the argument got heated. They got into a fight, and, unfortunately, Dinero killed this man. New Mexico was at that time a territory that was trying to become a state, and because of this, they had more controls on the Apache, on the Mescaleros, and on the way they traveled. The government had elements of the army stationed among them. At this time, Mescalero was no longer a camp, but was becoming a reservation. They had agents of the U.S. government who set up within the tribe their own judicial system. It might not have been as sophisticated as we know it, but it was more or less set up after the court system of that day. They would have a judge, and they would conduct a little court. So that's where they sent Dinero. They had built a jail a Mescalero, and Dinero had been in the jail; they sent him to court and found him guilty.

The agent, however, thought it might be bad publicity and that Dinero's actions might reflect badly, so he referred the case over to the next jurisdiction of the judicial system, which was the territorial circuit judge. So, they had a regular trial. The judge had all the information about how the Indian court had found Dinero guilty. He was found guilty again and sentenced to be hanged.[1]

As Dinero waited on his execution date, Chevato's ebb was very low. His only brother was going to be hanged. Chevato had heard that there was this Comanche chief from the Oklahoma Indian Territory who was in New Mexico hunting deer. He was going to be hunting at the Mescalero Reservation. The chief was Quanah Parker; by this time, he was the chief of all the Comanche. It was said that this Indian chief had a lot of clout, and that he was very highly thought of by both Anglo and the Indian sides. Chevato heard all of this and thought, "It can't hurt," so he went to see him. He told the chief what his desires were—that if Quanah Parker would save his brother from being hung, Chevato would appreciate it.

Unbeknown to my grandfather, this chief, Quanah Parker, was facing his own problems in Oklahoma. He had become the chief of all the Comanche and his people warmly loved him, but, as you know from today's society, there *were factions. There were those who spoke against him. So animosities had built up against this man, Quanah Parker, and they had sworn to kill him.*

All this was unknown to Chevato back in New Mexico. He went to see Quanah Parker and pleaded his case. He said, "I was told that you have a lot of influence and that you might be able to help my brother." He told about the incident that led to Dinero's death sentence. Quanah Parker said, "I happen to know the New Mexico territorial governor; he came to Oklahoma to hunt quail. Let me go to see him. I'm not making any promises, but let me go and see." So Quanah Parker went to visit the territorial governor, and they had a meeting. Quanah Parker came out and returned to see Chevato, telling him, "I have some good news and some bad news. You and your brother can leave New Mexico Territory, but for the rest of your life, you both have to stay out of New Mexico. If, by any chance, you come back, or your brother comes back, they will carry out the execution." So my grandfather said, "That's fair enough."

Quanah Parker also said, "I promised that I would give you both gainful employment when you come up to the Indian Territory [in Oklahoma]. So, that's another part of the agreement—that you will have to work for me." And Chevato said, "Fine, that's good." So Dinero was spared from being hung, and he and Chevato prepared to move to Oklahoma to work for Quanah Parker.

§

By 1877 Chevato had married a woman from among the group of Lipans living with the Mescaleros. Although her name is not known, she was born in Mexico and must have been a part of the Zaragosa band of Lipans.[2] Their first child, a daughter named Mineha, was born that year. A son, Susco, was born in 1878. Another son, Alguno (also spelled Alguino), was born in 1881. A final son named Jo-Co was born in 1888.[3] The children must have also been given names in the Lipan language; however, only several of those names have been preserved.[4] The family was also given two sets of English names by two different Indian agents, which confused the matter even further.

Names Given to Chevato and His Family, 1869–90

Name Known By	Lipan Name	Mescalero Name	English Name #1	English Name #2	Relationship
Chevato		Chivato	Jasper Antrim	William Goat	
		Billy Chiwat		William Heath	
		Chi-wa-ta			
		Chi-ten-de			
Carrie Heath	Ches-chilla	Mineha	Cora Antrim	Carrie Heath	Daughter
				Lola Heath	
Cora Heath				Corine Heath	Granddaughter
Susco		Susco	Wayne Antrim		Son
Harry Heath	Be-che-ide	Alguno	Joe Antrim	Harry Heath	Son
		Alguino			
		Jo-Co			
Chenoco		Chenocha		Fred Heath	Son
Dinero		Dinero Boy	Money's Boy	Clara Heath	Second wife
Chalita		Se-le-kia		John Dinero	Brother
				Jane Dinero	In-law
Blacita	En-a-ga-na	Blacita		Bessie Chilito	Niece

A glimpse of the Mescalero Reservation in 1884, which included at that time the Mescaleros, Lipans, and Jicarilla Apaches, is provided by the inspection reports made to the Bureau of Indian Affairs. Inspector E. S. Ward, who toured the reservation in July 1884, noted that there was enough land to give each family a small farm, yet the "Indians live in tents and dress in semi-barbarous fashion, and very few have any fixed habitation." Only about 500 acres out of a total of 500,000 were under cultivation. The agency "was poorly provided with buildings. Schoolhouse too small . . . [with only] nine boys in attendance." The inspector recommended that the Indians be encouraged in raising horses and that they be furnished with stock horses, although he noted that the Jicarillas alone had 3,000 horses. One final note casually mentioned a problem that would grow in severity over the next few years: "Some of the Jicarillas want to return to the old reservation. . . . [T]hey must be told to stay where they are."[5]

The Jicarillas had been forced to move to the Mescalero Reservation in 1883 as part of the Bureau of Indian Affairs' consolidation plan, but the reality seemed to be that the bureau had no idea what to do with them, and moving them to Mescalero seemed to be the simplest solution. Their wanderings had begun in 1873, when the New Mexico superintendent of Indian Affairs informed them that "the lands they were living on [i.e., their ancestral homeland in the Four Corners area of New Mexico] now belonged to a company over which the government had no control and that the country was being rapidly settled by people whose actions could not be predicted."[6] Since federal regulations required that the Jicarillas be placed on a reservation, it was first proposed to move them to the Mescalero Reservation. After consultation, however, the Jicarilla leaders proposed an area in northwest New Mexico on the San Juan River. This land was secured and established as a reservation by executive order in 1874. However, this order was never implemented. The government dragged its feet, and the Jicarillas themselves were not anxious to move from the area in which they were then living (near Abiquiu and the Cimarron Agency). The government foot dragging had to do with geological surveys that showed that the San Juan River area was rich in ore; thus Indian Affairs was not anxious to finalize a reservation on land that would later prove valuable. In addition, the citizens of the San Juan area were petitioning the "President, Secretary of the Interior and Indian Commissioner requesting that the Order be annulled and the Jicarillas be moved to Mescalero."[7] In 1880 a second area was set aside for the Jicarillas near Tierra Amarilla in northern New Mexico. Although this area was acceptable to part of the tribe, there were several groups who opposed the move and scattered. Primary among the groups resisting the move by using delaying tactics was the Jicarilla band led by San Pablo. The new reservation area, called Amargo, proved untenable. The agent reported that the land was so barren that it could not sustain humans or beasts, although the Jicarillas still preferred this land to being moved to Mescalero. However, since the Jicarillas were still divided into factions, with some wanting to stay at Amargo and others wanting further negotiations with the Indian agency for new land, they were unable to present a united front when the bureau finally decided to revert to its original position and move the entire Jicarilla tribe to the Mescalero Reservation. So on August 20, 1883, the Jicarillas began their "Long Walk" to Mescalero.[8]

Once at Mescalero, "the Jicarillas made the best of their situation ... carrying out their promises to cultivate the land."[9] The 500 acres of cultivated land found by Ward in his 1884 inspection at Mescalero were cultivated by the Jicarillas. Although they continued to express to the Mescalero agent their desire to leave, they had learned some valuable lessons from their previous experience with the government that would stand them in good stead. They had learned that when their tribe was divided by factionalism, their objectives were defeated. They had learned that when they tried to delay the implementation of a government order by scattering, their delaying tactics could backfire.

> Their first extensive interactions and negotiations with the government were beginning to teach the Jicarillas just how it operated. They saw that there was no "Great Father" who directed all the action, but a bureaucracy that wielded powerful influence. In their initial dealings, the Jica-

rillas seem to have put all their faith in the federal government to protect their interests, but when they lost their reservation in 1883, they were disillusioned. Within the next few years, however, they successfully gambled by playing off one group against another. . . . They also found out that the agent was really the low man on the totem pole, and within the coming years they often appealed to higher authority, sometimes with good results.[10]

When Inspector Pearsons toured the Mescalero Reservation in December 1885, he found the agency school attendance had risen to twenty-five children who were "making good progress . . . [although] the clothing is too small for the children." Most of the 500 acres planted that year had been planted in corn. The schoolchildren had also raised 3 acres of vegetables, although "owing to the carelessness of Agent Lewellyn in protecting the land by a proper fence, the crop was all destroyed." Pearsons reported that the Indians now wanted to live in houses, to which the Indian Division of the Office of Indian Affairs responded by authorizing two windows and two doors to be furnished to all Indians wishing to build a home.[11]

The 1886 inspection report, made by Inspector Gardner, found a number of deficiencies. The amount of land under cultivation was estimated to be only about 300 acres. The inspector continued to stress that little land was under cultivation, ignoring the actual terrain of the area, which was more amenable to livestock raising than to the raising of crops. "Some few of the Indians gave their crops good attention, while others almost entirely neglected their fields, and the labor of cultivating them fell upon and was done by the Agency employees."[12] However, it was noted that most of the Mescalero men were enlisted as scouts at Ft. Stanton and thus unavailable for farming chores.[13]

The Jicarilla problem had escalated by the time Inspector Gardner made his tour in October 1886. He observed that four Jicarillas had enlisted as scouts, yet

> those remaining upon the reserve did very little toward farming, practically nothing, and I am very sorry to say, as I firmly believe, that they

will never do anything upon this reservation. A certain portion or band of the Jicarillas under one Augustine have not worked or will not work within the reserve. They were brought upon this reservation against their free will some four years ago, and since which time they have done no good towards self-support, but have consumed most of their time in idleness, visiting, and devising means whereby they could get away from this reservation. About one hundred Jicarillas are now absent from the reservation.[14]

The housing situation showed no improvement over that reported in July 1884; Gardner stated that "they all live in tepes [sic] and wickiups. Although some few of them have houses yet they prefer to live in tepes." A total count of all livestock yielded the following figures: 550-600 head of cattle and 2,500 horses and ponies.[15]

What Gardner did not know when he wrote his report in October 1886 was that the balance of the Jicarilla tribe was planning their escape from the Mescalero Reservation. In November 1886 a second group numbering about one hundred stole away in the night while a violent snowstorm raged. They went to the agency school and took their children (with the passive support of the Mescalero children, who did not alert the school personnel), cut the telegraph lines from the agency to Ft. Stanton, and stole away in the night. "The escapees were well on their way when Col. Grierson [at Ft. Stanton] was informed about the second exodus. An interpreter was sent to interrupt the Jicarillas and to try to persuade them to go back to the Mescalero Agency. They refused absolutely, saying that they would rather die than return. Grierson allowed them to join the other Jicarillas who were already near Santa Fe."[16]

The final lesson learned by the Jicarillas in their odyssey to find a permanent home was that it paid to enlist the help of powerful persons. When the first group of Jicarillas had run away from the Mescalero Reservation in October 1886, the Mescalero agent, Col. Fletcher J. Cowart, requested that the military bring them back. Fortunately for the Jicarillas, Gen. Miles was informed and was given additional information as to the reason for their wanderings and became sympathetic to their cause. He was able to bring the Jicarillas' grievances to the attention of the proper authorities in Washington, helping to secure for them a final home back in Amargo.[17]

As the Jicarilla grievances became common knowledge among the Mescaleros and Lipans living with them on the reservation, the Mescaleros and Lipans were compiling their own set of grievances. These complaints were based on nonsensical and contradictory actions by the Indian Affairs bureaucracy as well as on the conduct of an ever-revolving parade of Indian agents after 1886, each of whom seemed more oblivious to the welfare of the Indians than the last. One bureaucratic example left the Indians perplexed. Since the Bureau of Indian Affairs had decreed, in its peace policy of 1872, that the Indians be taught agriculture, the bureau furnished each agency with wagons. However, the bureaucrats in Washington "knew nothing about selecting wagons for the mountain districts. [They] did not know that the mountain roads [were] six inches wider than the plains country roads. So when the wagons came they were six inches too narrow for the roads and were not satisfactory. . . . [So] the Indians abandoned the wagons whenever possible."[18]

One agent particularly disliked by the Mescaleros and Lipans was Col. Cowart (1886-89). The dislike stemmed from Cowart's heavy-handed attempts to regulate every aspect of the Indians' lives, with the view of turning the Mescaleros and Lipans into model Anglocized residents. While other agents railed at the Indians for their inability to become farmers, Cowart attempted to change the very fabric of their lives. The story of the Lipan Boneski and the new suit is illustrative:

> The Agent, Colonel Cowart, had a suit of clothes which was too small for him, so he gave it to Boneski and paid him five dollars to wear it. Boneski came to the agency several times with the suit on and then discarded the coat, explaining to the agent that it was too hot to wear a coat. The agent accepted the excuse. On his next appearance at the agency he had on the vest and the pants, which appeared to be all right. However, the agent soon noticed that Boneski watched his every move and wondered why Boneski

never allowed his back to be toward the agent. Finally, the agent's curiosity overcame his politeness. He seized Boneski, turned him around, and saw that the seat of the trousers had been entirely cut away. Boneski explained that he was not accustomed to wearing trousers but only a gee-string, so he had cut away that part of the pants which seemed to him useless. From then on only the vest was in evidence.[19]

Cowart also outlawed plural marriages, decreed that the tribal police force wear their uniforms at all times, and required that the policemen keep their hair cut short.[20] Then Cowart turned his attention to the matter of names.

Chevato's daughter, Mineha, had been forced to attend the agency school from about the age of seven, where she was renamed Carrie Heath. Soon, many of the Mescaleros and Lipans were given English names, causing consternation, but the English names bestowed prior to 1889 at least bore some relation to the translation of a person's Indian name, and the naming policy was only applied to about one-third of the population. When Cowart took over as agent, however, he decided that everyone must have an English name, and most of the names he chose bore no relation whatsoever to any translation from an older, Indian name. When Chevato was informed in 1889 that his name was now to be Jasper Antrim, he absolutely refused to be recorded in this way on the agency rolls. Prior to 1889 Chevato's name had simply been translated from Spanish to English, and he was recorded as William Goat or Billy Goat. After his refusal to be known as Jasper Antrim, he did acquiesce to the name of William Heath, since his daughter had been given the surname Heath at the agency school. Thus Chevato's Mescalero family was forever after known as the Heath family, with his two surviving sons, Alguno and Jo-Co, known as Harry and Paul Heath, respectively.[21]

Cowart's unhappy tenure as agent at Mescalero also coincided with private sorrow within Chevato's family. His Lipan wife and eldest son, Susco, had both died in late 1888. His middle son, Alguno, had been taken to live at the agency school with his sister, Mineha, while his youngest son,

Jo-Co, was just a year-old baby. Chevato remarried in 1890 to a Mescalero woman, Chenoco, daughter of Camisa. Dinero had married a Mescalero woman named Chalita sometime before 1885; their daughter, Blacita, was born in 1889.[22]

Chevato had paid close attention to the maneuvers of the Jicarilla Apaches in their struggles with the Indian Affairs bureaucracy. Their final escape from Mescalero was still fresh in his memory, as was the unexpected championship of their cause by a powerful general, causing the Jicarillas to reach a successful outcome in their search for a reservation on which they wanted to live. Chevato must have taken these lessons to heart, because in early 1886 he reached out to a powerful protector and old acquaintance, imploring his assistance in enabling Chevato and other Lipans to leave the Mescalero Reservation.

Quanah Parker had visited the Mescalero Reservation with a delegation of Comanches the year before Chevato reached out to enlist his aid. In October 1885 Parker had visited for ten days, making "a very favorable impression on these Indians" as well as on the agent, W. H. Llewellyn. While at Mescalero, Parker had "given [the Indians] much good advice and council."[23] No evidence survives as to the exact advice and council Parker gave to the Mescaleros and Lipans, but the result of his council was seen within a year. In 1886 a man named Chi-ten-de and his brother Enriques, or Ta-ha-shin-de, wrote to Parker at the Kiowa Agency, requesting his assistance in relocating the Lipans from the Mescalero Agency to the Kiowa Agency. Parker turned the letter over to the Kiowa agent, explaining that the letter writers were Comanches, "some of them nearly related to him, and that they had become separated from the Comanches twenty or twenty-five years since [i.e., circa 1861–65]."[24] The letter writers were none other than Chevato and Dinero. Since Parker made the assertion that Chevato and Dinero were related to him at least twice in talks with the Kiowa agent, it makes one wonder whether his Mescalero wife, Ta-ho-yea, was possibly a Lipan. Alternatively, Parker could have made these assertions simply to lend weight to his argument for moving the Lipans to Oklahoma. Once the Kiowa agent received the Chi-ten-de and Ta-ha-shin-de letter, he forwarded it to Washington; Indian Affairs then queried the Mescalero agent as to what was going on. The Mescalero agent replied that "the Indians referred to by Chi-ten-de were not Comanches but Lipans and that the party who wrote Chi-ten-de's letter for him claimed land upon their reservation, [suggesting] that such party was more anxious to have the Indians removed than they were to go."[25] And there the matter stood for three years, in a bureaucratic limbo, with no action taken either to force the Lipans to stay at Mescalero or to adopt Quanah Parker's suggestion and allow them to move to the Kiowa Agency in Oklahoma.

Chevato and the Jicarilla Apaches were not the only Indians learning how to deal with the Washington bureaucracy. Quanah Parker had become an influential chief within the Comanche tribe and by 1885 was the leader of a faction that wanted to open Comanche lands for lease to Texas cattlemen. Parker was in favor of the Comanches granting leasing rights since he believed that the cattlemen would only take over these lands anyway, and it would be in the best interest of the Comanches to be paid for the grazing rights. The Kiowa agent agreed with Parker's position, but there were factions within the Comanches who opposed the proposal. The Texas cattlemen began to move their animals into the Comanche grasslands, building pens and fences; when they began to pay Parker for his support, resistance stiffened among the older, more conservative Comanche leaders. Opposition also arose among the Kiowas, whose lands were too far north of the Red River to be of much interest to the Texans.[26] When Parker and a delegation of Comanches and Kiowas who favored opening the grasslands to leases visited Washington DC in March 1885 to lobby the secretary of the interior, approval was given for the lease arrangements with the Texas cattlemen, much to the displeasure of many of the Comanches and Kiowas.[27] The Chi-ten-de and Ta-ha-shin-de letter sent to Parker in 1886 from the Mescalero Reservation was acknowledgment of the fact that Parker had become adept at lobbying to obtain a result favorable to Indians. The letter was merely requesting his aid in using some of those same lobbying skills on behalf of the Lipans at Mescalero.

Chevato did not give up when the commissioner of Indian Affairs did not act upon his request to Quanah Parker to assist in a move to the Kiowa Agency. One year after the Chi-ten-de and Ta-ha-shin-de letter was sent, Chevato and other Lipans attempted to escape from the Mescalero Reservation. In late July or early August 1887 a delegation of four Comanches, led by Parker, visited the Mescalero Reservation; the visit was probably made in order to participate in peyote ceremonies. When the Comanches left to return to their reservation in Indian Territory, they were followed by seven Lipans.[28] The seven Lipans included Chevato and probably Dinero and their families (which totaled seven persons in 1887). When the Mescalero agent, Col. Cowart, discovered their absence, he requested military assistance. Lt. J. S. Scott and Troop D, Sixth Cavalry, were dispatched from Ft. Stanton to chase them down. Parker and the Comanches were allowed to return to Oklahoma, while Chevato and the other Lipans were returned to the Mescalero Reservation.[29] The report of the escape made its way up the chain of military command via the general who had championed the cause of the Jicarilla—Gen. Miles. The result in this instance, however, was not as favorable. When Miles passed on information about the Lipan escape, the secretary of war recommended that no further visits be allowed between any Indians in Oklahoma and those at Mescalero.[30]

Not deterred, Chevato tried again in 1888, writing again to Parker on October 25, 1888:

My dear friend:

Will you please send me two dollars worth of the medicine named Hooch [i.e., peyote; the Lipan word for peyote was *hoosh*]. I want to come to see you and the camanche [*sic*] country, but the Agent here, Col. Cowart, will not let me go. I started to come to you last year but the Agent sent the Soldiers after me and brought me back. I would like to have you write to Washington and get permission for me to come to you. Please have the papers made out good so that my brother, my brother's wife, my sister and my little boy can come to you. I have a correl [*sic*; corral] and plant for corn in the Camanche [*sic*]. I am very sad to come to you. Please send me a paper <u>soon</u> to come and my family also. I am much sorry here—here the Mescalero care for *tiswin* [an alcoholic brew] and are often crazy. I want to be with friends.

I do not want my boy to grow to be a man here where there is much *tiswin* and no money. If you will send me good papers, I will like to come and talk to you about Washington—Be sure and write to me any way so that I may [know] how it is. . . . I long to come. Please send you [*sic*] letter to L. J. Gans, Las Cruces, New Mexico. I am afraid the Agent will not let me have the letter if you send it to me at the Agency. L. J. Gans will send it to me.

Your friend—*Chi-wa-ta*[31]

Quanah Parker wrote back to Chevato as he had requested, but Chevato did not receive the response until early 1889. Evidently, his connection with Gans was not as firm as Chevato had originally believed, because Gans received Parker's letter but was afraid to forward it to Chevato at the agency, fearing it would be confiscated. On January 3, 1889, Chevato wrote back to Parker:

My dear friend—

I know that you are a good man and a friend, that your talk is strayht [*sic*], that you talk day and night the same. If you say we can come to you we <u>can</u> come. <u>We want to come.</u>

Please send us a paper <u>quick</u>. We are much sorrowful here. My home and John's home (Roan Horse) is at the Camanche [*sic*] country. I've been here a long time and we long to come home.

We are poor but we want to come to you soon. We want to work, to raise corn. Here we do not have land. I have a wagon and horses and a few cows. Could I bring them[?] I would like to but I want to come if I leave all but my family.

Please write to me soon. Write in care of Andy Wilson, Mescalero Agency. My friend do what you can for me.

—*Chi-wa-ta*[32]

Chevato's mention that he wanted to "come home" seems to be a reminder to Parker that Chevato and other Lipans had accompanied Parker to Ft. Sill, Oklahoma, after turning over Herman Lehmann in 1877. Evidently, Chevato regretted not staying in Oklahoma after 1877. If he had, he and his family would have been enrolled as Comanches and would have had a voice in tribal issues regarding land usage, a feature of reservation life available to residents of the Kiowa Agency but one not as readily available to those at Mescalero, where the amount of arable land was significantly less than in Oklahoma. Parker must have inquired in his letter just how many people Chevato was planning to bring to Oklahoma, if permission were granted. Chevato attached to his letter a list containing the names of thirty-four Lipans who also wanted to move from the Mescalero Agency to "Camanche" country (see appendix 1). After attaching the list, Chevato continued:

> These people long to come to you—they are very unhappy. The Mescaleros <u>are not good</u> friends to us and are one people while we are not many [and] are another people. The Mescaleros make much *tiswin* and are drunk much of the time and all want to make trouble and fight. We want to raise our children where they have friends all around. And our old woman [*sic*] want to come home to die—our Agent wants us to stay close to the Agency—he does not want us to go and hunt deer and there are many deer to be killed out a little way—and he does not give us enough meat.[33]

When Chevato had not heard from Parker by March 1889, he wrote for the third time, saying, "Please write me soon and let me know about what they say at Washington about our people returning to the Camanche [*sic*] country. If we can go back we want to know, and if we can not please write to us just the same."[34]

Parker turned Chevato's three letters written over to the Kiowa agent, W. D. Myers, in 1889. He asked Myers to forward the letters to the commissioner of Indian Affairs with the following explanation:

I enclose you herewith a number of letters he [Parker] has received from some relations of his who live in New Mexico, at the Mescalero Agency. He says that these people are all Comanches and some of them nearly related to him (possibly a sister and brother) and that they are entitled to homes on this reservation and among these people. He says that they were captured and taken to New Mexico 20 or 25 years ago, before the Comanches were located here and for that reason . . . [unreadable] . . . separated from their people and have never been able to get back to them.[35]

Parker was able to make that assertion because two Comanches were living at the Mescalero Reservation, and both men had been recorded as Comanches in the Mescalero census records. The two men were brothers, enrolled among the Mescaleros using the names Blue Knife's Boy (aka Comanche John) and Noltha (aka Pack-a-be). The Mescaleros had captured them when they were young men; they had grown up with that tribe and had married Mescalero women. Now they also wanted to "come home." When Chevato had sent his October 1888 letter to Parker, he had also enclosed a letter from Blue Knife's Boy, who had evidently sent several previous letters to Parker:

Mr. Quanah Parker
Dear Friend:

I have written two letter [sic] to you and have received no answer. This is the third letter I have written. I want very much to hear from you. You said that if my brother—*Nana-shu-yon*—wanted to come home you would send him money to go with. He wants very much to come to you but has no horse and no money. I also want to come to you but cannot come with out money. Please send us a letter, and money soon. The Mescalero Agency is not good now. There is much *tiswin* and many drunken men. Please send us a way to come to you. I have no horse and my brother has no horse. It is cold here and much snow, no grass and my brother's horse died. . . . I wish *Tabico* to send me some *hoose* [sic; peyote], a medicine. . . .

I wish to know if my dear friend *U-e* is alive and my friend *Pe-e-na* is

153

Comanche John (aka Blue Knife's Boy, Roan Horse). National Anthropological
Archives, Smithsonian Institution/#00454200.

he well? Also my friend *No-u-sha*, is he well? I wish to know if my friend *Ko-sop* is alive and well. And my friend *No-a-she* and my friend *Qua-ra*. I wish to find old *Wish-a-wa*, is he dead or alive? These are all dear friends and I care for all of them. Please name them to me in your letter.... My brother wishes to know if all his children are alive and well. He fears one of them is dead—

Camancha [*sic*] John, Roan Horse[36]

Quanah Parker turned over Chevato's three letters, as well as the letter from Comanche John, to the Kiowa agent. Parker also added his explanation, claiming a family relationship with Chevato and Comanche John in the hopes that this claim would prove such a strong argument that the commissioner of Indian Affairs would have no choice but to allow these persons to "come home," along with their extended families. Unfortunately, the acting commissioner of Indian Affairs did not agree with Parker's argument. In his reply to the Kiowa agent, dated June 5, 1889, he recalled the Chi-ten-de and Ta-ha-shin-de letter written in 1886 and the Mescalero agent's assertion that this earlier letter was a sham, that the persons writing the letter were not Comanches but Lipans, and that the whole affair was only a scheme by an unscrupulous unnamed person to steal land belonging to the Mescaleros. Therefore the acting commissioner also saw Chevato's 1888 and 1889 letters as fraudulent and refused permission for anyone living on the Mescalero Reservation to move off of that reservation, reaching back to an 1879 Indian appropriation act to find statutory justification for the decision. After dealing with the New Mexico end of the problem, the acting commissioner turned to deal with Parker, stating that even if these Indians were blood relations, they had been separated from the Comanche tribe for so long that even if Indian Affairs wanted to move them to Oklahoma, it would require congressional approval.[37] With the final roadblock thrown up, the Indian Affairs office and the Kiowa agent assumed the matter was concluded. For Chevato, however, that was not the end of the matter. Perhaps he, with the help of Quanah Parker, would have continued a letter-writing campaign with the bureaucrats for permission to move to Oklahoma, but a crisis intervened at Mescalero that required more desperate measures.

As was apparent from Chevato's and Comanche John's letters, conditions on the Mescalero Reservation in 1888 and 1889 were not peaceful. Drunkenness, caused by a homemade brew called *tiswin*, and fighting were creating problems. The Lipans seem to have held themselves somewhat aloof from these problems, but in 1890 all that Chevato had been working for—the chance to move with his family and other Lipans to Oklahoma so that they could farm and live in peace—was placed in jeopardy by the actions of his brother, Dinero.

Dinero had married a Mescalero woman, Chalita, by 1885. She had been married before and had two children from her previous marriage. In 1889 Dinero and Chalita had a daughter, Blacita. Dinero's Lipan foster mother, also named Dinero, remained a figure in his life, living nearby. Dinero joined the tribal police force in 1889 and was made a sergeant of police, receiving a salary of $10.00 per month. The police force seems to have been somewhat inclusive, adding heads of some of the larger Lipan households, such as Boneski and Magoosh, to the ranks, as well as some of the Mescalero subchiefs, such as Roman Chiquito (son of Chief Roman), Patricio, and San Puer.[38]

Around 1890 Dinero allegedly began an affair with a married woman. Although the identities of the woman and her husband are not conclusively proven by census data, there is evidence that indicates the woman was Guerdo, a fifteen-year-old who had been given the English name of Agatha Wyeth. She was the wife of Mariana, or Charles Wyeth, a twenty-one-year-old man who had indicated that he wanted to go with Chevato to Oklahoma in 1889. When that plan fell through, Mariana had married Guerdo, the daughter of Chiquita.[39] When Mariana confronted Dinero about the affair, Dinero killed him. After the murder, Dinero was arrested by the same police force on which he had once served and brought before the tribal court. Established only in 1889, the Court of Indian Offenses had as its judges Natzili, the Mescalero chief, and Jose Torres, a Lipan.[40] Dinero

Joseph Bennett, Mescalero agent, with Chevato (standing, far left) and Dinero (standing, second from right), 1889. Courtesy of the Mescalero Cultural Center, Mescalero NM.

was found guilty, sentenced to be hung, and remanded back to the agency jail to await the execution of his sentence.

The primary reason the Mescalero Agency was in such chaos in 1890 was because of its agent, Joseph F. Bennett, a creature of the "notorious Santa Fe Ring, which was running New Mexico for its own benefit at this time."[41] While sending sunny, optimistic reports to Washington, Bennett had let the reservation slide into chaos and disrepair, suspending the schoolteacher and shutting down the agency school. Bennett's 1890 report to the commissioner was the product of much wishful thinking, when he stated that "drunkenness is of rare occurrence."[42] Yet the chaos and disorganization at the agency did work to the benefit, for once, of one group of Indians. It allowed Chevato to contact Quanah Parker one final time and plead for his help in saving his brother's life.

There are no letters that exist detailing this plea, just as there are no documents detailing how Parker was able to spirit Dinero out of jail and bring him to Oklahoma. Perhaps Bennett was bribed to look the other way; perhaps the tribal judge who was a Lipan (Jose Torres) was prevailed upon to quietly help. Or perhaps Dinero was spirited away from Mescalero in the interval between Bennett's departure and the arrival of his successor, Hinman Rhodes, in early 1891. Antonio Apache, another Lipan living at Mescalero at the time, only related that "Dinero got in trouble here [i.e., at Mescalero]," but didn't go into detail regarding the type of trouble or how it was resolved.[43] The only two documents that exist to prove the tale are Comanche census records. At the end of the 1891 Comanche census, taken at the Kiowa Agency in Oklahoma, there is a loose scrap of paper with the heading "Lost Tickets." This paper lists those Comanches who had lost their ration tickets and needed replacements; the ticket system (where each family was assigned a ticket number) was also used to take the annual agency census, and families were listed by ticket number. The scrap of paper titled "Lost Tickets" contains six names; ticket #694 is the family head named Penaro, which is the Comanche version of the name Dinero. A second verifying document is the Comanche census for 1892-93, which lists under ticket #694 the family of two persons; the husband is named Penaro, and the wife is named Ad-do-che-nah.[44] This is the woman with whom Dinero probably had the affair, Agatha Wyeth; she had to leave Mescalero, or she would have been killed because of her adultery. In the remarks section next to the names of Penaro and Ad-do-che-nah is the notation, "From Mescalero Agency."[45]

14. The Bodyguards

When he finished his business in New Mexico, Quanah Parker was ready to leave, to go back home to Oklahoma. He told Chevato to tie up his family ties and to immediately follow him. Quanah Parker had told him in a general way where Ft. Sill was located, and that was where Chevato and Dinero were supposed to go.

So Chevato went to his wife, and Dinero went to his wife. They told them that they had gotten a reprieve and that they were going to Indian Territory.

This didn't sit too well with the wives, because they would have to leave their culture and go to a new culture, so the wives said no. They were released from their matrimonial agreements, and both wives stayed in Mescalero. I don't know if Dinero had any children with his Mescalero wife, but Chevato had three children—two boys and a girl.

Chevato and Dinero bought supplies and packhorses or mules with money given to them by Quanah Parker; they also dressed in western attire. Being from Mexico, Chevato was accustomed to this western dress. So they set off for Oklahoma, going through the panhandle of Texas.

On reaching Oklahoma, the first place they stopped was at a firing range adjacent to the old post at Ft. Sill. There were some army troopers there target shooting when Chevato and Dinero rode up on them. There was also a civilian there who later got acquainted with Chevato. The civilian later told me this story when I was a young boy. He told me, "Here comes these two men on horses leading these pack mules. They come up on the range, and I took them for scouts because they were dressed in western apparel rather than being dressed in the Native American way. Your grandfather came up to me and asked where Quanah Parker lived. He told me that they were hunting him. The army officer got suspicious and asked what they wanted to see Parker for. Your grandfather answered that Quanah Parker hired them in New Mexico and that they were supposed to work for him. This seemed to satisfy the officer, and he gave them directions to Quanah Parker's house."

They traveled on about seventeen miles west of Ft. Sill to a little town called Cache. It's a French name, but the native people around pronounce it "Cash" instead of "Cachet" and get very perturbed if you say "Cachet." They'll quickly point you to your error. Near Cache is where Quanah Parker had his home, called Star House. It was a two-story building with a porch all the way around. It was painted all white. Built by the government with government money, and it was quite a nice house for that time and that era. The roof was painted with a large white star. And they called this Star House.

My grandfather reported there. Quanah Parker had more than one wife, and his wives and the rest of the family were sitting on the porch when Chevato rode up. Quanah Parker told him, "You'll be working for me," and called a man to show Chevato where they would live. "But first I want to set some rules. This is my family. I have a niece sitting over there on the porch. She's nineteen years old, and she's been married once. She was in a failed marriage, and her husband would beat her. So they're divorced. But she's not a worldly woman, so you treat her with lots of respect." So Chevato said, "Don't worry. I'll tell my brother, and we will respect your wishes."

Quanah Parker had called the young woman his niece, but you have to think now in the way of the customs of the Comanche people. Our kinship does not have first, second, or third cousins. We don't call them cousins; we call them brothers and sisters. So, a fourteenth cousin is like my sister, even though they are removed a number of times. With the Comanche, it is strictly taboo to marry someone you would call a cousin. You only marry outside your family. You don't have any kind of relations with your relatives, no matter how far down the chain of heredity.

Getting back to Quanah Parker's niece, the reason I go this long in explaining the relationship is because Quanah Parker didn't have a living sister (his sister Topsannah had died as a small child), and so he didn't have a niece in the way you might understand. But you have to remember that he had a Comanche side to his family. The woman he pointed out to Chevato was from Quanah Parker's family; the same people that took Cynthia Ann Parker when she was young and raised her were also relatives of the woman he pointed out to Chevato. Also, in the Comanche language, when you claim relationship to a person, the exact translation says you are "crying relations" to that person. In other words, Quanah Parker was indicating that this woman was from a family that was close to him, a family that was related to his family. That's why she was living in his house. Her father had already passed away, and she had no brothers or sisters, so Quanah Parker had taken her and her mother in as family, whether they were blood kin or not.

After Quanah Parker gave Chevato the rules on how they were to conduct themselves around his family, they were shown where they could live. They were shown to a little house away from Star House, and that is where Chevato and Dinero lived. Their names were also translated into Comanche; Chevato became known as Che-bah-tah, and Dinero became known as Pinero.

The two brothers always stayed together. Even after they married again, they stayed in close proximity.

The day after they arrived at Star House, they went out to get their duties from their boss, Quanah Parker. He told them, "The other people around here in Cache, the other Comanches—we are going to tell them that you are work hands, cowboys. But that's not really your job. Your job is to be my companions and to see that I grow to be a ripe old age and that I become an old man. That's your job. I don't care how you do it. I have spoken to the local authorities here, and the local law knows you can carry firearms and that you are my bodyguards. But other than the local law, I don't want anyone else to know that you are my bodyguards." So, Chevato and Dinero agreed and acted as bodyguards for Quanah Parker.

Some of the Comanche knew about this, some of them didn't. But they readily got the idea, because one day Dinero heard some of the Comanche splinter groups were going to harm Quanah Parker. He walked up on them as they were being very bold and rash and told them, "Look, I know what you are saying. You'd better take those ideas out of your head because you're not going to hurt the Old Man." That's what Chevato and Dinero called Quanah Parker—the Old Man. "If you do, then I'm coming after you!"

By that time, word had gotten around about what Chevato and Dinero were. They weren't just the regular run-of-the-mill horse herders and cowboys. They had lived pretty hard lives, and when they said that they were coming after you, they were coming after you! So, this got around, and most everybody walked a wide berth around them. But the splinter group kept planning to harm Quanah Parker, so Dinero gave them a choice, saying, "We can just settle it here." One of the group said, "I don't want to fight and hurt my pride," and Dinero said, "Your pride's not going to get hurt because you're going to be dead. We're going to settle this right now." This is an old story among the Comanche.

By that time, people had gathered around, and Dinero said, "If you've got the silly idea that you're going to harm the Old Man, we can settle it here. Either I'm going to be lying down and you're going to be walking away, or vice versa. Or you can get this idea out of your head." So, they got the ideas out

*of their heads and walked away. They swallowed their pride. And that's the
way Dinero was.*

*So Chevato and Dinero worked for Quanah Parker for a number of years.
When they weren't watching over Quanah Parker, they would herd the horses
and work the cattle. Quanah Parker thought that Chevato was a good worker,
and Chevato kept Quanah Parker alive.*

§

After Dinero was successfully spirited away from the Mescalero Agency in
1891, Quanah Parker began a lobbying effort aimed at bringing Comanche
John, Chevato, and others to the Kiowa Agency. In November 1892 Parker
was in Washington to speak to the commissioner of Indian Affairs about
the renewal of the Comanche grassland leases to Texas cattlemen. While
there, "he also broached the subject of several Comanche warriors who,
rather than surrender at Ft. Sill after the Red River War, had taken up residence among the Mescalero Apaches. They now had families on that reservation, and Quanah wished to arrange the transfer of these people to
Oklahoma, over Mescalero objections to the removal of the wives and children."[1] In spite of an earlier decision in 1889 by the commissioner refusing to allow anyone at the Mescalero Agency to move to the Kiowa Agency,
Parker's lobbying was effective. He received permission to visit the Mescalero Reservation (a visit that must have occurred in December 1892) "to
bring those parties who desired to go to the Kiowa &c. Agency.... [Parker]
stated that every one who wanted to leave at that time belonged to the Comanche tribe, and that they were anxious to leave."[2] In early January 1893
the commissioner recommended that "Comanche John, Chevito [*sic*] Lipan, and Big Comanche" be ordered to the Kiowa Agency, but that "no
expense accruing out of the journey will be borne by the Government."[3]
Comanche John's brother, Nol-tha, had died by 1892,[4] so the "Big Comanche" referred to was a Mexican Lipan named Sanavoy, who had appeared
with his wife at the Mescalero Agency in 1890. This is the same Santavi who
had fought with Chevato and Dinero in their battle with the Kickapoos in
1868; Santavi/Sanavoy had stayed in Mexico after the Zaragosa massacre,
moving to join the rest of the Lipans in New Mexico in 1890.

Quanah Parker was able to receive permission for only the three men to relocate to the Kiowa Agency; their Mescalero wives and children had to remain in New Mexico in deference to objections raised by Mescalero leaders. The main source of objection to relocation must have come from the families of the wives of Comanche John and Chevato. Comanche John had three children with his wife, Lumbre, who was a Mescalero woman. Chevato and his second wife, a Mescalero woman named Chenoco, had no children together, but Chenoco was the daughter of Camisa, a Mescalero of some influence within the tribe. Both Mescalero and Lipan custom dictated that any children of a marriage were to be considered members of the mother's tribe, but since the Mescalero woman Chenoco was a second wife and the deceased mother of the children had been Lipan, the children of Chevato fell into a gray area in terms of tribal affiliation. For the moment, Mescalero objections prevailed, although all of Chevato's surviving children eventually rejoined their father in Oklahoma.

Once Comanche John, Chevato, and Sanavoy reached Oklahoma in January 1893, they were enrolled in the Comanche census records. The three men were recorded under the names by which they would be known henceforth:

Ase-ah-tamy (Comanche John)—"Comanche from Mescalero"
Che-bah-tah (Chevato)—"from Mescalero Agency"
Sah-nah-bah (Sanavoy)—"from Mescalero Agency"

Next to each man's name in the remarks column of the census was the notation "Quanah," acknowledging Parker's role in the transfer.[5]

Once the men had settled in at the Kiowa Agency, rejoining Dinero who had fled to Oklahoma in 1891, they began a letter-writing campaign directed at disaffected persons at the Mescalero Agency who wished to join them in Oklahoma. By September 1893 the Mescalero agent began to complain to the commissioner. Agent Levi Burnett reported that, while trouble had been anticipated when Chevato, Comanche John, and Sanavoy left the agency in January, by February matters had "been amicably adjusted and . . . nearly all those who wanted to go had changed their minds

Transfers from Mescalero to the Kiowa Agency, 1891–1910

Name	Name at the Kiowa Agency	Date Arrived at the Kiowa Agency
Dinero	Penaro	1891
Agatha Wyeth	Ah-do-che-nah	1891
Chevato	Che-bah-tah	1893
Comanche John	Ase-ah-tamy	1893
Sanavoy	Sah-nah-bah	1893
Carrie Heath	Carrie Heath	1894
Cora Heath	Corine Heath	1894
Mrs. Sanavoy	Tah-ne-we-kin	1894
Harry Heath	Harry Heath	1900
Paul Heath	Paul Chebahtah	1907

and [would] remain where they are." By September, however, the letters from Oklahoma had caused "a feeling of discontent among these people [the Mescaleros], and . . . the removal of the Comanches from this reservation, with their Mescalero Apache wives, would cause serious trouble."[6] Burnett requested that the commissioner order the Kiowa agent to stop the troublesome letters being sent by "Quanah Parker, Comanche John, Chivato & Sanavoy, of the Kiowa Agency."[7]

The letters stopped, but the lobbying continued. By 1894, Chevato had been joined by his daughter, Mineha (Carrie Heath), and granddaughter, Cora Heath.[8] They had been brought out of Mescalero by Quanah Parker himself, who visited that reservation on March 16, 1894.[9] By September 1894 the commissioner of Indian Affairs had reached the limit of his patience with the situation. When Parker requested even more family members be allowed to join their relatives at the Kiowa Agency, the commissioner put his foot down. He wrote the Kiowa agent, Maury Nichols, "You will therefore inform Quanah Parker that . . . this matter is definitely settled and he will not be again allowed to visit Mescalero Agency, nor will this office permit any more of these Indians to be transferred to the Kiowa, &c. Agency."[10]

When Chevato and Dinero rode out of Mescalero, on their way to Oklahoma Territory, they left their wives and a total of four children behind.

Dinero left a three-year-old daughter named Blacita in Mescalero along with her mother, Chalita, fleeing to Oklahoma with Agatha Wyeth.[11]

Chevato left three children (a daughter and two sons) along with his Mescalero wife, Chenoco. His daughter, Mineha (Carrie Heath), was sixteen years old when her father left and had a child of her own, Cora (or Corine). Chevato's eldest son, Alguno (Harry Heath), was twelve years old, while Chevato's youngest son, Jo-Co (Paul Heath), was five years old.[12]

The story of the children who were left behind is not always easy to track. Carrie and Cora Heath were brought to Oklahoma in 1894. They lived with an eighty-year-old Comanche woman named Tah-su-a-cau for several years. Carrie was officially enrolled in the Comanche tribe on June 8, 1896.[13] By 1899 she had married a Comanche, Owen Too-a-nippah. Carrie remarried in 1903 to Claude To-cah-wa-he-mah.[14]

Sons Harry and Paul Heath continued to live with their mother in Mescalero until 1895. By 1896 she had died, and the two boys were sent to live with their maternal grandparents—Camisa and Mama Camisa. This practice was in keeping with Mescalero and Lipan custom, where the residence and care of the child were determined by the tribal affiliation of the child's mother, not the father.[15] In 1897 Camisa died, and Harry, now sixteen, left Mescalero. His whereabouts are unknown until 1900, when he arrived at the Comanche Reservation in Oklahoma and began living with his father. After the death of his grandfather Camisa in 1897, Paul Heath continued to live with his grandmother until 1900, when his elderly grandmother moved in with Dinero's wife and daughter. Mama Camisa died in 1901, and Paul was bounced around, living with several relatives until 1907, when he, too, left New Mexico to join his father on the Comanche Reservation in Oklahoma.[16]

Quanah Parker's decision to bring Chevato and Dinero to Oklahoma as his bodyguards was a prescient one. He had already faced opposition over leasing Comanche grasslands to Texas cattlemen. His critics, primarily centered in other tribes such as the Kiowas and among Comanche bands other than the Kwahadas, had accused him of "selling out" to the cattlemen. In truth, his actions in negotiating the grassland leases had actually benefited the Comanches, giving the tribe a source of income at a time (1880s and 1890s) when other tribes across the nation were being impoverished. His critics might have had a point in stating that the Comanches had reaped the benefit to a greater extent than had the other tribes, but to be fair, the grasslands in question were Comanche, not Kiowa, lands.

While Parker negotiated for renewal of the grassland leases, and negotiated his way among the various Comanche and Kiowa factions opposed to this course of action, another threat arose: "the allotment of Indian land in severalty and the sale of surplus lands for eventual opening to settlers. In March 1889, a three man commission, chaired by David H. Jerome . . . was appointed by the federal government to negotiate with those tribes claiming land west of the 96th meridian in Indian Territory with the purpose of extending allotment to them and opening 15,000,000 acres of surplus lands to settlement."[17] Parker, already a focus of dissent in the grassland lease issue, was expected to play a prominent role in the negotiations with the Jerome Commission, a fact that only increased the anger of those already opposed to him.

When negotiations opened with the Jerome Commission in September 1892, Parker was faced with the difficult task of negotiating the best price possible for Comanche Reservation land scheduled to be opened to white settlement. The commission members arrived at Ft. Sill in a strong position, having already negotiated nine contracts with other tribes to open up portions of their lands to white settlement. As much as some of the more conservative Comanches and Kiowas would have wished otherwise, Parker had to face the reality that their lands were going to be carved up and that lands given to tribes under treaty were going to be opened up to white settlement. His task was to strike the best deal possible for the Comanches, Kiowas, and Kiowa Apaches. With so much at stake, it was not surprising that some tribal members were angry with Parker, afraid he was going to "sell them out." Unfortunately, the dissenters' wishes for a return to the old status quo was unrealistic; they had only to look at the sad treatment of the Cheyennes and Arapahos to see what would happen to tribes that resisted these negotiations and fought against opening their lands to settlers. After signing their agreement with the Jerome Commission, their lands were open to white settlement, and they were paid for ceding their land rights; however, within a few years of the agreement, the Cheyennes and Arapahos had spent all of their money and faced not only poverty but no longer possessed much of their original land.[18]

The strategy settled upon by Quanah Parker was one of delay, while also recognizing that an agreement would ultimately be reached, and Parker wanted the final agreement to contain the best terms possible for the tribes under his responsibility. "So, in the same breath in which he asked for a delay, Quanah asked how much the government was prepared to give for the land."[19] The negotiating tactic used by the commission was to bluntly confront Parker and the other leaders with the cold facts. The government had decided to open up all land west of the ninety-sixth parallel to white settlement, with the only exception being the small amounts of land necessary for the Indians' homes.[20] These small homesteads would be one 160-acre allotment per Indian, leaving thousands of acres open to white settlers. Parker and the other leaders had no choice; they signed the agreement on October 6, 1892.[21]

As Quanah Parker assumed leadership of the Comanches in the grassland leases issue and in negotiating with the Jerome Commission, he also assumed a leadership role in other aspects of tribal life. His persistent efforts resulted in the "repatriation" of Comanche John, bringing him home to join the rest of the tribe in Oklahoma. But what motivated Parker to make such extraordinary efforts to bring three Lipan Apaches (Dinero, Chevato, and Sanavoy) to Oklahoma? These three men formed the nucleus of the peyote religion that Parker wanted to establish among the Comanches, the form of religious practice that later became known as the Native American Church. Parker himself explained the Indian view of peyote in an address he made to the Oklahoma Senate around 1900:

> The Comanche Indians use this Peoti [sic] 50 years ago (ca. 1850). They
> got it from the Apaches in Mexico. I use Peoti 40 years ago Myself [ca.

1860]. . . . I know two ways—white way and Indian way—and I Understand the good. . . . Now I tell you what kind of use Peoti is. Every Saturday night there is somebody sick . . . [seven or eight men go into a peyote tipi with two or three sick people] . . . and eat [peyote] for the sick people. That is their devotion to God. They say, "I give you this Peoti and you [i.e., God] will help me make sick man well"—just the same as you people go to church.[22]

In bringing Chevato, Dinero, and Sanavoy to Oklahoma, Quanah Parker introduced to the Comanches a form of religious practice that would provide an alternative to Christianity. This religious alternative was more culturally compatible and familiar to the Comanches and would prove very popular after 1890. Peyotism gave a religious solace that was more appealing to many Comanches than the beliefs being preached by the Christian missionaries on the reservation. The peyote religion was a unifying factor for the Comanches, probably one of the few unifying ceremonies available to them. When a group of men entered a peyote tepee, they could come together as a group, worshipping the Great Spirit as their ancestors did; once they left the tepee, they walked outside into a world that required them to act as individuals, not as a tribe. They lived on individual allotments and went to Christian churches, where emphasis was placed on individual salvation. The peyote religion provided a sense of group, a sense of community rarely found in other aspects of Comanche reservation life.

15. Pi-he

Chevato continued working for Quanah Parker, who could see, after many years, that he was a good man. One day, Quanah Parker came up to Chevato and asked, "Do you have a wife?" Chevato answered, "I had one in New Mexico, in Mescalero, but she didn't want to come to the Indian Territory, so we were divorced." Quanah Parker asked, "You're not going back to New Mexico, are you?" Chevato replied, "I can't go back, you know that! We are di-

Pi-he, wife of Chevato, cousin of Quanah Parker.
Courtesy of William Chebahtah.

vorced; our relationship is split. I hope one day that all my children can come to Oklahoma, but she will never come. My wife in New Mexico told me that she will die in Mescalero." Quanah Parker said, "The reason I am asking you these questions is that I want you to marry my niece, the one you've seen sitting on the porch." At this time, Chevato was some years older than Quanah Parker's niece, who was in her late twenties. She had been married before, but never had any children. Quanah Parker continued, "So I would like for you to marry her. And, by the way, her name is Pi-he." Chevato agreed, saying,

"I like her, but what do you think she is going to say?" Quanah Parker said, "Come with me and see how the Comanche custom works."

So he took Chevato, and they went to Star House to eat. One of Quanah Parker's wives told Pi-he that her uncle wanted to speak to her, so she was waiting on the porch for him. When they got to the porch and sat down, Quanah Parker said, "This man is a good man. His name is Billy. I told him your name is Pi-he, and I want you to marry him. He agreed to marry you. I want you to marry him, live as a wife, have children, and have a happy home life of your own. Billy is a man that can give that to you." So Pi-he looked, and she looked at Chevato, and she didn't say anything. But my mother told me that Pi-he could see that Chevato was an older man. Then Pi-he looked at Quanah Parker and said, "Uncle, if this is what you want, I'll be happy to do this." Her relatives even asked her later, "Are you sure you want to marry this man? He is so much older." But Pi-he answered them, saying, "I love my uncle, and if this is what he wishes, then this is what I will do." And that's the Comanche custom.

Even to this day, a Comanche uncle has great influence on his nieces, and they look at him, in today's custom, as an uncle but also as a father figure. Whenever he desires something of them, he asks them, and they do not refuse the request, but the uncle always uses his ability to make a request with great discretion. That's the essence of the Comanche way.

So Pi-he married Billy Chevato, and they had four boys: James Hezekiah Chebahtah being the eldest, Thomas David Chebahtah (my father) being the second eldest, Moonie Sunrise Chebahtah being the third, and the youngest being Leonard Chebahtah. To that point is the origin of my life.

§

Pi-he was the daughter of Noki and Nas-su-tipe (b. 1827), members of the Noconi (People Who Return) band of Comanches. The Noconis territorial range before 1875 "centered on the upper reaches of the Red River and the headwaters of the Pease River" along the current Texas-Oklahoma border.[1] They had sporadic contact with Americans before 1860; after that date, they took part in some treaty negotiations but did not es-

Chevato and family, circa 1903 (front left to right): Chevato, James Hezekiah, Pi-he,
Thomas David (held in mother's lap), Harry Heath (standing in background).
Courtesy of William Chebahtah.

tablish consistent or prolonged relationships with the U.S. government. "After 1866, the most prominent Nokoni was Terheryaquahip ('Horseback'), who continued the policy of peaceful but not submissive coexistence with Americans. The Nokonis were probably never very numerous and by the late 1870s there were only two local bands that could be identified as Nokoni."[2] Terheryaquahip had signed the Medicine Lodge Treaty of 1867 and brought the Nokoni band onto the reservation near Ft. Sill, Oklahoma, by 1870.

Pi-he and her family were not among the Nokonis moving onto the reservation. Her father, Noki, was the son of Peta Nocona's older brother (see appendix 3). Since Quanah Parker was Peta Nocona's son, he and Noki were cousins, in the Anglo way of reckoning familial relationships. Pi-he and Quanah Parker were also cousins, but in the Comanche way of looking at familial relationships, Quanah Parker was the "uncle," and Pi-he was deemed a "niece."[3]

After the recapture of his mother (1860) and the death of his father, Peta Nocona (ca. 1863–65), Quanah Parker joined with a Kwahada band of Comanches, accompanied by other relatives such as Noki and his family. The Kwahada band that took in the Noconi group had not signed the Medicine Lodge Treaty of 1867 and continued to raid into Texas from their base area located on the Staked Plains. By 1875, when the remaining Kwahada bands were brought onto the reservation, Pi-he and her mother, Nas-su-tipe, were counted, along with Quanah Parker, as part of Isatai's band, which surrendered in June 1875.[4]

Pi-he's father, Noki, died at some point before 1879, a date that represents the first extant Comanche census data that has survived.[5] She and her mother remained members of the group of Kwahadas associated with Quanah Parker, in some years listed with Parker's band, in other years listed in bands led by men associated with Parker, such as Tah-hau-vi-yah (High Lifter).

As a cousin to the deceased Noki, Quanah Parker assumed familial responsibility for the welfare of Pi-he and her mother. Under Comanche custom, "brothers with their sisters formed a marriage group, which established relationships with another marriage group on the basis of inter-family exchange marriage. . . . A man called his brother's children his own, since they were descendants of his marriage group, but distinguished his sister's children, because they were in another marriage group."[6] Since Pi-he was the child of Quanah Parker's father's brother, he assumed responsibility for her as if she were his own child. Additionally, "a woman who lost her husband by death was inherited by a brother of her husband. Thus brothers were potential husbands of a woman whether they ever became such in actuality. Hence, there was no separate word for brother-in-law, only . . . 'husband.'"[7] As the patriarch of the family, Quanah Parker, under Comanche custom, assumed responsibility for Pi-he and also "inherited" her mother, Nas-su-tipe. Thus Parker had the duty not only to care for Nas-su-tipe but also to arrange a marriage for Pi-he.

Pi-he was born between 1865 and 1867 and was in her late twenties when she married Chevato. Family tradition states she was born at the great Comanche camp in the Palo Duro Canyon of Texas. Her marriage to Chevato took place in late 1895. Their first child, a son named James Hezekiah, was born September 1, 1896. In 1900 a daughter named Emily was born; she died, however, by 1901. On January 10, 1903, a second son named Thomas David (the father of William Chebahtah, the narrator of Chevato's oral history) was born. Moonie Sunrise was born in 1907, and Leonard was born in 1910.[8] For a complete family genealogy, see appendix 4.

16. Quanah Parker and Wild Horse

To understand Quanah Parker, you have to look back to the capture of his mother, Cynthia Ann Parker. Our people say she was five years old when she was captured in a raid. The two men that captured her were brothers, and they were Pi-he's grandfather and uncle. One brother was much younger than the other. After they kidnapped Cynthia Ann, they fled north. When they reached the Texas side of the Red River, they found that they had a problem. The Red River was flooded from bank to bank. I questioned my parents, "Was the river really up that high?" because when I go across it, the river is not that big. My parents said that they were told that the winter of 1835 carried a lot of snow, and the area had received a lot of rain. The Comanche raiding party had already crossed the river going south before the snow had melted—that's how long they were gone—and when they came back the same way, they found the river was flooded from bank to bank. You have to remember that these men were expert horsemen, and for them to have doubts such as, "Can I make it across?" well, it must have been a bad situation.

When the raiding party came to the banks of the flooded Red River, they told Peta Nocona's older brother (Peta Nocona was the younger brother) to put Cynthia Ann Parker on the ground. One man even got off his horse and sat her on the ground. But Peta Nocona's brother said, "Give her to me. I didn't tell you to put her on the ground." And he took Cynthia Ann and placed her against his chest, with her face facing toward his chest so that the water wouldn't get in her mouth, and tied them both together. Then he said, "I'm going. If you want to stay here and face the 'taivos' [i.e., Anglos; they were being chased by the Texas Rangers], then you can. But I'm going across." He jumped his horse into the river, and the rest of the raiding party followed. Their pursuers stopped at the Red River and never could figure out how the raiding party had gotten across without drowning.

The story that my mother told me is that the Comanche family that captured Cynthia Ann raised her. When she became a young woman and started looking for a husband, for you know how young girls are, the mother said to the father, "We raised her, we put time and effort into raising her, and I'd hate to see her marry just anybody." So they married Cynthia Ann to the younger brother, Peta Nocona, because they wanted to keep her in the family. It was Peta Nocona's brother who had kidnapped her.

Many years later, after Quanah Parker was born, Peta Nocona and Cynthia Ann were camped some distance from the rest of the tribe. Quanah was almost grown and was with others when the Texas Rangers attacked and recaptured Cynthia Ann and her younger daughter Topsannah. Our people say that Peta Nocona was not shot in that battle, but was shot by a sniper as he slept. Other members of the tribe took Quanah Parker into their care. Cyn-

thia Ann was taken back to Texas, where she pined away, always remember-
ing her Comanche home.

Some years went by. Wild Horse became a Comanche chief. He had three
wives at one time. The women were not related to him in any way, but two
of the women were sisters, and the other was a cousin. I think that perhaps
the husbands of one sister and the cousin were killed in battle, and they had
no brothers to care for the widows. This is the Comanche way—the husband
of the other sister would take them in. My sister-in-law would call me "little
husband." At first, I was confused because I was very young, but I was told
that she was quoting tradition to me. If anything happened to my brother, I
would have to marry her or provide for her. I couldn't turn her out; it would
be a disgrace to our family.

Wild Horse lived happily with his three wives. He had nine daughters and
one son. The son was the youngest. Comanche lore says that the son had a
blue pony, and he rode it very fast. They were always horse racing. The son
was about ten years old, and he was racing with some other boys. On the prairie, they have a lot of prairie dogs and prairie dog holes. As they were racing
full speed, his horse stepped in a prairie dog hole and rolled over on him, killing him. That is why my father always beat it into my head the proper way
to come off of a falling horse.

Wild Horse was left with nine daughters and no sons. The Comanche way
goes with hereditary leaders—leadership is passed from father to son. His
daughters couldn't lead, and his only son was dead. He later had another
son, but by then, he was no longer leader of the Kwahadas.

All Wild Horse's daughters were good horsewomen—all Comanches were
good with horses. His youngest daughter came to him one day, and I guess
the incident with his son was still fresh in his memory. The youngest daughter had been given a mare to ride, but she didn't like this. This was not to
her liking. So she went to her father and said, "I would like a spirited horse;
I don't want to ride a mare." Her father said, "I will give you a gelding," but
the daughter said, "No, I want a stallion." She was very young when she said
this, maybe sixteen or seventeen. Her father told her, "You can't handle a stallion." She insisted she could, so he got her a stallion thinking it was going to

throw her. He watched her very closely, but she jumped on the stallion, and she handled that horse from that day forward. If it was a spirited horse, she loved that and she could ride him.

All of Wild Horse's daughters were like that. His oldest daughter was "Weck-ea-woonard" (pronounced Weck-ye-o-wan-ee). He gave her that name because leaders would name their children after deeds they had done, events they remembered with pride. Her name means "Charging Up Close to the Enemy." My mother was her first daughter and Wild Horse's eldest granddaughter.

When my great-grandfather Wild Horse was a younger man, he could see how smart Quanah Parker was. He could see that Quanah had foresight, even as a young man. My mother's side of the family always said that Wild Horse thought highly of Quanah Parker. When he was getting older and getting frail, he called Quanah in and said, "I have no sons to inherit the leadership. But I like you because you show me a lot in your thinking. I want you to take care of The People." So Quanah Parker agreed.

Wild Horse died, and an odd thing happened. Among the Comanche, when someone died, especially a chief, they would kill his horse and destroy his things. But Wild Horse had told The People and Quanah Parker before he died, "You'll have my things." And that's what happened. Wild Horse's power transferred to Quanah Parker through the inheritance of his horse and personal possessions. And that's how Quanah Parker took leadership of the Kwahada, or Antelope Band of Comanche.

§

The Comanche attack on Parker's Fort in late May 1836 has been viewed as a terrible atrocity. Nine men, ten women, and fifteen children were suddenly attacked by 500 to 800 Comanche warriors who swooped down upon the isolated outpost, murdering seven of the men, raping and stabbing Granny Parker, and capturing Elizabeth Kellogg and her niece, Rachel Plummer, as well as another young girl and two young boys.[1] The young girl, Cynthia Ann Parker, was to remain with the Comanches, adopted by the family of the warrior who had captured her. When she grew older, she was married to a war chief, Peta Nocona, and had several children, one of whom, Quanah Parker, rose to head the Comanche tribe in the critical years after 1875, as they adjusted to life on the reservation.

The 1836 attack on Parker's Fort cannot, however, be viewed in isolation. When considered in a wider context, the attack not only occurred at a pivotal point in the midst of the Texas revolution against the government of Mexican president Santa Anna, but the attack was part of a larger effort by the Comanches to protect the boundaries of their domain. The attack on Parker's Fort was a tragic event, but one that occurred against the backdrop of the tempestuous events swirling throughout Texas and along the Red River in the 1830s. One common thread, however, woven throughout the tempest—whether one looks at Texan relations with the Mexican government or Comanche relations with Anglos—is the seeking of some sort of accommodation, through treaty or through force, that would recognize the existence and boundaries of the various groups involved in the struggle.

From 1830 to 1836 in east, central, and south Texas, all eyes (Comanche, Anglo, and Hispanic) were focused on political and trade issues with the Mexican government. The struggle between two political movements— the conservative movement led by Anastacio Bustamante that wanted a centralized government, and the liberal movement led by Santa Anna that wanted decentralization—was much like a kettle sitting on a hot stove. One primary issue between the two factions—that is, the spot where the bottom of the kettle met the heat of the stove—was customs duties, which were the primary source of governmental revenue. Bustamante wanted close government control of the customhouses, sending troops to patrol the border of Texas and Louisiana and nab smugglers. The northern provinces of Mexico, particularly the province of Coahuila y Tejas, wanted free trade with the United States, and riots ensued when Bustamante's troops arrived at the east Texas customhouses in 1830. Santa Anna, on the other hand, was hailed as the liberator of the Veracruz customhouse, wresting control of that port from the Spaniards, who had attempted to collect claims owed to foreign nations by Mexico, through the use of force. As odd as it sounds today, when Texas history from that period is dominated by tales of the Texans' fight against Santa Anna, in 1832 both Hispanic and Anglo Texans supported Santa Anna in his struggle to gain control of the Mexican government from Bustamante, petitioning Santa Anna to abolish the customhouses and border patrols along the Texas-Louisiana border. When Santa Anna denied the Texans' petition, adopted the old conservative position of governmental centralization, and sent Gen. Martin Perfecto de Cos and Mexican troops to Texas to ensure that import duties were collected, the fire under the kettle was turned up. In December 1835 a "Tejano" army, composed of Texas Hispanics and Anglos, intercepted Gen. Cos at San Antonio and drove him back south of the Rio Grande. The steam had escaped the kettle, and the water was about to boil out in a series of battles that would later be known as the Texas Revolution.

The Comanche bands that lived in central, east, and south Texas were also focused on trade and political issues in the years from 1830 to 1835. Many Comanche leaders of southern bands tried to maintain peaceful relations with the Mexicans in Texas, and in the early 1830s many attempted to trade, but there were also incidents of violence.[2] Fueled by the chaotic political situation, Mexican Indian policy was also contradictory. "Although earlier Spanish policy had been to remain neutral in intertribal wars, in 1832 it was decided to encourage the Shawnees in their Comanche war. . . . [However], in May [1832], General Martin Perfecto de Cos ordered the renewal of presents for the Indians, and particularly for the Comanches. In August, 300 Comanches came to Béxar and then continued on to Matamoros to arrange a treaty with the general."[3]

The northern Comanche bands along the Canadian and Red rivers (primarily the Yamparika and Nokoni bands) also faced trade and political issues in the early 1830s, yet their struggle with other groups was predicated on their desire to force acceptance of their territorial boundaries. Throughout the 1820s and into the early 1830s groups of eastern Indians had been moving into the Arkansas Territory, pushed from the east by ever-westward Anglo settlements. Many of the new groups (Cherokees, Chickasaws, Creeks, and Shawnees) clashed with the Comanches and other plains tribes who had traditionally inhabited the territory.[4] Feeling increasingly vulnerable, the Comanche bands alternately fought back and sought accommodation. "In 1830, Sam Houston, then a trader with the Cherokees, proposed that he, Osage agent Auguste P. Chouteau and Colonel Matthew Arbuckle be commissioned to make peace among the Osages, Pawnees, and Comanches."[5] The result was the signing of a treaty at Ft. Gibson in 1835. One article was to have specific implications for the family of John Parker. The fourth article stated that the Comanches were to have "free permission to hunt and trap in the Grand Prairie west of the Cross Timbers, to the western limits of the United States."[6] The Comanches repudiated the treaty one year later, angered over the insufficient presents as a reward for signing and angered that they had now opened their territory to eastern Indians.[7] The full fury of the Comanches was also turned against the small group of Anglo settlers who had appeared on the eastern edge of the area of north-central Texas known as the Cross Timbers.

In 1834 John Parker, along with a small group of family and friends, had settled on the Navasota River in an area known as Cross Timbers, which later became Limestone County, Texas. Parker was unaware that his settlement was one of the first American settlements made far inside the bounds of the Comanche domain. He was also unaware that his choice of settlement area placed his family and friends right in the middle of what the Noconi band of Comanches considered to be their territory. The Comanches also considered the timing of the settlement suspicious. Appearing in their territory just at the time other eastern Indian tribes were moving onto the plains, Parker's Fort appeared to the Comanches as just one more manifestation of incursion from the east. When the Comanches repudiated the Ft. Gibson treaty in 1836, and the residents of Parker's Fort showed no intention of going away, the Comanches declared war.

Parker was following an Anglo-American settlement pattern that had proved successful for at least one hundred years, first in Virginia, then later in Kentucky and Tennessee. A small group of settlers composed of related families and friends would set off into the wilderness and stake out a settlement area, building a small, fortified settlement. Relying on their own defense, they also had available (if word could be sent in time) the assistance of local militia, who would ride out from a more settled area to assist in the defense of the fort if trouble with Indians arose. Parker and his family were among the flood of Anglo settlers pouring into Texas in the early 1830s. Most settled in east and south Texas, although a few hardy souls followed the rivers north into the prairies of east-central Texas. Parker was probably counting on assistance in times of Indian trouble from local militias, known later as the Texas Rangers, from areas east of the Parker settlement. Unfortunately, when Indians appeared on the prairie horizon in May 1836, no help was available. All available Texas military forces had been gathered along a bayou at San Jacinto a month earlier, surprising the Mexican army and capturing Santa Anna. The Anglo settlers in Texas found themselves, in May 1836, trying to organize a republic; all of the men who had fought at San Jacinto had been sent home, and settlers in such far-flung areas as Parker's Fort were forgotten in the rush of events.

The 500 to 800 Comanches who appeared over the horizon on the morning of May 16, 1836, were no raiding party, bent on stealing livestock from Parker's Fort, if the estimates of their numbers are correct.[8] This was most certainly a war party, and the oral history passed down from Pi-he makes it clear that the war party had been on the move since at least February or March 1836, as they had crossed the Red River before the snow had melted. In the winter of 1835 Maj. Paul Chouteau had visited a combined camp of Comanches, Kiowas, and Apaches located on Cache Creek, Oklahoma. He was told at that time that the Comanches were angry over what they had been promised in the way of trade goods, which had proved to be inadequate. In addition, the Comanches were angry because they now realized that they had not fully understood the implications of their signature on the treaty that had opened up their lands.[9] Pi-he's oral history would indicate that the Noconi band was part of the unsatisfied group of Comanches who had repudiated the treaty and declared war on Texas by the early spring of 1836.

The isolated Parker's Fort must have seemed an obvious and easy target. The five captives taken after the attack were split up soon after they were captured: "Elizabeth Kellogg went with an allied band, Mrs. Plummer and James Pratt with one band of Comanches and Cynthia Ann and [her brother] John Parker with another."[10] All except Cynthia Ann were eventually ransomed and returned to their families, although the young John Parker (age six when captured) was not ransomed from the Noconis until he was a teenager. Traders had tried to ransom Cynthia Ann four years after her capture, but she refused to speak with them, and her adoptive Comanche father refused any amount of money to let her go.[11]

The oral history passed down by Pi-he states that Cynthia Ann was five years old when she was taken at Parker's Fort. The Parker family and later historians have stated that she was nine years old.[12] Since her younger brother, John, was also taken captive in 1836 and was said to be about three years younger than his sister, it would seem that the older age for Cynthia Ann is probably more correct. However, children taken by the Comanches did tend to be from five to eight years old. "Children capable of easy assimilation fit into the traditional pattern of adoption and acculturation. ... [A]ge was a tangible factor."[13]

Virginia Webster was another Anglo child captured only a few years after the Comanche attack on Parker's Fort. She was taken from an area about one hundred miles southwest of the now-abandoned Parker settlement. Virginia was about four years old when Comanches captured her in 1839; as an adult, she recounted the tale of her captivity, although many of her memories must have been augmented by information told to her by her mother and her brother, also captured in 1839. Virginia's father, John Webster, had come to Texas in 1836 from West Virginia:

> He made up a company of 44 picked men and induced them to come to Texas with him, all being like himself, ready for adventure, and expecting to assist Texas in gaining her independence from Mexico. Captain Webster, with his family, consisting of my mother, one brother 10 years old, and myself, 2 years old, and two or three Negro servants and his company of 44 men, landed at Galveston in November 1836. The fighting with Mexicans and Indians was still going on and my father and his company was [sic] in service of Texas from January 1837 until the first of March 1839, and 21 of his men were killed in battle and many of them wounded. . . .

After my father's service in the army he went to Bastrop county in the spring of 1839, where [he] had bought some three hundred beeves and cows, intending to start to the home he had selected [in Burnet County] and build a fort as a protection against the Indians. About June 13 [1839], the party started, consisting of our family, my father, my mother, my brother and myself, a Negro servant and twelve men of my father's company, making fourteen men. There were four wagons with four yoke of oxen to each wagon. We also had one cannon. The wagons were loaded with provisions, ammunition, guns, clothing, and other supplies. . . . When the . . . party got within six miles of its destination, Indians were discovered in great numbers and it was thought that the party was not strong enough to engage the Indians in battle, so it was determined to turn back, as Col. Burleson was expected to follow us in a few days with a hundred men. The party turned back, but the axle on one of the wagons broke as the party reached a point on Brushy Creek in Williamson County.

When it was seen that the Indians were going to attack, the wagons were formed into a small square and immediately the battle began. . . . My mother often told me that the number of Indians was estimated by my father and his men to be fully three hundred, my father's party being only 14 men. The battle lasted from sunrise until 10 o'clock at night, when the last man of the Webster party fell.

By the time the battle was ended, six hundred or more of the savages had arrived, swelling the number to nine hundred, the Indians leaving the scene of the massacre after dark. There were ten sacks of coffee in the wagons and they poured that out on the ground. They smashed the crate that contained my mother's fine china and silver, that she had brought with her from home in Virginia, taking the silver and making trinkets out of it with which they ornamented themselves, stringing them around their necks, their arms and their ankles. My father had his sword with him, and they broke it up into three small pieces, breaking the hilt into three pieces for the three chiefs—Guadalupe, Buffalo Hump, and Yellow Wolf. While I was very young, scarcely four years old, yet I can well remember these old Comanches breaking up the sword, and cutting up the silver that awful day.[14]

The only survivors of the Comanche attack on Brushy Creek were Virginia, her brother, and her mother. All three were taken as captives to the Comanche camp, where their clothes were taken from them. Mrs. Webster was given the clothing of an Indian woman; Virginia's brother was similarly clad in Indian clothing. Virginia, however, "never had a stitch of any kind of clothing at any time," the one thing that seemed to be of great importance to her, as she lamented this a number of times in her narrative. She also said that the Comanches "burnt me and whipped me because I cried," and "tied me on the back of a wild horse and turned it loose. . . . They treated me worse than they treated my mother, and God knows they treated her cruelly. They treated my brother much better than mother and I for some reason, and he would fight them whenever the occasion offered."[15] As cruel as the Comanche treatment seemed to the captives, there was some logic involved. A Comanche band on the move could not be betrayed by the cry of a child, hence the whipping Virginia received for crying. A Comanche band on the move also had to be assured that all members were proficient on horseback, hence the cruel game of tying someone to a wild horse and turning it loose. If a captive were able to ride a spooked horse, he or she could be trusted to keep up with the band. The Comanche "training of [their own] children consisted almost entirely of precept, advice, and counsel. He was told what to do, or warned to refrain from doing, certain things, not because they were right or wrong, but because they were to his advantage or disadvantage."[16]

Virginia, her mother, and her brother were split up after their capture, with separate bands taking each of the Webster captives. Virginia estimated that there were about thirty women and children captives in the band in which she was held, but that she was the only Anglo child. Virginia was given to a Comanche woman, who was to be considered her "mother." The different Comanche bands only came together three times, and Virginia was able to see her brother and mother on these occasions. The first gathering occurred "at the head of Devil's River" in west Texas. At each reunion, Virginia's mother would attempt to gather her two children and escape, but was unsuccessful at the first two attempts. At the third gathering on the Devil's River (which Virginia said occurred in February 1840), Mrs. Webster learned that

> the Comanches were preparing to make a treaty with the white people, and had promised for a certain amount to deliver all the captives they then held, and the delivery of the captives was to be made at San Antonio. Mother told me that at that time they had thirty-three white prisoners, including my mother, my brother and myself. During the time the tribe was together on the Devil's River, previous to starting to San Antonio, mother said she saw the Indians murder six white girl prisoners and, being able to understand and speak the Indian language and Spanish too, she learned that, under certain circumstances, all the captives were to be killed.[17]

Fearing the same fate, Virginia's mother was able to secure Virginia and escape from the Comanches, arriving in San Antonio. Virginia's brother was "brought in by the Indians about six days after we reached San Antonio. I think this was in March 1840, and about the time of what is known as the 'Council House Fight.'"[18] The "Council House Fight" occurred when about fifty Comanches, bringing a large number of furs and horses along with Virginia's brother, rode into San Antonio apparently assuming that they could trade. The Comanches were told they would be held hostage until more captives were turned over, at which point they resisted. Thirty-five Comanches were killed, and twenty-seven Comanche women and children were taken prisoner.[19]

The Comanches held four-year-old Virginia Webster captive for about a year. She was never fully assimilated into the band, as was Cynthia Ann Parker, although Virginia does refer to the Comanche woman who cared for her as "mother," which would seem to indicate Virginia's acknowledgment of the Comanche woman's care. The three times when the Comanche bands came together afforded Virginia's Anglo mother an opportunity to renew contact with her child, actions that the Comanches did not seem to forbid. This would indicate, in the context of political negotiations that were being undertaken at the time in order to force the Comanches to give up their captives at Béxar, that Virginia's status at that point was not that of an adoptable child, but rather that of a potential object of trade, since she was too young to have been considered a servant. Virginia's later memories of her experience were colored by the prevalent Anglo-Texan attitudes toward the Comanches: "They were always on the warpath and would not keep a treaty with the white people. They were bloodthirsty and savage, and did not want to remain at peace."[20]

These attitudes went to the core of the Anglo-Texan fascination with the case of Cynthia Ann Parker. Anglo Texans assumed the Comanches captured children simply because the Comanches were a savage and bloodthirsty people. What they could never understand, what confounded Anglo Texans, was why such a captured child would choose to stay with her captors, when cash offers were made for her redemption.[21] They never saw that the "volatile matrix created by the borderland economies" was operating within the Comanche bands.[22] Anglo Texans had formed an army with their Hispanic neighbors in order to drive Gen. Cos back across the Rio Grande, all in the cause of free trade with the United States. They couldn't see that the Comanches were raiding settlements and stealing livestock in order to support their economy. That the Comanches considered captured women and children as economic currency would not have been a foreign idea to a slave owner such as John Webster, had the captured women and children been any other race than white. When Comanche raiding parties sought out "replacement children" for adoption into the band, they were following customs of "reciprocal adoption that usually fostered intergroup exchange" among Indian tribes in the past.[23] These exchanges, although emotionally volatile because they were seldom voluntary, laid "groundwork for multiethnic enterprises toward subsistence, military, and even ceremonial collaborations."[24] Thus instances such as the Lipan capture of Comanche children and their integration into the Lipan tribe in the early 1800s made it easier for the Lipans, Mescaleros, and Comanches to trade together at a trading spot such as Muchoque after 1860. The problem that arose with the Comanche capture of young Anglo children and their integration into the band as a "replacement child" was the emotional volatility and violence of the capture that occurred, as with the capture of Hispanic children or children from other Indian tribes. Yet most Anglo Texans before 1850 viewed these child captures as a particularly cruel Comanche war tactic, one that had to be met in equal measure. They would allow for no possibility of eventual collaboration.

By around 1850 Cynthia Ann Parker had become the wife of Peta Nocona, a war chief of the Nokoni band. According to Pi-he's oral history, she thus remained within the same family that had captured her, since Peta Nocona was the much younger brother of her captor. Cynthia Ann's first child, Quanah, was born around 1850 "on Elk Creek, just below the Wichita Mountains."[25] A second son, Pee-nah, was born by 1851. A daughter named Topsannah (or Prairie Flower) was born early in 1860.[26] In the late summer of 1860 a group of Texas Rangers, trailing a raiding party of Noconis who had attacked the Sherman farmstead, came upon a Comanche camp on the Pease River. The Rangers made a surprise attack on the camp, killing a number of Comanches and capturing some Comanche women, one of whom was Cynthia Ann Parker.[27] Peta Nocona was not at the battle site on the Pease River, but was several miles away hunting, accompanied by sons Quanah and Pee-nah. Peta Nocona's death several years after the recapture of his wife, Cynthia Ann Parker,[28] set their son Quanah on a path that would eventually intersect with that of Chevato, who in 1860 probably considered the Comanches merely as ancient enemies of the Lipans and fierce raiders, but who did not possess any of the supernatural power naturally bestowed upon the Lipans.[29]

The connection between Chevato, Quanah Parker, and the Comanche chief Wild Horse was not made until after the Comanches were brought onto the reservation in 1875. Wild Horse (Kobi) first appears in the historical record in Santa Fe on March 4, 1869, when he, along with six other Comanche and Kiowa chiefs, presented themselves at District Headquarters "ostensibly for the purpose of making a treaty of peace."[30] Wild Horse was joined by four other Comanche chiefs, all leaders of the Kwahada or Kotsoteka bands—Quaippe, Buffalo Robe, Venturas, and Mow-way—as well as two Kiowa chiefs. The Comanche chiefs claimed "to represent 8,000

Wild Horse (Kobi), Comanche, 1880. National Anthropological Archives, Smithsonian Institution/#06300401.

people scattered along the edge of the Staked Plains in Texas,"[31] with the Kiowa chiefs representing about half of all the Kiowa bands, who were "mixed in" with the Comanche bands on the Staked Plains. The military authorities in New Mexico, however, refused to discuss a peace treaty with the group, since the chiefs had been instructed to present themselves to Gen. W. B. Hazen at Ft. Cobb, "who would receive them and assign them places of safety."[32] The chiefs were willing to travel to Ft. Cobb, but were instructed to wait at Santa Fe until arrangements were made. Two days later, however, they stole away in the night. They were arrested by cavalry troops at Chaparita and taken to Ft. Union, New Mexico, where they were placed on a train and sent to Ft. Leavenworth, Kansas.[33] After being held over the summer of 1869, the captive Comanche chiefs were sent to the Kiowa Agency in Oklahoma, where they soon rejoined their Kwahada and Kotsoteka bands on the Staked Plains.

Wild Horse and his band of Kwahadas did not surrender at Ft. Sill until April 19, 1875. On that date, Wild Horse and his small band of Kwahadas, joined by the Kotsoteka leaders Mow-Way and Long Hungry, turned themselves in along with thirty-six men, 140 women and children, and 700 ponies.[34] Quanah Parker, along with Isatai's band of Kwahadas, surrendered at Ft. Sill two months later.

The transfer of leadership from Wild Horse to Quanah Parker was accomplished after both men had long been on the reservation, but it illustrates much about Comanche culture involving inheritance and the transfer not only of estates but also of power. The Comanches had long made a distinction between a "peace chief" and a "war chief." The function of a war chief was an obvious one; a peace chief was not formally recognized by the band, "but genuine recognition of his powers was reflected in the attention given to his advice and in the general subordination to his influence. . . . A peace chief rose to his position of leadership by combining generosity, kindness, evenness of temper, wisdom in council, and knowledge of his territory with good sense and the ability to speak persuasively on matters at issue."[35] Although it sounds contradictory, when Wild Horse presented himself at Santa Fe in 1869 seeking to sign a peace treaty on behalf of his band of Kwahadas, he was not acting as a peace chief per se. He was merely relaying the decision made by his band's council that they wanted to seek peace at that time. Once on the reservation, however, Wild Horse was acknowledged not only by the agency authorities as a chief of his band, but he was also acknowledged by the members of his band as their peace chief. What was unusual, however, was his transfer of nominal power, before his death, to Quanah Parker, since the Comanches did not "elect" or choose a man for the office of chief. Under custom, a man gradually emerged as a leader; in other words, he became a leader by consensus without the endorsement by another prominent leader. In the case of Wild Horse and Parker, however, the endorsement was made at a time (1890-91) when Parker was already an acknowledged leader. Perhaps Wild Horse thought his endorsement of Parker was needed in order to cement Parker's leadership over a number of Comanche bands. Regardless of the ramifications of a transfer of power, the two men were certainly friends. "Quanah Parker was one of Wild Horse's best friends. When he saw that Wild Horse was gravely ill, he brought him a new suit of clothes and a gold watch. They dressed Wild Horse in the new suit and hung the gold watch on him and held a mirror before him to show him how he looked in his funeral clothes. Wild Horse was exceedingly proud and impressed with his appearance. Two days later [July 15, 1891] he passed away."[36]

In the matter of inheritance, Wild Horse also broke with Comanche custom, leaving his estate to Parker. In the past, Comanche custom had dictated that a man's personal possessions were destroyed upon his death. Because the Comanches reckoned wealth by the possession of horses, and to destroy large numbers of horses would be prejudicial to tribal interest, usually only the deceased's favorite mount was killed, with the balance of the herd dispersed among relatives and friends. Once on the reservation, however, Comanche "practices in regard to inheritance were in a chaotic condition. Apparently the whole problem of inheritance was so new to their culture that no established norms had evolved."[37]

One aspect of Comanche culture seen in the life of Wild Horse was the practice of polygamy. "By the beginning of the nineteenth century, women probably outnumbered men . . . in Comanche . . . society, given the extent of casualties among men in raids and warfare. But where social prestige expressed in horse-wealth provided men the ability to gain wives, men who either by military excellence or social rank were preferred husbands could almost always outcompete their juniors by age or rank."[38] Wild Horse had been a Kwahada chief since at least 1869, giving him a high social rank, but he also seems to have possessed a military reputation for bravery, as exemplified by the translation of the name of his eldest daughter, Charging Up Close to the Enemy. The fact that two of his three wives were sisters was not uncommon. "The Comanche thought sisters made better multiple

Emily Weckahwoonard (left) and cousins, granddaughters of Wild Horse.
Courtesy of William Chebahtah.

wives. There was less possibility of friction developing because a younger wife challenged the supremacy of an older one."[39] In the early reservation period, most of the Comanche leaders had polygamous households. By 1900 this was no longer the case for most Comanches, but as Quanah Parker continued to add wives, the practice began to cause considerable friction with the Kiowa agent.[40]

In New Mexico, the Mescalero and Lipan political leaders also practiced polygamy before 1900.[41] Apache shamans such as Chevato might have gained some measure of political power through their forecasts but generally remained without the social status required to maintain a household with multiple wives. This fact also held true once Chevato moved to Oklahoma. Having a leader such as Quanah Parker arrange a marriage to one of his relatives was a mark of honor and esteem for Chevato, but it did not confer wealth or social rank. However, the connection between Quanah Parker and Wild Horse, both Kwahada leaders, was cemented through Pi-he and Chevato's son, Thomas David Chebahtah, who married the eldest granddaughter of Wild Horse (Emily Weckahwoonard). Through his marriage to Pi-he, Chevato was fully integrated as a Comanche; through his son's marriage into the Wild Horse family, Chevato's children were fully integrated.

17. Warriors

Books have been written about the Comanche—about how ruthless they were, about how so many people, especially in Texas, dreaded them. Many have wondered how they could go so far and go for so long without food or water. As long as their horses had water and grass, that was good enough. They knew where the water holes were for the horses and knew where the grass was plentiful, especially in north Texas. You can get on plateaus where there is no water, and, at certain times of the year, there is no foliage for the stock. So, the Indians took care of their mounts very well, and they provided for them.

The Comanche were able to go for days with very little food when they were on raiding parties because they carried beef jerky with them. They took meat that was seasoned and cured, cut it into strips and ground it into a fine powder. Then they mixed the powder with drippings or lard, making it co-hesive and giving the jerky a good flavor. They would carry the ball of jerky, called ta-a-o, in a little bag on their belt or sash, and they could go for days without any other food.

In 1958 I went into the Marine Corps. We would go out on "problems," which were training exercises sending us out into the brush for up to forty days. I had my father send me some ta-a-o in a small bag and was able to go about three quarters of that time with just the jerky and some water.

They trained us in the Marine Corps right after the Comanche way. In the Marine Corps, if you are pursuing your objective and you're in hot pursuit of the enemy, if your best friend gets hit and knocked down, you don't stop for him. They tell you that there is a corpsman behind you who will come up and help your friend. It's very severe punishment for you to stop once you're in hot pursuit of the enemy. They even do this today in Iraq. I was looking at a pic-ture of some young marines from my old unit, Second Battalion, First Ma-rines, and they looked pretty exhausted. I can understand why, because of the way they fight in battle. That's just the way Comanches believed that fighting should be—relentless. And that's why they suffered so many casualties.

Have you ever seen old western movies where the Indians have painted handprints on both sides of the front chest of the Indian's horse? That custom comes about in this way. When the enemy of the Comanche is on the ground, and the warrior knows he has the enemy pinned on the ground, the warrior will ride over the man with his horse. Almost always, the man on the ground will instinctively hold up both hands to protect himself as he is about to get run over by the horse. The Comanche would ride over him, and then turn around very quickly and stick the enemy on the ground with a lance. So, the handprints on the horse's chest meant, "I'm going to get you; you're going to surrender on your back." If the Comanche painted their horses in this man-ner, it meant that they had killed an enemy in this way before.

In combat situations, where it is a no-win situation, what you are trying to protect is in back of you, and you have to give them time. Much like the story of the Alamo; Travis had to buy Sam Houston time, thirteen days, and they paid it out, paid the ultimate price. It was the same way with Comanche warriors, except that they would signify that they were in a no-win situation. They would have a little rope tied up to them, and they would use an arrow, knife, or a lance. It's symbolic after this point. They would throw one end of the rope down on the ground and run an arrow or lance through the end of the rope. The other end of the rope was tied to themselves. Then they would say, "I stake myself on the battlefield." When the enemy came, they would stand right there and fight, because if they didn't they could never live it down. Others could run, but once you staked yourself to the battlefield, you fought to win or fought to die.

Today we have Special Forces, Navy Seals, and Green Berets, but the Comanche also had something similar. They were called warrior or clan societies. The way to get into these societies was to be battle-hardened with a lot of experience. When you look at a war bonnet, each eagle feather in the war bonnet signifies the same thing that the ribbons on the chest of a military man signify today. The Comanche called it a "coup," or an act of bravery, and an eagle feather would be put on the war bonnet to signify each act of bravery. Today we might think that their acts were senseless, but you have to remember that the Comanche honored a man who had a lot of moxie. If you had a lot of faith in yourself and you were fearless in combat, you were honored and highly valued because you had "counted coups." That is why the Comanche were so tenacious in fighting. You had to be battle-hardened, and you had to have a war bonnet full of your exploits; then you could be part of a warrior society, but only if you were invited. In a tribe of 20,000, there might be only ten or twelve men who would qualify.

When it was a no-win situation, these men would be called up. They would send the rest of the warriors home, and they would go on by themselves. They knew what they were doing, and they didn't want the rest of the warriors to get in their way. Sometimes they faced insurmountable odds, but because of what they were, sometimes they prevailed.

The "coups" might seem to some people as senseless, but if you think as they thought, the "coups" would add to their notoriety and show their valor in combat. An example of a "coup" would be this: if a warrior was fighting on his horse, and it looked like an even match between he and his enemy, the warrior might jump off of his horse and undo the horse's cinch. Now, the Comanche had bone saddles and buffalo hide blankets, but they still had cinches for the saddles. They used hackamores for bridles because they did not have metal for bits. They would uncinch the horse and drop the reins, and the horse would just stand there. This was a way in which they would say to their enemy, "Look, I'm not scared of you. This is how much I fear you. And when I re-saddle my horse, I'm coming after you and you'd better be gone!"

It's hard for me to read in books and hear from old-timers in Texas how ruthless the Comanche were. It's hard for me, because I look at how I was raised and at how genteel my folks were. I was eight years old when I was taken to meet this gentleman who was my first recollection of my kinfolks. He was kin to my mother, and his name was Oscar Yellow Wolf. At that time, when I was eight, he must have been about seventy-five. I was introduced to him, and, I guess, he looked down at me, as a man of seventy-five who had lived all these things and had been in the heat of battles. He was quite impressive to me. He was dressed in Comanche attire; he wore earrings that were like thunderbirds on each side. He had his hair combed so neatly; he had it braided, and the braids were decorated with yarn. He looked down on me, and I guess he was thinking, "So this is one of my relatives." I think in much the same way when I look down on my young relatives. Here I am, hitting my seventies, and when I look at them I think, "This person is the future. This person is going to carry on when I am gone."

Oscar Yellow Wolf reached down and shook my hand. He told me in Comanche, "Tocoh," which means nephew, *"come on, I'll show you my horse." So we went to the barn. He had the horse saddled, and he put me on the horse's back and led me to the house. He would only talk in Comanche, and I could only answer back in English, but he was bilingual and he knew. He said, "Some day, come over when you get older, and we'll go horseback riding. I'll show you how the old ones used to ride." He took me back to my mother, but I remember it to this day. He impressed me very much. Here was a man* seventy-five years old, didn't have a stomach, was thinly built, about five feet eight inches or five feet nine inches—very impressive.

My grandfather, Chevato, was also impressive and had been a warrior in his day. He always prized two things—his weaponry and his horse. He had a Winchester Model 1873 rifle that used a .44-.40 caliber cartridge because that ammunition was interchangeable and could also be used in his Colt revolver. He also carried a derringer with him all of his life, strapped with a piece of rawhide to his left wrist. It had saved his life in his fight with the Kickapoo, and he always wanted to be prepared.

Chevato was a good horseman and was good in working with horses and cattle. I was told that even in his later years, when he was at least eighty years old, he could still control a fresh horse. One day, he was riding into India-homa, Oklahoma, and was riding a fresh, young horse. The horse spooked and reared, throwing him off. He picked himself up, disciplined the horse, climbed back on, and rode on with no ill effects. He passed on to my father a bit of wisdom about horses—around the mouth of the horse are small hairs, and the area is very sensitive to the horse. Chevato told my father to take a small hair from around the horse's mouth and don't waste around, just take the small hair and pull it out quickly. As soon as you do that, blow into the horse's nostril. If you do this, the horse will never leave you.

My grandfather, Chevato, also passed on much of his wisdom about being a warrior to his sons. He passed along lessons he had learned as a young Lipan warrior in Mexico and lessons he had learned while raiding with the Mescalero.

His oldest son with Pi-he was James Hezekiah Chebahtah. When World War I broke out, Jim wanted to enlist as a soldier. Chevato didn't think he should enlist because he felt that this war was not a fight that concerned the Indian. He thought it was a foreign war, one that did not concern us. In fact, he went so far as to tell all of his sons that if they were drafted, they could claim exemption because they had been enrolled as Mexican citizens. Chevato said that he had gone to Mexico City years ago and had filed papers with information that he had been born in Mexico, making him a citizen there

James Hezekiah Chebahtah, Camp Mills, Long Island, New York, February 20, 1919.
Courtesy of William Chebahtah.

and that this also applied to his sons. But Jim wanted to enlist and he did so, even with his father's blessing. He was assigned to Company G, Thirteenth Infantry, and sent to Camp Mills, Long Island, New York.

Jim Chebahtah served with other Comanches from Oklahoma. One friend, Owen Yackey-on-ny, was blinded by mustard gas in battle and lost his eyesight. When he got home, his wife was very devoted to him and always went with him, helping him find his way. I have to take my hat off to those men from my tribe who served in World War I. After they came back home, they were very stable; they didn't hold a grudge. Owen was always very jovial, pleasant, and never felt sorry for himself. Jim was also the same way, and they were good examples for everyone else who didn't go through the rigors of war.

In the same unit with Jim was a Ft. Sill Apache. They were fighting in France, and this man was awarded the Silver Star for bravery. But one month later, they came to him and told him, "Your medal has been rescinded; we have to ask you to give it back to us. We think it might be a misunderstanding, and we are working to fix this, but you have to give it back." So the Apache gave the Silver Star back. The man was wondering why this happened. Some time later, they came back to him and told him that they were going to re-award the medal to him. They explained that his parents or grandparents were prisoners of war with Geronimo and had never had that status officially removed. If his parents were prisoners of war, then he was considered a prisoner of war and not a citizen. But the army was able to have all this straightened out in his case, and he was not only made a legal citizen, but was re-awarded the Silver Star.

Chevato also had some specific advice for his grandsons when they went to war. My older brother was in the Marine Corps, First Raider Battalion, and fought in the battle of Iwo Jima. Before he left for boot camp, Chevato sat him down and gave him some advice on being a warrior. He said that if he was ever to go into combat, he must carry a second weapon other than the weapon that he normally used or that he was issued. So my brother, Clifford Chebahtah, always kept a hunting knife underneath his fatigue or utility jacket. Underneath, he had a leatherworker make him a holster that fit like a pistol holster but where he holstered his knife. He had a sharp hunt-

ing knife that he always carried in this way as a marine, and, in this way, he carried out the wishes of our grandfather, who had told him to always have a second weapon, going back to the Kickapoo Incident.

Chevato also told his sons and grandsons that if they ever went to war, the worst enemy a warrior could have would be hesitation. He said, "You've got this little thing. A lot of people call it a conscience. A lot of people call it instinct. I call it instinct. What you have to do is listen to that voice within yourself. If you ever go into combat, you must listen to that voice. And never hesitate."

My brother Clifford related to me that his knife saved his life in the battle at Iwo Jima. He was completely out of ammunition when a Japanese marine accosted him, and they had to fight hand to hand. My brother had the upper hand because he had his knife. It saved his life. He also heeded his inner voice and moved from where he had taken cover. That move saved his life, for he had been hiding behind a tank of airplane fuel. An artillery shell was dropped on the tank shortly after he had moved away.

So Chevato's wisdom was heeded even unto his grandchildren, for he had taught the family to always stay prepared so that you could take care of your own life in a dangerous situation.

§

The Comanches had a well-deserved reputation as fierce warriors. In December 1870 interpreter Horace Jones submitted a report on the Comanches to Laurie Tatum, the Kiowa agent, where he endeavored to explain to Tatum why the Comanches were always raiding:

> It is then to their education and traditions that we must look for a true solution to these causes for war. The Indian boy is taught from infancy to believe that the only true road to honor or destruction is the warpath. An Indian who cannot look from his lodge and behold a herd of horses or ponies and a few scalps dangling from his shield, as the results of his exploits, is branded among the tribe as an old woman, a coward and a fit subject for ridicule.
>
> It is well understood by any one who is conversant with the manners

and customs of the Indians of the Plains that the influence of the old chiefs is merely nominal. When they attempt to restrain their young warriors from war, they are at once given to understand that theft, rapine, murder were the means which they themselves had become head men or chiefs. Until these ideas are thoroughly eradicated from the minds of these young warriors, we may expect a repetition of these outrages every Spring, if not in the immediate vicinity of their respective Agencies, at any rate upon the frontier settlements of Texas, New Mexico and Kansas.[1]

Warfare provided, for the Comanches, the "basis of the whole system of rank and social status in Comanche society. Consequently, the life of the male came to be centered around warfare and raiding."[2] Oscar Yellow Wolf (Peet-su-vah) was born in 1877, only two years after the last of the Comanches had entered the reservation. He was the son of Yellow Wolf (Esa-hau-pith, b. 1851) and Her-kay-yah. His father, Yellow Wolf, was a Yamparika in Howling Wolf's band, and the family was the same family that had produced the chief named Yellow Wolf, who had broken up the sword of Virginia Webster's father in 1839.

Because the Lipan Apaches were not a plains Indian tribe, they did not place the same emphasis on warfare as the basis for social status as did the Comanches. For the Lipans, warfare was for revenge; raiding was a means by which their economy was sustained:

> A few Lipan were going out to hunt antelope. They came upon some Co-
> manche. The Apache men went back to their camp. They told that they
> had seen eight Comanche men and one woman. A young Apache had
> been killed by the Comanche just a few days before and the Apache were
> still thinking about this and were very angry and sorry. The scouts told
> the relatives of the dead boy what they had seen and the Apache got ready
> to fight. This time they were going to start it.
>
> [The Apaches attacked the Comanches, and the Comanches fought
> bravely, wounding a number of Lipans. The Lipans were able to capture
> two of the Comanches.] They took the two prisoners back and killed
> them that night. They turned them over to the women who stabbed them

in the throat. They killed them because the Comanche had wounded so many Apache. They threw the bodies out somewhere. They don't bother to bury the enemy.[3]

Several Lipan stories have been preserved where war with the Comanches was averted because someone on either side recognized a kinsman in the opposing group, indicating the number of kinship relations that must have existed between the two tribes, whether those kinship relations were forged through captives or through marriage.[4] The Lipan warrior also seems to have made a much sharper distinction between warfare and raiding than did the Comanche warrior. A story tells of a group of Lipans who were trapped by the Comanches inside a corral that the Lipans had strengthened by adding their spears to the wooden corral wall. The Lipans fought bravely, but the Comanches had them surrounded and were about to kill them all. Suddenly, one Comanche remembered that a relative had married a Lipan woman and recognized his kinsman as one of the cornered Lipans. The Comanches let all of the Lipans go free, but in doing so, one of the Comanches took a Lipan spear. "The Lipan walked up to the man and said, 'My friend, that is my spear.' 'No, it is mine,' [said the Comanche], 'I took it away from you during the fight.' 'No, you never took it away from me,' [answered the Lipan]. 'If you had taken it out of my hand while we were fighting, it would belong to you. But the way you got it was to take it from in front of our corral at a time when I was out fighting. That is nothing but stealing, so give it back to me.' The Comanche had to give it up and went off ashamed."[5]

The Lipan warrior did not "count coup," as did his Comanche counterpart, but the Lipans did scalp their enemies. According to Lipan myth, the tribe was given instructions on scalping from the Coyote People. After a battle, they were to go to the bodies of their dead enemies, where they would "cut around the tops of their heads, and scalp every one of them. ... Treat the scalps in this manner: hold all the hair, build a fire, turn the flesh side toward the fire, burn and dry off the flesh, being careful not to burn the hair, then put a stick through two holes made in the scalp."[6] The

Lipans were to carry the scalps on poles back to their camp. Before they reached the camp, however, they would line up and carry the scalps into camp while singing a victory song. Once back in camp, the people would celebrate with a scalp dance. The victorious warriors would sit in a circle, slapping their thighs in time to singing. Later, a special sage-filled buckskin pillow was held in the warrior's lap and slapped while songs were sung. After this, the scalp dance would begin.[7]

18. The Lost Sister

Now, remember the sister of Chevato and Dinero who was kept by the ranchers? Well, here is her story.

One day, Chevato and Dinero decided to go visit their sister, but Chevato did not feel there would be good prospects of finding her. He felt the ranchers had misled him when they told him where they lived, and he told his younger brother, "Don't be disappointed."

So they rode to the place where the ranchers said they lived. Sure enough, their sister was there! They got to see her and visit with her, and they remained in touch with her for the rest of their lives.

In their sister's life, she had grown to be a young lady, and she looked at her adopted parents as her parents, but she always remembered that she had two brothers. The lady of the house never tried to hide the fact that she had brothers and never tried to hide the facts of her adoption. She grew up happy, and later, her adopted parents even sent her to school. She got her education and even took a nurse's training.

I myself got to see her. She fit the way our family was built, a slender woman about five feet six inches to five feet eight inches. Her name was Ruth, and she had married a prospector named Arthur Hill. They had moved to the west and had lived there many years. When I saw her, she was an elderly woman, past eighty, but she could get around well. She was always caring about our diet; you know, the diet of Native Americans is mostly meat. She

would tell my mother that we shouldn't eat so much meat and eat more veg-
etables. She visited with us about two weeks and then went back home. Later
she passed away.

§

Tracing Chevato's sister, Pe-chá, is much like trying to find a phantom, and
is illustrative of the many problems in researching the lives of individual
Lipan Apaches, who seem to float like ghosts on the edges of the historical
record after 1800. There are two oral histories and one piece of documentary evidence in which she appears. Her brother spoke of her in his oral
history, indicating that she was "five" at the time of the Zaragosa massacre. It is unknown whether that number indicated five months of age or
five years of age, but using Chevato's information, we are able to extrapo-
late a possible date of birth for Pe-chá from 1863 to 1869. Antonio Apache
spoke of her when Morris Opler interviewed him at Mescalero during the
summer of 1935. As a preface to his story about the Kickapoo Incident of
1868, Antonio Apache explained, "They [Chevato and Dinero] have a sister in California named Ruth Hill. She was here in April and visited her
brother. She is married now so her name is changed. She is about fifty-five
years old. She was not born yet when her brother was stabbed by the Kickapoo [1868]."[1] As is the case with Chevato's information regarding his sister, contradictions abound. Was she known as Ruth Hill but had married
by 1935 and had a different name by that date? An age of fifty-five would
yield a year of birth of 1880, yet all other evidence shows that her parents
had died by 1870. If she was not yet born in 1868, however, that fact from
Antonio Apache would lend weight to the theory that she was five months
old, rather than five years old, at the time of her parents' deaths in 1869.

Chevato's grandson, William Chebahtah, met Ruth Hill around 1940,
when she visited his family in Oklahoma. He remembers being told that she
was a nurse and that she had married a prospector named Arthur Hill.

The one piece of documentary evidence regarding this woman is found
in two letters written by Chevato to Quanah Parker. The first letter, dated
October 1888, asked Parker to "please have the papers made out good so

that my brother, my brother's wife, my sister and my little boy can come to you."[2] In January 1889 a second letter from Chevato to Parker contained a list of thirty-four Lipans who wanted to come to Oklahoma, and among those persons listed was Pe-chá, whom he called "my sister."[3]

The phantom, however, disappears at this point, and the trail goes cold. A check of Mescalero and Comanche census data reveals no Pe-chá or an equivalent name. A check of the federal census data from 1870 to 1930 for Texas, New Mexico, California, and Oklahoma reveals no nurse named Ruth Hill married to a prospector named Arthur Hill and born between 1863 and 1880. Going back to the beginning of the story, however, might provide a few more clues.

Antonio Apache, in speaking of the Zaragosa massacre, stated that his group of survivors made their way to the Mescaleros by crossing the Rio Grande near Eagle Pass and traveled northwest until they reached Madzil (Coyote Mountain), a site near Ft. Davis in west Texas.[4] If Chevato and Dinero followed a similar route, then they probably met the couple in a buckboard wagon at some point between Eagle Pass and Ft. Davis. A survey of the 1870 and 1880 census data from the Texas counties that bordered the Rio Grande in that region provides an interesting clue. The 1880 census for Presidio County, which included the Ft. Davis region, lists a Santus Mean and his wife, Carmella. Santus was a fifty-two-year-old Mexican shepherd whose wife worked in the laundry at a hospital. A ten-year-old girl named Francy Reno lived with the Mean family as their adopted daughter. Francy worked as a nurse at the same hospital where her adopted mother worked as a laundress. However, at age ten, her duties were probably not those we would think of today as nursing duties; nonetheless, she is listed in 1880 as being a nurse. The census states that Francy was born in Texas, but both of her natural parents had been born in Mexico. Francy represents someone who would be a likely candidate as Chevato's sister, assuming the oral history information is correct. The Mean surname is not a traditional Hispanic surname, although both Santus and Carmella Mean were born in Mexico. There were, however, a number of persons of Sephardic Jewish origin living in Coahuila and Nuevo Leon; perhaps the surname is connected with that population. Another family listed as neighbors of Santus Mean in the 1880 Presidio County census was the family of Jose Joshone (Jose and Pirolosa and infant son David), who also had an adopted ten-year-old daughter named Puntabeta Sousodone.[5]

Chevato's sister next appears at the Mescalero Reservation from October 1888 through January 1889, although she does not appear on any census taken during this time. She obviously had come to assist her brother in the care of his children, since his Lipan wife had died in late 1888, and Chevato did not remarry to Chenoco until 1890. There were a number of gold prospectors working claims next to the Mescalero Reservation from 1883 on; perhaps Arthur Hill was among that group. The Lipan woman known to her brother as Pe-chá vanishes after January 1889, and any further information on her life is of a speculative nature; she remains another Lipan phantom dancing on the pages of history.

19. The Revolutionary

As Chevato got older, he began to travel back home to Zaragosa every year to visit with old friends, particularly Mr. Rodriguez—his friend from the bandit days. Mr. Rodriguez had done quite well for himself and owned a large hacienda; he always treated Chevato with the utmost respect and hospitality.

Chevato would ride the train from Oklahoma to south Texas and then go over the border into Mexico. On one trip, as he was nearing his old home of Zaragosa, the train was forced to stop. Everyone on the train was asking what was going on when, all at once, a group of young men came onto the train. They told everybody to get their valuables out. They had a sack, and they were going from seat to seat down the aisle of the train. They asked everyone for their money, their valuables, and anything they had of any worth. When they got to Chevato, he asked why they were robbing the train. "Well," one young man said, "we are revolutionaries. We're raising money for Pancho Villa, and that is why we are taking all these valuables."

Chevato started to give what he had in his pockets, for at this time, he was an older man, and he knew the value of not arguing with revolutionaries. He was about to give his valuables when one young man said, "Where are you going in Mexico?" Chevato told him, "I'm going home. I'm going to visit my old home in Zaragosa." The young man said, "I'm from Zaragosa, too. Who do you know?" They started swapping stories, and the young man told him, "When I was a boy, I heard stories about you and what you have done. I remember hearing songs [corridas] about you." Chevato answered, "I hope they were good." So the young man told Chevato, "You keep your money. We don't want your money. You're like us—a revolutionary!" And the bandits went on robbing everyone else on the train.

Chevato went on to Zaragosa, but always remembered this event with fondness, for anyone who was fighting against the Mexican federal government, as he had done, was someone he applauded.

20. The Peyote Singer

When I was a young boy, a Kiowa man named Vandal Apauty asked me if I knew about my grandfather's powers as a healer. Mr. Apauty had known my grandfather, and he related this story to me:

> *I was there when this person was very sick, and they called your grandfather. After a few days, he came, and when he got there, he came into the room and looked at the person who was lying there. He said he would find out what was wrong with the person. Your grandfather had a black kerchief around his neck. The kerchief was threaded through a bolo, a little ornament that held the two ends of the kerchief together. He took off the kerchief and put the ornament in his pocket. He unraveled the black scarf; it was black silk, and I have never seen a black scarf like that before or since. Your grandfather laid the black scarf on the person's chest and looked down into the scarf. Your grandfather said, "I see what your problem is," and he began to tell the person what was wrong. The people who were standing by looked at the black scarf, but couldn't see anything.*

My grandfather used his kerchief as a seer would use a crystal ball. He could see inside the kerchief. He also took roots and remedies that he was always attuned to, and he made some medicine out of these herbs. And the person got well.

Chevato was very much in tune with peyote because he was an Apache. Nowadays, young people misuse peyote. It's a hallucinogen, and it's very strong, as we all know. But it can also be used in medicinal ways, and it is a very good medicine. Chevato used it, and he also used other herbs. He would take my father out, when my father was young, and they would walk through the pasture. Chevato would say, "You see that flower over there? It looks like a flower, but it's an herb. It's good for this kind of sickness." Then they would walk some more. He would take my father and his brothers on long nature walks through the trees and the creeks, and he would point out different flowers or weeds that were medicinal. He would tell them, "You can use this for a gunshot wound. You take it, you cure it and dry it and sprinkle it on a wound. It will keep infection away." He knew a lot about curing with herbs. When he got his powers, he also gained knowledge of these herbs and roots.

I have personal knowledge that using the old ways can heal a person. When my mother was in her older years, she suffered a stroke. My sister and I took her to the Indian hospital where she was examined. The doctors told us that the only thing that could be done for my mother was diet and exercise therapy. The doctors told us that she would never recover, but with a good diet and exercise, she might show some improvement. My sister did not accept what the doctors had told us, since she believed in the old ways. The elders told us of an old Kiowa shaman who might take our mother's case, but there was a strict protocol in how we were to approach him. Since my older brother Clifford was not living at home and my father had passed away, I was the family patriarch. It would be up to me to go and approach the shaman. I was to take a gift of tobacco to him—he smoked a certain brand of cigarettes— and I was to strictly follow a certain protocol. So I drove to his house with my mother and sister.

As I turned into his driveway, I could see an old Kiowa man standing on his front porch, as if he were waiting for us. I parked the car, and he walked up

and introduced himself to me. He said "Good day" to my mother and sister,
but did not touch the car door to open it for them, nor did he have any other
interaction with them. He motioned to me to follow him as his wife came out
of the house to greet my mother and sister. I got out of the car and followed
him some way across the yard to a tree, where we both sat down. "I hear you
have a problem," he remarked. At this point I knew that I must present him
with a present of tobacco before the conversation could go any further; this
must be done in a certain way, however. I took the package of cigarettes out
of my pocket—I had been told that his favorite brand was Pall Mall—and
tapped one end of the package against the palm of my hand. I then carefully
tore off a small square of the package top and removed one cigarette. I put
the cigarette in my mouth (even though I did not normally smoke) and lit it
with a wooden match. Taking three puffs and blowing each puff into the air,
I then handed the lit cigarette to the shaman without saying a word. He took
it and also took three puffs, blowing each puff into the air. After handing the
cigarette to the shaman, I took the cigarette package and wooden matchbox
and placed them in front of him. As the shaman continued to smoke, I knew
we could now begin to talk about my mother's problem.

I explained that she had suffered a stroke and that we wanted to use the old
ways to see if she could be healed. The old shaman then said, "I believe I can
help her." He went on to explain his ritual. For three weeks, he would fast on
water and live alone in the hills behind his house. During this time, he was
to have no contact whatsoever with women—not my mother, nor my sister,
nor his wife. What he was doing was very serious, and he was forbidden to
touch any woman during this time. During his fasting time, he would pray.
At the end of our first meeting, he would give me a small amount of a liquid
that looked like dark tea; it was peyote. My mother was to drink this. I was
to come back the next week to get another small cup of liquid for my mother.
The third week, I was to come back for further instructions.

I did as the old shaman had asked. When I came back the third time, he
told me that the ritual was complete. He explained that he did not ask for
payment for what he did, but he would accept items to replace things he had
used to help heal others. I was to bring him the following things—an eagle

feather, a white doeskin bleach-tanned on both sides, and a white silk scarf.
I found these items at an Indian store; the eagle feather was placed in a box,
while I carefully folded the scarf, placing it in the middle of the doeskin. I
then wrapped the doeskin into a neat bundle, tying it up with a string. My
sister had made a nice cloth to cover these things. I presented the cloth-cov-
ered bundle with the boxed eagle feather resting on top. This was acceptable to
the shaman. He then gave me three quart jars of peyote-steeped tea. This tea
was to be used as a medicine. My mother was to take about three teaspoons a
day, and the liquid was to be kept cool until it was all gone. My mother, who
understood the old ways, began taking the tea. After her stroke, my mother's face was drawn down on one side, and she had much difficulty walking because of the paralysis on one side of her body. After she had completed
the shaman's treatment, she could walk and talk as before. All our neighbors
were amazed, and they could not understand what had caused her to make
such a complete recovery.

My sister had a friend who also used the old ways to recover from a stroke.
This friend, a young woman named Gloria, had suffered such a bad stroke
that she wore a hat with a veil every time she went out of the house because
people would stare. Her face was so distorted. She went to the hospital, and
the doctor told her that there was nothing they could do, so she sought treatment in the old way. Several months later, she went back to the hospital and
requested to see the same doctor who had told her there was no hope. When
he came into the room, she was sitting in a chair; she was not wearing her
veil. The doctor was startled and at first could not recognize her. When he
saw how she had completely recovered, he was amazed and told her, "Tell me
what you did to recover so completely. I could make a lot of money, if only I
knew your secret!" Gloria then stood up and told the doctor, "That's why I
will never tell you how I recovered. I only came back to tell you that there is
more to healing than what you know here in this hospital." With that, Gloria walked out of the room.

The old Kiowa shaman had known and respected my grandfather, Chevato. He told me that Chevato was also able to heal people through the use
of peyote. As a shaman, it was important that, when practicing his rituals,

he not have any contact with women. My mother told me this story about my grandfather:

> Chevato was leading a peyote meeting. The men were sitting inside the te-
> pee, while my mother, aunt, grandmother Pi-he, and other women were
> outside preparing the breakfast that would be served at the completion of
> the ceremony. The women did not enter the tepee until the all-night meet-
> ing was over. When they brought in the food, the men were sitting in a semi-
> circle; most of the women passed in front of them, setting down the dishes.
> One woman, however, was walking behind the men, looking to see what
> additional things they might need to eat. One of the men became very un-
> easy, and after the women had finished, he whispered to Chevato, "There is
> a woman here who is in her menstrual cycle." Chevato got up and went out-
> side, where he asked my mother, "I want you to call together all the women.
> One of them is in her menstrual cycle, and it is forbidden for her to be here.
> She must leave immediately." My mother did as he asked, and, sure enough,
> one of the women had to leave. Peyote rituals had very strict rules that had
> to be followed exactly, in order for the ritual to be done properly.

§

To discover the roots of the peyote religion as practiced by the Comanches and Kiowas, one has to trace Chevato's footsteps back in time to the
land and people of his birth. James Mooney, the ethnologist who first
reported on the ritual use of peyote in a speech to the Washington Anthropological Society in 1891, attributed the beginnings of the ritual use
of peyote to the Carrizos, a Coahuiltecan-speaking people whose territory covered both south Texas and the peyote-growing areas of northern
Mexico.[1] However, Mooney came to believe that the Mescalero Apaches,
rather than the Lipans, had transferred the knowledge of the peyote rituals to the Comanches and Kiowas, citing the similarity in the tribal name
(Mescalero) to the mescal plant from which he believed the peyote buttons were taken. In actuality, the mescal cactus, or agave, was a staple food
used by the Mescaleros and did not produce the peyote used in religious

rituals.[2] In November 1897 Mooney paid a visit to the Mescalero Reservation, where he interviewed several men about peyote rituals, taking careful notes as well as making a comparative vocabulary of some Lipan and Mescalero words. Unfortunately, Mooney misunderstood his primary informant, Nayoka (Andy Miller), a Mescalero who gave Mooney information about Lipan peyote practices, even though Nayoka was a Mescalero. Mooney assumed that Nayoka was telling him about Mescalero peyote practices, and the misunderstanding grew from there. If Mooney had just looked back over his 1897 notes, he had the answer written there all along, but he just didn't realize it. Scribbled at the end of some notes regarding locations where peyote could be found, Mooney wrote, "Chibata has been there. The *Tu-etin-imi* or *Tu-etin-inde* = No Water People, a part of Mescaleros, used to live there."[3] The No Water People was another name for the Uplander band of Lipans who had lived in southern New Mexico, a designation later confirmed by Opler.[4] The man Chibata cited by Andy Miller was none other than Chevato. How, then, did the Comanches and Kiowas come to adopt rituals associated with the use of peyote (*hosh-chezhál*; Lipan for "cactus to eat"; colloquially known as "hoosh") if they didn't learn those rituals from the Mescaleros? The answer lies in the historical migrations of the Lipan bands.

As the Lipan Apaches were pushed out of Texas and into Coahuila, Mexico, after 1750 by the aggressive Comanches, and as the Lipans were coaxed into Spanish missions in both southwestern Texas and northern Coahuila, they came into contact with the Carrizos, adopting many elements of their peyote rituals. There was even a Spanish mission named for peyote, which grew so abundantly just south of the Rio Grande. Named the Mission del Dulce Nombre Jesus de Peyotes (Mission of the Sweet Name of Jesus of the Peyotes), it was founded in 1688 by Franciscan friars about thirty miles south of the missions later used to shelter and protect the Lipan Apaches (San Juan Bautista, Monclova Viejo, and Agua Verde).[5] Also located within close proximity to the Mission del Dulce Nombre Jesus de Peyotes was a mission founded for the Carrizos; the first mention of the mission San Jose del Carrizo can be found in 1773.[6]

The Indians of Coahuila found a ready supply of peyote for their ceremonies, since the region contained one of the largest source areas for peyote in the Western Hemisphere. The Lomerío de Peyotes, an area of small
hills just west of Zaragosa, was a rich source of supply. Peyote could also
be found in the Bolsón de Mapimí, the rugged mountains of the Sierra
Madre. In these areas, peyote—small, spineless cacti "with a flat, fissured
top, hardly rising above the ground"—grew in abundance.[7] It produced,
from the fleshy part of the plant, small "beans," or buttons, of peyote that
were cut off and used in the rituals. The peyote buttons could be chewed,
processed through fermentation to make a slightly inebriating drink, or
boiled and infused to make a healing tea.

The first peyote ceremony mentioned in the historical record can be
found in a 1788 Spanish report from a spy who surreptitiously witnessed
a joint Western Lipan/Mescalero peyote ritual celebrated near Zaragosa.
The ceremony lasted all night and consisted of eating and smoking. The
substances eaten and smoked are not named, but the spy reported that he
had experienced "extraordinary visions without end."[8]

The first European to describe the Lipan use of peyote was Jean Louis
Berlandier, who noted in his 1830 journal after his visit to Texas:

> Thus the Lipans and Carrizos, and almost all the rest of the peoples who
> live along the Rio Bravo del Norte [Rio Grande] are the ones who con-
> sume the most hard liquor. . . . Before the time of the conquerors, several
> of the Anahuac nations used to get drunk by chewing a plant known in
> Mexican as *peiotl* and in Creole as *peyote*. The coastal peoples, the Tanca-
> hues [Tonkawas], the Lipans, and several other native groups of the north-
> ern reaches of Tamaulipas still use this intoxicating plant in their feasts.
> Each year, they gather a store of it and . . . they make a sort of rosary of it,
> and keep it by them to use as need be.[9]

Chevato was born in 1852 in an area rich in peyote; he was born into a
Western Lipan Apache culture whose primary feature was a refined peyote ritual adopted from the Carrizos at least seventy-five years earlier. As
the 1788 Spanish spy reported, the Western Lipans had originally eaten the

peyote buttons in an all-night ceremony that only included the smoking of tobacco. As practiced by the Carrizos, the ritual use of peyote consisted of a ceremonial dance while chewing peyote to enhance the religious experience and provide a closer spiritual connection between the celebrant and the Great Spirit. Several musical instruments were associated with the Carrizo peyote dance—a drum, a gourd rattle containing *usachito* seeds, and tinkle bells attached to the legs of the dancers just below the knee.[10] By 1800 the Lipans had refined the Carrizo ceremony by adding the element of song, rather than the use of dance, while keeping the drum and gourd rattle as instrumental accompaniment to the song.

According to a statement made by Chevato's brother, Dinero, their great-grandfather had been the first Lipan to use peyote:

> My name is Pa-na-ro. I am a Lipan Apache. I live five miles northeast of Indiahoma, Oklahoma on my own allotment. I am about 57 years old.
>
> I knew about peyote before any of these Indians in the Oklahoma country knew about it. I first ate peyote in Mexico. My great-grandfather was the first [Lipan] to make use of it in Mexico, and it was brought among the Indians here years after. It was used as a medicine at first, and no women or young people ate it as they do now. It is called mescal-peyote in Mexico; here in Oklahoma it is called peyote.[11]

Dinero's statement seems to indicate that his great-grandfather was the first to use peyote as a "medicine," but this term is misleading, bringing to mind the use of plants or herbs as war-medicine. What Dinero seems to be referring to is the particular peyote ritual, as practiced by Dinero, Chevato, and later many Comanches, which was both a religious ritual and a healing ceremony. A Methodist missionary to the Comanches in Oklahoma, A. E. Butterfield, described such a ceremony, as he witnessed it in 1893:

> Their custom was to clean a spot of ground of all trash and erect a tent in which to hold the service. The door of the tent faces the east. In the center is a hole where a fire is kept burning. A mound of dirt is on the west side of the fire. There is a trench leading from the hole to the door of the

tepee. Observing their rule, I turned to the left and walked completely around the tepee before entering. Then going in through the door, I again turned to the left and sat on the ground at the south side. Inside were twenty-two Indian men (there were no women because they believed the women had no soul and were therefore not a fit subject for worship). On a pallet some distance from the door, and on the south side, there lay a sick boy who was there to be prayed for. A bucket containing many mescal or peyote buttons, to be eaten during the night, sat near the middle of the north side of the tepee. Big Looking Glass [a Comanche] sat on the west side facing the door with a large mescal button on the elevated dirt in front of him.

The worship was begun by beating the tom-tom or drum, shaking a gourd with beads in it, and singing a most weird kind of song with no harmony or melody. [This was the essence of the Lipan peyote ritual.] . . . An old man who sat at the right of the door held in his hand a bunch of eagle feathers. If the devil should get into the buttons, all the prayers offered would be in vain. They prayed to the button on the mound as they sang and beat the drum and shook the gourd. The bucket was passed around occasionally and each took and ate as many of the buttons as he wanted. This was continued all night, the men sitting in one position, never standing all night.

About 2 a.m. I went home and returned about 7 a.m. Soon after this a woman put a pan of food in the trench, and then three other women did likewise. Four men kneeled around this food and for nearly an hour they had some kind of thanksgiving service. After this all came around and ate this food and then went out and lay down on the scaffolds under the arbor. In a very short time they were all asleep and the first one to awake had been asleep for about twenty-four hours. Then for three or four days their bodies were so sore they could do but little.

The effect of the peyote is like opium. It dilates the pupils of the eyes until vision is so changed that the ugly may appear beautiful and the pretty may look horrid. The mind is also visionary and wonderful, and glorious mental pictures pass before them.[12]

Chevato and Dinero had lived at the Mescalero Reservation for almost twenty years, so if they were influential in the spread of the Lipan peyote ritual from Mexico northward, that same ritual should have been found at Mescalero during the period of their residence there. Morris Opler found, in his study of the Mescaleros, that "the peyote cult became established among [them] about 1870 or a little before," precisely at the time the Mescalero tribe took in the Lipans who fled Mexico after the Zaragosa massacre.[13] Opler maintained that the peyote cult existed among the Mescaleros after 1870, but that the Mescaleros had adapted it to their own ritual because "some common plains features of the sect never took root, and [the peyote cult] was virtually abandoned by [the Mescaleros] by 1910."[14] It should be noted that the period in which Opler believed the peyote cult flourished at Mescalero coincides with the approximate period of Chevato's and Dinero's residence. Opler also observed that the use of peyote heightened the Mescalero fear of witchcraft. A heightened Mescalero paranoia fueled by peyote was not evident during the years Chevato and Dinero lived at Mescalero, but in 1908 Mescalero paranoia did erupt into violence. Three elderly Lipans—Shosh, Manuel, and Manuel's wife—were accused of witchcraft and killed by the Mescaleros. Shosh was shot while sitting in his tepee one night, while the Mescalero agent asserted that "this man has always lived here and he told everybody that he was a witch doctor. He claimed that he was able to make people sick and to make them die and this is the reason, so the Indians tell me, that he was killed."[15] This outbreak of violence seemed to signal the end of the Mescalero peyote cult.

The Comanche use of peyote is verified through the statements of Quanah Parker, who noted that he had used peyote since about 1860.[16] The growth of the peyote cult among the Comanche tribe, however, did not occur until around 1884. when "a Mexican named 'Sit-tees-toque' or 'Chi-wow-wah,' having been a captive of the Comanche . . . escaped punishment by remaining with the Apache in New Mexico. He returned to this reservation [the Kiowa Agency in Oklahoma] . . . bringing with him quite a sack full of these Opium Buttons . . . and traded them to the Comanches for several head of horses and cattle. . . . He is still one of the ring leaders in the use of the Medicine."[17] Other "ring leaders" in the new peyote cult among the Comanches were "a few Quahadis [Quanah Parker's band] who happened to be associated with the Lipan Apaches. These Apaches having practiced the use of the *Wok-wave* [peyote ritual] for the last 20 or 30 years."[18] Counting back twenty years from 1888, when this information was conveyed to the Bureau of Indian Affairs by the Kiowa agent, would give a date of 1868; one year later, some survivors of the Kúne tsá band of Lipans who lived at Zaragosa, Coahuila, were fleeing across the Rio Grande to safety with the Mescalero Apaches. Thus a straight path can be traced from the Western Lipan Apaches of Coahuila, through Chevato and Dinero, through the Mescalero Apaches of New Mexico, to Quanah Parker, to the peyote rituals adopted by the Comanches and Kiowas by 1890, and finally to the beginnings of the Native American Church. This path reveals Chevato and Dinero to be two of the founders of the Native American Church.

Those Lipans who practiced the peyote rituals did not have to announce to the world their belief system. To those who knew what to look for, the announcement was made in the manner in which they dressed. The earliest photograph of Chevato, containing the photographer's notation, "Chevato-Apache," contains numerous clues as to Chevato's role in the peyote cult. The feathers held in the right hand, the small gourd rattle tied to the end of the otter skin, and the vest were all signals that he was a peyote singer, or one of the leaders of the ceremony. His necklace contains a cross, but the beads were those of the mountain laurel, a bean considered sacred by peyotists. The crescent was also a sacred symbol in the peyote ritual. Although the photograph of Chevato does not show his earrings in close detail, the use of the crescent as ornament can be seen of the picture of the Mescalero shaman named Chino. The photo of this shaman, taken in 1886, shows his necklace containing a crescent; this indicates that he also participated in the peyote rituals at Mescalero.

The Lipan gift of their particular style of peyote ritual to the Comanches was reciprocated when the Lipans adopted elements of Comanche and Kiowa shamanism. The story of the black handkerchief, as told by Vandal Apauty, is an illustration of "black handkerchief shamanism." The Comanches believed that a shaman wearing a black handkerchief around his neck was indicating that he had *puha*, or medicine power, through the black handkerchief, much in the same way that Chevato's wearing of a necklace of mountain lion claws would indicate that he was a shaman who had received his power through the mountain lion.[19] The Lipans recognized the Comanches' use of black handkerchief shamanism, telling a story of an incident that probably occurred sometime between 1850 and 1870:

> Two Comanche were camping with the Lipan.... They thought they had more supernatural power over the shield than the Lipan men. One Comanche had a war shield. He said to a Lipan, who had a muzzle loader gun, "No gun will go off when it is aimed at my shield." The Lipan was an old man and he began to load his gun. The Comanche meanwhile was working on his shield. He took the cover off. He pushed it out so that it curved. He put a black silk handkerchief over it and sang and prayed, made his medicine. Then he set it over there.
>
> The Lipan took his gun and aimed it. At the signal, "Ready," he shot. You could see the dust over there. The Comanche owner went to his shield. There was a big hole in it; the feather was shot away, too.
>
> The old Lipan man said, "I wouldn't have shot at it if I had known that your power was that weak. You might as well throw it away. It's no good. There is no use for you to brag about your power; there is not much to it."[20]

In spite of the rivalry in supernatural powers seen in the Lipan story, Chevato must have integrated and used aspects of Comanche shamanism. The Comanches, however, were always a bit afraid of Chevato and his power since he had come to Oklahoma from Mescalero; they just didn't know if his shamanism was tinged with witchcraft since his powers seemed so mysterious. As a Comanche neighbor of Chevato's in Oklahoma expressed to his son, "We never wanted to cross him because we were afraid he would 'put the hoo-doo' on us."[21] Chevato always stressed to his family, however, that his power dictated that he only use it to help people; his shamanism had to be used in a beneficent manner or all his supernatural power would vanish, and without supernatural power, he would be at the mercy of evil forces and would perish.

21. The Community on the Creek

In spite of the kind of life Chevato lived, he did have certain morals. I credit that to his mother and father. He had to do certain things in order to stay alive—for his brother and sister. But he was always compassionate.

As an adopted member of the Comanche tribe, he had been given a 160-acre headright. His sons and his wife were also given headrights, so they had a big spread. They were lucky enough to get their headrights close together, a mile away from a little town called Indiahoma, Oklahoma. There was a large creek running through Chevato's headright with banks about twelve feet high. There was nice sand down by the creek, where you could dig down and hit water that was drinkable. On the east side of the bank of the creek were sprinkled numerous blackjack and pecan trees. It was just like a shelter down by the creek. Chevato had his house sitting just off the creek.

When hard times came to Indiahoma, one thing that proved to be a blessing to a lot of Indians was the fact that they were wards of the government. Chevato didn't hold title to his land because the government kept the deed. He didn't have to pay tax, and everything he got off of the land was tax-free. That is the way it also is today. So, when hard times came to Indiahoma, creditors could never take an Indian's land, because the government held the deeds.

Chevato was always a farmer at heart. He had cattle and horses, and he had farmed the land back in Zaragosa. Now, the land around his headright in Oklahoma was very fertile because it was just off that creek bottomland.

So Chevato was successful in raising crops. We always had a large garden with all kinds of vegetables.

I was told this story by my parents, as well as by other older people, about an incident that happened when hard times came to Indiahoma. Some people were losing their homes and their town lots; they had nowhere to go. Chevato traded in Indiahoma and bought supplies there, and he knew people there—both Indian and Anglo. The good thing about Indiahoma was that, after the 1874 Buffalo War (also known as the Red River War, 1874–75), relations between Comanches and Anglos were very good. It was a place that was optimistic, hopeful, fruitful, and there was always a good atmosphere. When Chevato went into town, he noticed that some people were losing their homes because of the hard times. He asked one of them, "Where are you going to live? What are you going to do?" The person replied that he and his family were now homeless, and they would have to live on the road. So Chevato said, "Let's find you a tent; you come on down to my place. I've got land down there, and the government will leave us alone. You can put your tent and your family there in the trees along the creek. There's water there for you. The only thing I ask is that you don't tear up the land. From time to time, I will provide for you. Maybe you could work for me, your family could work for me. And we will give you food."

He had over one hundred families living in that creek bottom when it was all over. They lived there happily, and they all worked together. That all got in the fields, and they all did the gardening. They split up what the land produced, just like a big community. This is one of the stories about Indiahoma, and I hope it never gets lost.

When I was a young boy, I was told, "Yes, my father lived on your grandfather's place down on the creek. We lived in tents, and your grandfather was a very good man." When they were naming the streets of Indiahoma, a small town of under 1,000 people, they named a street after him, Chebahtah Street. It runs in front of the high school. It was named for him because of what he had done for the people.

§

When Quanah Parker signed an agreement with the Jerome Commission in October 1892 opening up tribal lands to white settlement, his strategy was to try to delay its implementation for as long as possible, hoping that better terms could be negotiated at a later date. He was joined in his fight by the Philadelphia-based Indian Rights Association, which charged that the agreement had been made in a fraudulent manner and that the 160-acre allotments were insufficient.[1] Although Parker traveled to Washington DC several times with other Comanche and Kiowa leaders to protest the way in which the Jerome Agreement had been negotiated, the forces lobbying for the opening of Indian lands to white settlement were stronger. Eventually, a compromise version of the agreement became law in March 1900. In the eight-year period between signature and implementation of the agreement, Comanche life continued much as it had since the Comanches had come onto the reservation in 1875. Members of the Kwahada band lived around the town of Cache, Oklahoma, and throughout Comanche County, while other Comanche bands clustered on other parts of the reservation. The Kiowas were likewise scattered throughout the reservation area. Although some Comanches lived in "ID houses," built for them by the government, others still lived in tepees.

The 1900 federal census shows Chevato, Pi-he, and their children living in a tepee in Comanche County, while his occupation is listed as horse herder.[2] The Chebahtahs, along with the families of Kowena, Codopony, Saupitty, Tahmaker, and Asenap, had settled in the area between Big Sandy Creek and Post Oak Creek, south of Elk Mountain in the Wichita Mountains.[3] Situated along Post Oak Creek and acting as an anchor for the small community was an Indian mission church. "In 1894, Reverend Henry Kohfield approached Quanah Parker . . . and succeeded in obtaining a grant of land for a mission. . . . In 1901, Kohfield was joined by another Mennonite Brethren missionary, Reverend A. J. Becker and his wife."[4] The mission, named the Post Oak Mennonite Brethren Church, provided a Christian foundation for the community. Although many of the older Comanche and Kiowa men in the area attended church every Sunday, they still practiced the peyote religion as well as herbal and peyote healing.

Chevato found himself, after 1900, in a congenial setting. Surrounded by family and friends, he was respected and even feared for his knowledge of peyote rituals and healing powers by neighboring Comanches and Kiowas. In 1908 Quanah Parker asked his help in resolving a situation brought to Parker's attention by James Carroll, Indian agent for the Mescaleros in New Mexico. Carroll wrote Parker that two Lipan men, Julio Mendez and Pancho Venego, were demanding to be allowed to move to the Comanche Reservation, fearing their lives were in danger if they stayed in Mescalero. Mendez's father was Shosh (Bear), a Lipan who had left Zaragosa in 1869 with Caro Colorado's group and fled to the Mescaleros. By 1908 some in the Mescalero tribe believed Shosh to be a witch, and he was killed. Shortly after the killing, an elderly Lipan couple, also suspected of witchcraft, were killed. This violence threw all the Lipans at Mescalero into a panic. The Mescalero agent asked Parker to intervene with the Lipans, asking him to "talk to them and show them how foolish they are."[5] Instead of dissuading the Lipans from coming to Oklahoma, however, Parker asked Chevato for help, getting Chevato and Dinero to agree to give the two Lipans some acreage in Oklahoma so that the newcomers could farm for themselves.[6]

In 1901 a lottery was held to open Comanche lands not taken up by individual Indian allotments per stipulations of the Jerome Agreement. New Anglo settlers moved to the area along Post Oak Creek. Some early settlers were the Dillon, Potter, Brenton, and Jones families.[7] In 1902 a post office was established, and the small community that grew up around the post office became known as Indiahoma. "With a town name that symbolizes the unity of cultures, this community was meant to be different. Its common ground seems to have been a good natured acceptance of each one in its midst, a belief that there was room for all."[8]

The Dust Bowl conditions in the late 1920s and early 1930s had a severe impact on Indiahoma and Comanche County. The area had seen much cotton farming, but the drought conditions made that agricultural activity a thing of the past. Everyone—Anglo and Indian—experienced hard times but "in many ways, the community hung together. 'Often the community would kill a cow [remembered Rosie Eisner, a resident of Indiahoma] and do the work together. Everyone who worked got some meat.'"[9] The families who lived on Chevato's land along the creek were another manifestation of the community pulling together during hard economic times.

Chevato's place in Indiahoma and Comanche County history was recognized in 1978, when the town renamed its streets in honor of the first settlers, both Indian and Anglo.[10]

22. The Death of Chevato

Of all my grandfather's sons, my father was the only one who was very interested and cared about the older ways. So it also was with my brother and I; my older brother didn't care as much as I cared about the old things. So my father and I were always the ones attuned to our fathers.

One day, when Chevato was quite elderly, he approached my father and asked, "Would you like to have this power I've got?" Of course, my father agreed. So he told my father the rules that governed having this power—he couldn't accept monetary value for using his power, he had to use the power to help people. So my father was schooled in this power.

One day, Chevato caught pneumonia. He got very sick, so he called my father into the room and said, "Do you remember what we talked about? The power we talked about? Stay with me, I'm getting very weak. Just before I die, just before I take my last breath, my mouth will come open. There will be four things that come out of my lungs. They will rest on my lips just long enough for you to reach over and grab them. Put them in your mouth and swallow them. Four times, things will come up to my lips. Regardless of what they look like, just reach over, take them and swallow them. The fourth time, you will have the powers that I have. I hope you use the powers well." Shortly after that, Chevato fell into a coma.

The first day went by, then the night; my father sat in the room waiting. And Chevato still hung onto life. More time went by, and my father was getting very tired. He thought, "I'm just going to lean my chair against the wall."

My mother came into the room, and it was already daybreak. She tapped him on the shoulder and said, "I'd like for you to go get some rest. Your father has passed away." My father couldn't believe it. "Why didn't you wake me?" he asked. My mother said, "We did, but you were very tired." And so my father did not take possession of Chevato's power. He lived in the modern world where people were cured by doctors, instead of by black silk handkerchiefs, but he always held precious the things of the past.

§

After the death of Pi-he sometime between 1926 and 1927, Chevato lived his last years in the home of his son, Thomas David Chebahtah. On September 3, 1931, Chevato died at the age of eighty.[1] He was buried in the cemetery attached to the Post Oak Mission Mennonite Brethren Church, since his son, Thomas David, had become a Christian. A small handmade headstone marked his grave.

In 1956, due to an expansion of the Ft. Sill Artillery and Guided Missile Center, the cemetery was moved. Formerly located two miles east and three miles north of Indiahoma, Oklahoma, the cemetery was moved within the town, and many Indian graves were reinterred at the new location.[2]

So Chevato rests amid his Comanche family. He rests near his two Mescalero sons, Alguno and Jo-Co, who chose to follow their father to Oklahoma. He rests near his brother, Dinero, protecting him in death as he did in life.

As close as his relationship was with his family and children, his life was also interwoven, in a strange and unfathomable way, with that of the eleven-year-old boy whom he had helped kidnap in 1870. Herman Lehmann died on February 2, 1932, five months after the death of his friend, Chevato. In his book, Herman tells the reader that Chevato was almost one hundred years old at the time of the book's writing (1927). This is not true, although Herman must have considered Chevato a mentor and attributed his wisdom to Chevato's advanced years. In truth, Chevato was only eight years older than Herman Lehmann, but the hardships endured must have etched themselves on Chevato's face, making him seem much older. Herman visited Chevato often in the years between 1908 and 1926, when Herman lived with his wife and children on his 160-acre allotment received as an enrolled member of the Comanche tribe.[3] One can only speculate what they talked about, or if either had any regrets over the actions that wove their lives together. What seemed to differentiate Chevato from the other Mescaleros in that fateful raiding party was his compassion, a trait that shone throughout his life, a trait that was remembered by those who knew him, long after he had departed this life and joined the Great Spirit.

Appendix 1. Lipans at the Mescalero Agency, 1869–1903

Lipan survivors of Zaragosa taken in by the Mescaleros, 1869

Indian Name	Approximate Date of Birth	Also Known As	Date Taken in by the Mescaleros
1. Chevato	1852	Billy	1869
Wife	1859		probably 1869
(Four children born at the Mescalero Agency, 1877–88)			
2. Dinero	1860	Dinero Boy	1869
Wife: Chalita, Mescalero			
(One child born at agency, 1889)			
3. Caro Colorado	1825	(Lipan name: Ayris) Red Face	1869
Wife: Yanconi	1825		1869
Niece: Bis-han	1869	Louisa	1869
Daughter	1867		probably 1869
Grandson	1860	E-do-da Antonio Apache	1869
4. Shosh	1845	Bear	1869
Wife: Bolita	1852		1869
(One son born at agency, 1873)			
Great-grandmother: Viejo Cojo	1800	Great-grandmother of Shosh	1869
5. Bo-nes-kei	1835	White Tooth	1869
Wife: Con-tu-ja	1845		1869
Son	1869	David Boneski	1869
(One daughter born at agency, 1879)			
6. Dinero (widow)	1837	Sarah Money/Mooney	1869
(One grandson, Penn Scott, born at agency, 1873)			

(continued)

Lipan women captured at Zaragosa (1869) and taken in by the Mescaleros, 1885

Indian Name	Approximate Date of Birth	Also Known As	Date Taken in by the Mescaleros
7. Ye-yu			by 1885
8. Conejo	1864		by 1885
Husband: Big Mouth, Mescalero			
9. Liha			by 1885

Lipan members of the "Uplander" band living with the Mescaleros, 1850–85

Indian Name	Approximate Date of Birth	Also Known As	Date Taken in by the Mescaleros
10. Magoosh	1830	Lipan chief "Mogul"	1850
Wife: Co-sah	1849		by 1885
Wife: E-kid-a	1862	Medicine	by 1885
Son	1865	Mogul's Boy	by 1885
Son: Peshia	1880		
Son: I-sa	1887	John Mogul	
Son: I-cusco	1888	Jacob Mogul	
Daughter	1889		
Son	1890	Levi Magoosh	
11. Magill	1841	Madzil "Coyote"	by 1885
Wife	1846		by 1885
12. Big Chops	1840		by 1885
Wife: Henca	1850		by 1885

(continued)

13. Jose Torres			
Wife: Ezhuni, Mescalero	1832	Benta	by 1885
Wife: De-ge-ta, Lipan			
Daughter	1849	Secana	
	1873	Mollie Ohio	
Son: Nashtodil	1878	Czatu	
		Horace Greeley	
Daughter: Iteddy	1886		
14. Blanco	1846	White	by 1885
Wife: Chulinta	1851	Ztnac	by 1885
Daughter	1883	Bin-da-go-la	
Grandson		Es-kan	
Mother-in-Law		Che-an-na	
15. Che-pah/Chi-pan	1828	Manuel	by 1885
Wife: Dah-dis-cha	1850		by 1885
16. Peter	1869		by 1885
Wife: daughter of a Mescalero widow, Long Hair			
17. Chiquita	1856	Sally Wyeth	by 1885
Daughter: Guerdo	1875	Agatha Wyeth	
18. Mariana	1870	Charles Wyeth	
Wife: Guerdo	1875	Agatha Wyeth	

(continued)

Chevato's list of Lipans wanting to leave Mescalero, 1889

Indian Name	Approximate Date of Birth	Also Known As	Date Taken in by the Mescaleros
1. Chevato		Chi-wa-ta	
2. Ches-chilla		Chevato's daughter Mineha	
		Carrie Heath	
3. Be-che-ide		Chevato's son Alguno	
		Alguino	
4. Pe-chá		Chevato's sister	
5. Dinero		Chevato's brother	
6. Ec-o-da		Dinero's wife's son by previous marriage	
7. En-a-ga-na		Dinero's daughter Blacita	
8. Agilar/Aguilar		Uncle of Chevato	
9. Es-pon-sa		Wife of Aguilar	
10. Pe-lo-sa		Daughter of Aguilar and Es-pon-sa	
11. Charles Wyeth	1870	Mariana	
12. Blanco	1846		
13. Chu-len-ta	1852	Wife of Blanco, aka Ztnac	
14. Bin-da-go-la	1883	Daughter of Blanco and Chu-len-ta	
15. Es-kan		Son of Bin-da-go-la	
		Grandson of Blanco	
16. Che-an-na		Blanco's mother-in-law	
17. Jose Torres	1832	Judge of Tribal Court at Mescalero	
18. De-ge-ta		Second wife of Jose Torres	
19. "their small boy"			
20. Iteddy	1886	Daughter of Jose Torres and De-ge-ta	

(continued)

Indian Name	Approximate Date of Birth	Also Known As	Date Taken in by the Mescaleros
21. Chi-pan	1828	Manuel, aka Che-pah	
22. Dah-dis-cha	1850	Wife of Manuel	
23. "their aged mother"			
24. Shosh	1845	Bear	
25. Da-et-ta	1852	Wife of Shosh	
26. Na-oe-ka (female)			
27. Ya-oh	1863	Stella Lester	
28. Che-et-ta	1882	Frank Lester	
29. Do-et-sa		Son of Ya-oh	
30. Ca-ta-na (elderly female)		Daughter of Ya-oh	
31. Ma-la-na (female)			
32. De-e-hole		Son of Ma-la-na	
33. Co-sa	1849	First wife of Magoosh, Lipan chief	
34. Peshia		"a boy now at school"	
35. Et-se (elderly female)			

Zaragosa Lipans taken in by the Mescaleros by 1890

Indian Name	Approximate Date of Birth	Also Known As	Date Taken in by the Mescaleros
1. Sanavoy Wife	1845	Santavi Sah-nah-bah	by 1890

(continued)

Mexican Lipans taken in by the Mescaleros, 1903

Indian Name	Approximate Date of Birth	Also Known As	Date Taken in by the Mescaleros
1. Juan Villa	1869	Ska-en-to-en	1903
2. Pancho Venego	1864		1903
Wife: Teodora	1869		
Dau: Genavera	1887		
Son: Nicholas	1890		
Son: Felipe	1893		
Son: Fileman	1895		
Son: Julian	1900		
Daughter: Isabel	1902		
3. Miguel Zuazua	1844		1903
Wife: Josefa	1864		
Daughter: Rosa	1888		
4. Augustina Zuazua	1879		1903
5. Jesus Zuazua	1884		1903
6. Cardenal Rodriguez	1854		1903
Wife: Cuera	1864		
Son: Catarino	1889		
Daughter: Maria	1892		
Daughter: Encarnacion	1895		
Daughter: Ester	1898		
Daughter: Juanita	1902		
7. Teresa Rodriguez	1883		1903

(continued)

#	Name		
8.	Ricardo Rodriguez	1886	1903
9.	Juana (female)	1854	1903
10.	Pedro Mendez	1884	1903
11.	Julio Mendez	1876	son of Shosh	1903
	Wife: Otila	1884	
	Son: Eduardo	1901	
	Son: Lisandro	1902	
12.	Andrea (female)	1834	1903
13.	Coyota (female)	1824	1903
14.	Tanille (female)	1834	1903
15.	Jahe (female)	1864	1903
16.	Nicolasa (female)	1834	1903
17.	Concha (female)	1834	1903
18.	Rosa (female)	1879	1903
	Son: Ismall Carrillo	1899	

Sources: 1886, 1887, and 1903 census returns, Apache Reservation census rolls, Bureau of Indian Affairs, *Mescalero Reservation 1885–1914*, microfilm publication #M595, roll 254, National Archives.

Antonio Apache's oral history, Morris E. Opler, *Myths and Legends of the Lipan Apache Indians*, Memoirs of the American Folk-Lore Society 36 (New York: J. J. Augustine, 1940), 260–71.

Chevato to Quanah Parker, January 3, 1889, attached to a letter from W. D. Myers, Kiowa Agent, to the Commissioner of Indian Affairs, April 20, 1889. Bureau of Indian Affairs, *Letters Received by the Department of the Interior, 1881–1907*, record group 75, 11319-1889, National Archives.

Oral history regarding Magoosh, Eve Ball, *Indeh: An Apache Odyssey* (Norman: University of Oklahoma Press, 1988).

Appendix 2. Indian Scouts from the Mescalero Reservation, 1883–90

Name	Age	Height	Date of Enlistment	Place of Enlistment	Enlisting Officer	Date of Discharge
Agua	28	5'5"	May 17, 1886	South Fork	Lt. Davis	Sept. 20, 1886
Aqua Dos	22	5'6"	June 6, 1886	Ft. Stanton	Lt. Davis	Sept. 20, 1886
Ben Butler	35	5'6½"	Oct. 19, 1886	Ft. Stanton	Lt. Davis	no entry
Big Hunter	26	5'7"	Aug. 3, 1886	Ft. Stanton	Lt. Davis	Oct. 14, 1886
Big Mouth	25	5'6½"	Aug. 5, 1886	Ft. Stanton	Lt. Davis	Oct. 14, 1886
Blue Knife's Boy	27	5'7½"	Feb. 2, 1886	Ft. Stanton	Lt. Fletcher	Sept. 5, 1886
Can-o-can	40	5'6"	Aug. 3, 1886	Ft. Stanton	Lt. Davis	Oct. 14, 1886
Cay-a-tana	26	5'6¾"	Feb. 2, 1886	Ft. Stanton	Lt. Fletcher	Sept. 5, 1886
Charlie	38	5'7"	May 17, 1886	South Fork	Lt. Davis	Sept. 20, 1886
Chineal	28	5'7"	Feb. 2, 1886	Ft. Stanton	Lt. Fletcher	Sept. 5, 1886
Chivata*	27	5'10"	March 22, 1883	Ft. Stanton	Cavanaugh	Sept. 21, 1883
			Sept. 7, 1885	South Fork	Lt. Cruise	Dec. 18, 1885
Dinero*	27	5'8¼"	June 6, 1886	Ft. Stanton	Lt. Davis	Sept. 20, 1886
Domingo	35	5'5½"	Sept. 7, 1885	South Fork	Lt. Cruise	Dec. 18, 1885
			Aug. 3, 1886	Ft. Stanton	Lt. Davis	Oct. 14, 1886
Eclodenanton	35	5'7¾"	March 22, 1883	Ft. Stanton	Cavanaugh	Sept. 21, 1883
			May 17, 1886	South Fork	Lt. Davis	Sept. 20, 1886
Eiejo	21	5'6"	May 17, 1886	South Fork	Lt. Davis	Sept. 30, 1886
Espaja	25	5'6"	May 19, 1886	Ft. Stanton	Lt. Davis	Sept. 20, 1886
			Oct. 19, 1886	Ft. Stanton	Lt. Davis	April 18, 1887
Eyahien	22	5'4"	May 22, 1883	Ft. Stanton	Cavanaugh	Sept. 21, 1883
Frankalena	30	5'7½"	Aug. 3, 1886	Ft. Stanton	Lt. Davis	Oct. 14, 1886

(continued)

Name	Age	Height	Date of Enlistment	Place of Enlistment	Enlisting Officer	Date of Discharge
Hon-es-co	35	5'5"	Aug. 3, 1886	Ft. Stanton	Lt. Davis	Oct. 14, 1886
Horse Thief	40	5'8¾"	July 11, 1885	Hillsboro Camp	Wilson	Aug. 17, 1885
Jarambullo	27	5'7½"	June 6, 1886	Ft. Stanton	Lt. Davis	Sept. 20, 1886
Jimie	33	5'3"	May 19, 1886	Ft. Stanton	Lt. Davis	Sept. 20, 1886
Jo-Ca	23	5'6"	Aug. 5, 1886	Ft. Stanton	Lt. Davis	Oct. 14, 1886
Kahu	30	5'6½"	Aug. 3, 1886	Ft. Stanton	Lt. Davis	Oct. 14, 1886
Kedenshen	26	5'6½"	Aug. 3, 1886	Ft. Stanton	Lt. Davis	Oct. 14, 1886
Kitt	22	5'7"	June 6, 1886	Ft. Stanton	Lt. Davis	Sept. 20, 1886
Lewellyn	18	5'6"	May 19, 1886	Ft. Stanton	Lt. Davis	Sept. 20, 1886
Little Andrew	20	5'6"	May 5, 1886	Ft. Stanton	Lt. Davis	Oct. 14, 1886
Madison	34	5'7"	Aug. 5, 1886	Ft. Stanton		deserted Aug. 16, 1886
Magoosh*		5'7"	Sept. 7, 1885	South Fork	Lt. Cruise	Dec. 18, 1885
	30		May 4, 1886	South Fork	Rogers	Sept. 20, 1886
Maria's Boy	30	5'5"	Aug. 3, 1886	Ft. Stanton	Lt. Davis	Oct. 14, 1886
Muchacho Grande	35	5'8"	May 4, 1886	South Fork	Rogers	Sept. 20, 1886
Muchacho Negro		5'8"	May 17, 1886	South Fork	Rogers	Sept. 20, 1886
	22		Oct. 10, 1886	Ft. Stanton	Lt. Davis	no entry
Nautzilla's Boy	30	5'7"	Aug. 3, 1886	Ft. Stanton	Lt. Davis	Oct. 14, 1886
Na-yo-ka		5'3"	March 22, 1883	Ft. Stanton		deserted Aug. 1883
Old Boy	21	4'8"	Aug. 3, 1886	Ft. Stanton	Lt. Davis	Oct. 14, 1886
One Eye	30	5'9"	May 22, 1883	Ft. Stanton		deserted Aug. 27, 1883
Packawah		5'6½"	Feb. 2, 1886	Ft. Stanton	Fletcher	Sept. 5, 1886
Patricio		5'7"	Aug. 3, 1886	Ft. Stanton	Lt. Davis	Oct. 14, 1886

(continued)

Name	Age	Height	Date	Place	Officer	Date
Peganse	21	5'5½"	May 17, 1886	South Fork	Rogers	Sept. 20, 1886
			Oct. 19, 1886	Ft. Stanton	Lt. Davis	no entry
Peso	30	5'7"	May 4, 1886	South Fork	Rogers	Sept. 20, 1886
Pockmark	30	5'4"	May 17, 1886	South Fork	Lt. Davis	Sept. 20, 1886
Price, Hiram	23	5'6¾"	June 6, 1886	Ft. Stanton	Lt. Davis	Sept. 20, 1886
Red Boy	25	5'6"	June 6, 1886	Ft. Stanton	Lt. Davis	Oct. 14, 1886
Roman Chiquito	40	5'6"	Oct. 3, 1886	Ft. Stanton	Lt. Davis	Oct. 14, 1886
Running Water	22	5'7½"	Aug. 3, 1886	Ft. Stanton	Lt. Davis	Oct. 14, 1886
Sharpo		5'4½"	May 22, 1883	Ft. Stanton	Cavanaugh	Sept. 21, 1883
Shosh*	30	5'6½"	Sept. 7, 1885	South Fork	Lt. Cruise	Dec. 18, 1885
Sweetwater	22	5'6"	June 6, 1886	Ft. Stanton	Lt. Davis	Sept. 20, 1886
Tall Boy (The Jumper)	26	6'1"	Aug. 5, 1886	Ft. Stanton	Lt. Davis	Oct. 14, 1886
Thomas	27	5'1"	June 6, 1886	Ft. Stanton	Lt. Davis	Sept. 20, 1886
Toby	25	5'8"	June 6, 1886	Ft. Stanton	Lt. Davis	Sept. 20, 1886
			Oct. 19, 1886	Ft. Stanton	Lt. Davis	no entry
Torres, Jose*	35	5'9"	Oct. 19, 1886	Ft. Stanton	Lt. Davis	no entry
Torres's son-in-law		5'7"	Aug. 3, 1886	Ft. Stanton	Lt. Davis	Oct. 14, 1886
Trias, Jose	40	5'7"	May 4, 1886	South Fork	Rogers	Sept. 20, 1886

*Designated as Lipan in the 1886 and 1887 Mescalero census

Source: Records of U.S. Army Continental Commands, 1821–1910, Indian Scouts, 1878–1914, *Record of Enlistments for the 20th Regiment of Infantry, U.S. Army*, microfilm publication #M233, roll 71, National Archives.

Appendix 3. **Pedigree Chart: Chevato and Pi-he**

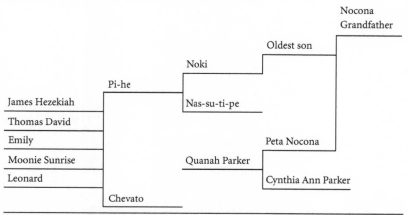

Source: Oral history of the Chebahtah family; information passed from Pi-he to her daughter-in-law Emily Weck-ah-woonard (wife of Thomas David Chebahtah).

Appendix 4 . **Descendants of Chevato**

1. Chevato (b. Feb. 2, 1852—Hacienda Patiño, Zaragosa, Coahuila; d. Sept. 3, 1931—Indiahoma, Comanche Co., Oklahoma)
|
sp: Lipan woman born in Mexico (b. unknown; m. about 1877; d. 1888/1889)
|
|---2. Mineha/Carrie Heath (b. 1877—Mescalero Reservation, New Mexico; d. about 1914—Oklahoma)
| |
| sp: Owen Too-ah-nip-pa (m. 1899)
| |
| |---3. Cora/Corine Heath (b. 1892—Mescalero Reservation, New Mexico)
| |
| |---3. Na-neet-sa-to/Katie Heath (b. 1900—Oklahoma)
| | |
| | sp: James Koweno (m. 1916)
| |
| |---3. Annie Heath (b. 1903—Oklahoma; d. 1904—Oklahoma)
| |
| sp: Claude To-cah-wa-he-mah (m. 1904)
| |
| |---3. Ella To-cah-wa-he-mah (b. 1904—Oklahoma)
| |
| |---3. Roy To-cah-wa-he-mah (b. 1908—Oklahoma)
| |
| |---3. Rollen To-cah-wa-he-mah (b. 1910—Oklahoma; d. by 1915—Oklahoma)
|
|---2. Susco (b. 1878—Mescalero Reservation, New Mexico; d. 1889/1890—Mescalero Reservation, New Mexico)
|
|---2. Alguno/Harry Heath (b. 1881—Mescalero Reservation, New Mexico; d. Feb. 14, 1929—Indiahoma, Comanche Co., Oklahoma)
| |
| sp: Tottie (m. 1900)
| |
| |---3. Maggie Heath
| | |
| | sp: Elmer Parker, grandson of Quanah
| |
| |---3. Mabel Heath
|
|---2. Jo-co/Paul Heath/Paul Chebahtah (b. 1888—New Mexico; d. May 1, 1918—Oklahoma)
|
sp: Chenoco (b. unknown; m. 1890; d. after 1914)

|

sp: Pi-he (b. 1867—Palo Duro Canyon, Texas; m. 1895; d. 1926/1927—Indiahoma, Comanche
   Co., Oklahoma)

|

|---2. James Hezekiah Chebahtah (b. 1896—Oklahoma; d. 1961)
| |
| sp: Topappy/Annie Blackstar (m. 1917)
|

|---2. Emily Chebahtah (b. 1900—Oklahoma; d. 1901)
|

|---2. Thomas David Chebahtah (b. 1903—Oklahoma; d. 1968)
| |
| sp: Emily Weckahwoonard (m. 1918)
| |
| |---3. Child Chebahtah (b. 1919; d. 1919)
| |
| |---3. Cleo Chebahtah (b. 1920; d. 1921)
| |
| |---3. Clifford Chebahtah
| |
| |---3. Marian Chebahtah
| |
| |---3. William Chebahtah
|

|---2. Moonie Sunrise Chebahtah (b. 1907—Oklahoma; d. 1976)
| |
| sp: Mollie Godsoe
|

|---2. Leonard Chebahtah (b. 1910—Oklahoma; d. 1974)
      |
      sp: Mary Ann Red Elk

Sources: Apache Reservation census rolls, Bureau of Indian Affairs, *Mescalero Reservation 1885–1914*,
microfilm publication #M595, roll 254, National Archives.

Jeff Bowen, *Kiowa, Comanche, Apache, Ft. Sill Apache, Wichita, Caddo and Delaware Indians, Birth and
Death Rolls, 1924–1932* (Signal Mountain TX: Mountain Press, 1996), 106.

Genealogy compiled by William Chebahtah.

Kiowa Agency Records, *Comanche Vital Statistics*, Genealogy Library microfilm #0576911, Church of Jesus
Christ of Latter Day Saints, Salt Lake City UT.

Kiowa Agency Records, *Census and Enrollments, Undated–1922*, microfilm #KA-1 through #KA-5, Oklahoma
Historical Society, Oklahoma City.

Post Oak Mennonite Brethren Church, *Post Oak Mission Centennial 1885–1995* (Indiahoma OK: Post Oak
Mennonite Brethren Church, 1995).

Post Oak Mission Cemetery in Indiahoma OK, Madeline S. Mills and Helen R. Mullenax, *Relocated
Cemeteries in Oklahoma and Parts of Arizona, Kansas, and Texas* (Tulsa OK: privately published, nd).

Notes

Abbreviations

AGM   Archivo General de Mexico

BIA   Bureau of Indian Affairs

CAH   Center for American History, University of Texas at Austin

KAR   Kiowa Agency Records

NA   National Archives, Washington DC

NAA   National Anthropological Archives, Smithsonian Institution, Washington DC

OHS   Oklahoma Historical Society, Oklahoma City

RACC   Records of the U.S. Army Continental Commands, 1821–1910

Introduction

1. For a detailed description of the Lehmann/Buchmeier family, see Perry and Focke, *A New Look at Nine Years among the Indians, 1870–1879*, 249–73.

2. The facts of Herman's kidnapping, as well as Herman's description, were detailed in an affidavit filed by his stepfather, Philip Buchmeier, on July 2, 1870. The affidavit was sworn before the justice of the peace, Precinct 1, R. Radeleff, Gillespie County, Texas, and was included as an attachment to a letter from Col. J. E. Tourtellotte, Headquarters, Fifth Military District of Texas, to Laurie Tatum, Indian Agent at Ft. Sill, Oklahoma, reporting the kidnapping of Herman Lehmann. Tourtellotte's letter was dated May 27, 1871. Tourtellotte to Tatum, May 27, 1871, KAR, *Military Relations and Affairs: Indian Captives, 1870–1934*, microfilm #KA-42, OHS.

3. Hunter, *Herman Lehmann*, 175.

1. The Lipan Apaches

1. Cobos, *Dictionary of New Mexico and Southern Colorado Spanish*, 32. The word *chivato* is derived from the diminutive for "goat" and also means "mischievous, rascal."

2. Opler, *Myths and Legends of the Lipan Apache Indians*, 13–15. Opler's informant for this creation story was Antonio Apache, a Lipan who knew Chevato in Zaragosa. Antonio was a young boy in 1869 when he fled Zaragosa with his grandfather, Caro Colorado. Antonio Apache became one of Opler's primary source informants in the summer of 1935.

3. Albert Samuel Gatschet, *Lipan Vocabulary Taken at Ft. Griffin, Texas, September–October 1884*, 64, MS 81-a-b, NAA. This is the Lipan linguistic form used to end a story.

4. Tiller, *The Jicarilla Apache Tribe*, 4. The other southern Athapascan tribes are the Chiricahua, Navajo, Western Apache, Mescalero, Kiowa Apache, and Jicarilla. In the Lipan creation myth, the different Apache tribes were scattered from west to east, with the

Lipans being the last tribe to end their journey. This tale reflects the fact that the Lipans were the easternmost group of southern Athapascans, as well as the fact that the Lipans allied with the Tonkawas in Texas during the nineteenth century. The Lipan bands that moved south into Mexico, however, were allied with the Mescalero Apaches.

5. Opler, *Myths and Legends of the Lipan Apache Indians*, 2n.

6. Opler, *Myths and Legends of the Lipan Apache Indians*, 5. Although Opler found a number of similarities between the myths of the Lipans and the Jicarilla Apaches, the most striking differentiation of these two groups from the Mescalero Apaches was in their creation myths. The Mescaleros did not have a creation myth similar to that of the Lipans or Jicarillas.

7. Opler, *Myths and Legends of the Lipan Apache Indians*. The Jicarilla Apache culture was heavily influenced by the Navajo and Pueblo cultures from the seventeenth century on, while the Lipan culture did not show these influences to that degree.

8. Tiller, *The Jicarilla Apache Tribe*, 4.

9. Kavanagh, *The Comanches*, 63–71.

10. Hoxie, *Encyclopedia of North American Indians*, s.v. "Lipan Apache."

11. Gatschet, *Lipan Vocabulary Taken at Ft. Griffin, Texas, September–October 1884*, 33, 55–56, 183. The Natagés were an Apachean-speaking group considered by most scholars to be affiliated with the Mescalero Apaches. See also John, *Storms Brewed in Other Men's Worlds*, 359–60, 503.

12. Dunn, "Missionary Activities among the Eastern Apaches Previous to the Founding of the San Saba Mission," 193–95.

13. Dunn, "Missionary Activities among the Eastern Apaches Previous to the Founding of the San Saba Mission," 193.

14. John, *Storms Brewed in Other Men's Worlds*, 297–98.

15. "Old Mission Acts as Highway Curbstone," *Eagle Pass News Guide*, August 11, 1994.

16. Report on the state of the missions under the presidency of the northern Rio Grande from October 1758 to December 1767, AGM, *Historia*, 2Q178, vol. 349, CAH; report of Fr. Diego Ximenez on the missions for the Lipans, December 26, 1764, AGM, *Historia*, 2Q178, vol. 349, CAH.

17. "How Long Is 100 Years—Relatively Speaking?" *Eagle Pass News Guide*, September 16, 1971. See also John, *Storms Brewed in Other Men's Worlds*, 380.

18. Betty, *Comanche Society Before the Reservation*, 53–54.

19. John, *Storms Brewed in Other Men's Worlds*, 439.

20. John, *Storms Brewed in Other Men's Worlds*, 441.

21. John, *Storms Brewed in Other Men's Worlds*, 503.

22. "How Long Is 100 Years—Relatively Speaking?" *Eagle Pass News Guide*, September 16, 1971.

23. Ball, *Indeh*, 267–70.

24. Berlandier, *The Indians of Texas in 1830*, 128–35. There are at least three versions

of Berlandier's diary. One is located at the Gilcrease Museum, Tulsa, Oklahoma. Another version is located in the Western Americana Collection at Yale University, and the third is in the Library of Congress. All are written in French and in Berlandier's hand. Another member of the expedition to Texas, Jose Francisco Ruiz, also left his impressions of the Lipans. He stressed their good horsemanship and disposition toward agricultural settlement, but noted their thefts and cruelty. See Ruiz, *Report on the Indian Tribes of Texas in 1828*, 6–7.

25. Kavanagh, *The Comanches*, 208.

26. Kavanagh, *The Comanches*, 208.

27. Basso, *Western Apache Raiding and Warfare*, 260–61.

28. RACC, *Special Files, Headquarters Department of the Missouri: Rio Grande Disturbances, March 1872–November 1875*, microfilm publication #M1495, roll 11, NA. See materials related to Mackenzie's raid on El Remolino. The quote is taken from the Mexican Report of the Commission Appointed to Investigate Matters on the Northern Frontier, July 2, 1873. This commission was appointed by the government of Mexico to report on the Indian situation in Coahuila that had led to Mackenzie's extralegal attack; the report was forwarded to the U.S. State Department as part of Mexico's protest.

29. William Schuhardt, U.S. Consul at Piedras Negras, Mexico, to the U.S. Secretary of State, May 7 and 14, 1878, June 7, 1878, Despatches 197, 198, 202, U.S. Department of State, *Despatches from the U.S. Consul at Piedras Negras, Mexico, to the U.S. Secretary of State* (vol. 2, 1873–81), microfilm publication #M299, roll 1, NA.

30. LaTorre and LaTorre, *The Mexican Kickapoo Indians*, 217.

31. Opler, *Myths and Legends of the Lipan Apache Indians*, 222–30.

32. It is often difficult to arrive at an exact year of birth when researching American Indians. In most cases, their births were not registered with an official authority until the twentieth century, and if individual Indians do appear in census records, in many instances their age or date of birth is often the result of a "guesstimate" made by an Indian agent. With Indians born in Mexico, however, the case is slightly different. If the tribes were attached to a mission, then children would be baptized and recorded in the Catholic baptismal records. Even for bands that rejected the Catholic Church, such as the Lipans living near Zaragosa, the Mexican government still required civil registration of births. Unfortunately, the complete Zaragosa civil registrations for the years of birth for Chevato and his siblings have not survived. Additionally, it seems that the Lipans probably would not have registered their children with the town council in any case, since they alternated between peace and war with the town.

Chevato appears in U.S. census data from 1885 to 1930, but almost every form shows a different year of birth. Almost all, however, show years of birth between 1850 and 1853, and a date of birth within that time frame does fit with other events in his life. His family believed that he was born early in the year (February), and he always insisted that he was sixteen and a half years old at the time his parents were killed. In addition, the oral history of Antonio Apache, another survivor of the Zaragosa massacre, states that the massacre occurred in 1869. Thus counting back sixteen and a half years from 1869 would give Chevato a date of birth of 1852.

Dinero's date of birth was determined using Chevato's oral history, which states that Chevato was eight years older than his brother and that Dinero was eight years old at the time of the Zaragosa massacre. In addition, U.S. census data was reviewed to determine a date of birth. The name Enriques comes from a letter written by Chevato to Quanah Parker in 1886 (see KAR, *Kiowa Agency Census and Enrollment: Undated and 1869–1883*, microfilm #KA-1, OHS). Ruth's date of birth was determined using Chevato's oral history (which stated that Ruth was "five" at the time of the Zaragosa massacre—five months or five years old? Her exact age is not known). Her name in Lipan was taken from a letter from Chevato to Quanah Parker, January 3, 1889, attached to a letter from W. D. Myers, Kiowa Agent, to the Commissioner of Indian Affairs, April 20, 1889. BIA, *Letters Received by the Department of the Interior, 1881–1907*, record group 75, 11319-1889, NA.

The U.S. census records in which Chevato and his brother appear are as follows: Apache Reservation census rolls, BIA, *Mescalero Apache Reservation 1885–1914*, microfilm publication #M595, roll 254, NA; KAR, *Kiowa Agency Census and Enrollment: 1890–1894*, microfilm #KA-3, OHS; KAR, *Kiowa Agency Census and Enrollment: 1893–1901*, microfilm #KA-4, OHS; KAR, *Kiowa Agency Census and Enrollment: 1902–1922*, microfilm #KA-5, OHS; and Bureau of the Census, *U.S. Federal Census for Oklahoma, Comanche County, Comanche and Kiowa Reservation* (years 1900, 1910, 1920, 1930), NA.

33. Diego de Lasaga, Governor of Nuevo Santander, to the Viceroy of Mexico, June 21, 1874, AGM, *Provincias Internas*, 2Q205, vol. 481, 272–73, CAH.

34. The information that Chevato's family had lived in northern Mexico for at least three generations comes from statements made by his brother, Dinero, in a November 1918 article on the topic of Lipan Apache influences on the Comanche use of peyote in religious rituals. The article was first published in the *American Indian YMCA Bulletin* 8, no. 4, and Dinero's statement is quoted in Stewart, "Origins of the Peyote Religion in the United States," 218.

35. Stewart, "Origins of the Peyote Religion in the United States." Opler believed that the Lipans had gotten peyote from either the Carrizos or the Tonkawas or both, but later anthropologists have traced the Lipan use of peyote back to the Carrizos (see Opler, *Myths and Legends of the Lipan Apache Indians*, 277).

36. S. S. Brown report on the Indians of Coahuila, Mexico, September 1868, explanatory letter A, RACC, *Letters Received by the Adjutant General: S. S. Brown Report on the Indians of Coahuila*, microfilm publication #M619, roll 642, NA.

37. Opler, *Myths and Legends of the Lipan Apache Indians*, 260–73.

38. Latorre and Latorre, *The Mexican Kickapoo Indians*, 6–11.

39. Latorre and Latorre, *The Mexican Kickapoo Indians*, 11–20.

40. S. S. Brown report on the Indians of Coahuila, Mexico, September 1868, statement C, RACC.

41. S. S. Brown report on the Indians of Coahuila, Mexico, September 1868, statement C, RACC.

42. S. S. Brown report on the Indians of Coahuila, Mexico, September 1868, statement C, RACC.

43. Rogers, "A History of the Cherokee Nation of Mexico."

44. S. S. Brown report on the Indians of Coahuila, Mexico, September 1868, statement C, RACC.

45. Letter, "Case of Fragments of Indian Tribes Inhabiting the Territory of Mexico, Bordering on the Rio Grande," Adj. Gen. to Secretary of War, October 7, 1868, RACC, *Letters Received by the Adjutant General: S. S. Brown Report on the Indians of Coahuila*, microfilm publication #M619, roll 642, NA. See also report abstract from S. S. Brown to Brevet Maj. J. J. Reynolds, September 1, 1868, RACC, *Letters Received by the Adjutant General: S. S. Brown Report on the Indians of Coahuila*, microfilm publication #M619, roll 642, NA.

46. Opler, *Myths and Legends of the Lipan Apache Indians*, 222–27.

47. Opler, *Myths and Legends of the Lipan Apache Indians*, 227–29. The fact that Chevato's older brother and father are not named reflects the Apache taboo on naming one who is dead. The Lipan adherence to this taboo is verified in Opler, *Myths and Legends of the Lipan Apache Indians*, 99.

48. S. S. Brown report on the Indians of Coahuila, Mexico, May 1868, extracts from official Mexican papers E, RACC, *Letters Received by the Adjutant General: S. S. Brown Report on the Indians of Coahuila*, microfilm publication #M619, roll 642, NA.

49. S. S. Brown report on the Indians of Coahuila, Mexico, May 1868, extracts from official Mexican papers E, RACC.

50. S. S. Brown report on the Indians of Coahuila, Mexico, May 1868, extracts from official Mexican papers E, RACC. It should be noted that there is a discrepancy between the report from Zaragosa and the report from Musquiz as to the number of casualties and the sex of the child captives. Zaragosa reported fourteen deaths and two young boys captured; Musquiz said that twenty-six scalps were brought in along with two female captives. Since Antonio Apache's story explains that one Lipan was scalped but survived, perhaps the lower Zaragosa number is closer to the true number of casualties. Another problem in the report is the mention of a Presidio de la Bahia—no such presidio existed in Coahuila in 1868. There was a presidio called la Babia, located on the other side of the mountains from the Lipan camps. It is probably the presidio referred to.

51. S. S. Brown report on the Indians of Coahuila, Mexico, September 1868, statement C, RACC.

52. S. S. Brown report on the Indians of Coahuila, Mexico, September 1868, statement C, RACC.

53. Opler, *Myths and Legends of the Lipan Apache Indians*, 230–34.

54. LaTorre and LaTorre, *The Mexican Kickapoo Indians*, 217.

2. The Massacre at Zaragosa

1. S. S. Brown report on the Indians of Coahuila, Mexico, June 15, 1868, correspondence C, extracts from official Mexican papers E, RACC, *Letters Received by the Adjutant General: S. S. Brown Report on the Indians of Coahuila*, microfilm publication #M619, roll 642, NA.

2. Report abstract Brown to Reynolds, September 1, 1868, RACC.

3. *Special Files, Headquarters Department of the Missouri: Rio Grande Disturbances, March 1872–November 1875*, RACC. See materials relating to Mackenzie's raid on El Remolino, Coahuila. The quote is taken from the report of the Mexican Commission Appointed to Investigate Matters on the Northern Frontier, July 2, 1873.

4. Opler, *Myths and Legends of the Lipan Apache Indians*, 260–61. Caro Colorado died at the Mescalero Reservation by 1890. His grandson, Antonio Apache, was a young boy at the time of the Zaragosa massacre. Antonio Apache is given the name Young Red Face in early Mescalero census entries (see Apache Reservation census rolls, *Mescalero Reservation 1885–1914*, BIA).

5. Opler, *Myths and Legends of the Lipan Apache Indians*, 262–73.

6. S. S. Brown report on the Indians of Coahuila, Mexico, letter from Gen. Canby to the Adjutant General, February 12, 1869, RACC, *Letters Received by the Adjutant General: S. S. Brown Report on the Indians of Coahuila*, microfilm publication #M619, roll 642, NA.

7. S. S. Brown report on the Indians of Coahuila, Mexico, letter from Gen. Canby to the Adjutant General, February 25, 1869, RACC, *Letters Received by the Adjutant General: S. S. Brown Report on the Indians of Coahuila*, microfilm publication #M619, roll 642, NA.

8. S. S. Brown report on the Indians of Coahuila, Mexico, letter from Col. Mackenzie, May 29, 1869, RACC, *Letters Received by the Adjutant General: S. S. Brown Report on the Indians of Coahuila*, microfilm publication #M619, roll 642, NA.

9. Gen. W. T. Sherman to Gen. C. C. Augur, February 5, 1873, RACC, *Special Files, Headquarters Department of the Missouri: Rio Grande Disturbances, March 1872–November 1875*, microfilm publication #M1495, roll 11, NA.

10. Scouting report from Col. Ranald S. Mackenzie to the Assistant Adjutant General, Department of Texas, May 23, 1873, RACC, *Special Files, Headquarters Department of the Missouri: Rio Grande Disturbances, March 1872–November 1875*, microfilm publication #M1495, roll 11, NA.

11. Lt. Gen. Sheridan to Gen. W. W. Belknap, Secretary of War, May 27, 1873, RACC, *Special Files, Headquarters Department of the Missouri: Rio Grande Disturbances, March 1872–November 1875*, microfilm publication #M1495, roll 11, NA.

12. Schilz, *Lipan Apaches in Texas*, 61.

13. Daniel Castro Romero Jr. (Nante Nde, General Council Chairman, Lipan Apache Band of Texas), phone interview by Nancy McGown Minor, March 18, 2005. See also Romero, *The Castro Family History of the Lipan Apache Band of Texas*.

14. Ball, *Indeh*, 270–72.

3. The Mescalero Apaches, Mexican Bandits, and Revenge

1. Ball, *Indeh*, 281.

2. Ball, *Indeh*, 200. Big Mouth (Mescalero scout), interview by Eve Ball. The Rio Bonito was also stated to be the place of haven for the Lipans in Antonio Apache's story of the massacre at Zaragosa.

3. Ball, *Indeh*, 211. Solon Sombrero (grandson of Natzili), interview by Eve Ball.

4. Farrer, *Living Life's Circle*, 28–29.

5. Opler, *Apache Odyssey*, 27.

6. Opler, *Apache Odyssey*, 27.

7. Opler, *Apache Odyssey*, 27.

8. Opler, *Apache Odyssey*, 12.

9. Apache Reservation census rolls, 1886, *Mescalero Reservation 1885–1914*, BIA.

10. Opler, *Apache Odyssey*, 11.

11. Ball, *Indeh*, 211, 285–86. Big Mouth, interview by Eve Ball. See also Pruit, *Santana*, 2.

12. John, *Storms Brewed in Other Men's Worlds*, 360, 439–40.

13. Ball, *Indeh*, 200–203. Big Mouth, interview by Eve Ball. Big Mouth was an infant (b. 1862) when these events occurred and accompanied his mother to Bosque Redondo in 1862. For Big Mouth's date of birth, see RACC, *Record of Enlistments for the 20th Regiment of Infantry, U.S. Army, 1878–1914: Indian Scouts*, microfilm publication #M233, roll 71, NA. Big Mouth first enlisted as a U.S. Army scout on July 13, 1883.

14. Ball, *Indeh*, 202.

15. Ball, *Indeh*, 202.

16. New Mexico District report, June 1869, prepared by Brevet Maj. Gen. George M. Getty, RACC, *Letters Sent; Ninth Military District, New Mexico, 1849–1890*, vol. 13, 393–94, microfilm publication #M1072, roll 4, NA.

17. Synopsis of Indian scouts and their results, January 17, 1863, RACC, *Special Files, Headquarters Department of the Missouri: Rio Grande Disturbances, March 1872–November 1875*, 2, microfilm publication #M1495, roll 11, NA. The list of Mescalero chiefs was obtained by contrasting the listed Mescalero chiefs in the Synopsis of 1863 with the Mescalero chiefs named in letters sent by the Ninth Military Department of New Mexico from 1869 on and with the Mescalero census rolls beginning in 1885.

18. New Mexico District report, September 1871, prepared by Col. G. Granger, Headquarters District of New Mexico, RACC, *Letters Sent; Ninth Military District, New Mexico, 1849–1890*, vol. 14, 266, microfilm publication #M1072, roll 4, NA.

19. Kavanagh, *The Comanches*, 429.

20. Kavanagh, *The Comanches*, 429.

21. Ball, *Indeh*, 213. Solon Sombrero, interview by Eve Ball.

22. "History of Coahuila after 1865."

23. Schuhardt to the U.S. Secretary of State, May 14, 1878, Despatch 198, U.S. Department of State.

25. Gill and Wegmann, *Streetwise Spanish Dictionary/Thesaurus*, 49.

26. Ball, *Indeh*, 296.

27. Apache Reservation census rolls, *Mescalero Reservation 1885–1914*, BIA. See census data for 1885–90; in almost every year Dinero is listed as Dinero Boy. For additional documents indicating Dinero was known as Dinero Boy, see his appointment as a member of the tribal police force, BIA, *Mescalero Reservation Inspection Reports*, 1889, microfilm publication #M1070, roll 25, NA.

4. The Vision Quest

1. Opler, *Apache Odyssey*, 29.

2. Opler, *Myths and Legends of the Lipan Apache Indians*, 74n.

3. Ball, *Indeh*, 62. Daklugie was from the Nednhi band of Apaches, allies of the Chiricahuas. His father, Juh, had fought with Geronimo. By 1913 the remnants of the Nehnhi, Chiricahua, and Warm Springs Apaches were transferred to the Mescalero Apache Reservation. It was there that Eve Ball interviewed him over thirteen years, from 1942 to 1955. Daklugie's description of how a young boy received his power was similar to the hints Opler found with the Lipans (i.e., receiving power from an animal through a vision; see Opler, *Myths and Legends of the Lipan Apache Indians*, 74n).

4. Opler, *Myths and Legends of the Lipan Apache Indians*, 74. The Jicarillas have a similar tale of people being saved by prairie dogs.

5. Opler, *Myths and Legends of the Lipan Apache Indians*, 9, 21n. "The myths of all Southern Athapascan tribes . . . include a story of a culture hero who slew the foes of the race. The Navajo, Western Apache, and Jicarilla name the chief protagonist Killer-of-Enemies and have him attended by a subordinate who is ordinarily known as Child-of-the-Water. By a curious twist the Mescalero and Chiricahua have just reversed the positions of these two; for them Child-of-the-Water becomes the intrepid hero and monster slayer and Killer-of-Enemies his weaker companion" (Opler, *Myths and Legends of the Lipan Apache Indians*, 3). The Lipans follow the pattern of the Navajos, Western Apaches, and Jicarillas in their culture hero myth, with the hero named Killer-of-Enemies, but his companion is a younger brother named Wise One.

6. Opler, *Apache Odyssey*, 147.

7. Ball, *Indeh*, 4. Eve Ball collected oral histories primarily from the Chiricahuas and several related bands as well as from the Mescaleros and one Lipan family. For the alternate spelling (*Yusn*), see Opler, *Apache Odyssey*, 142. For the Lipan word for Supreme Creator, see Gatschet, *Lipan Vocabulary Taken at Ft. Griffin, Texas, September–October 1884*, 3. The first term (*yatásetá*) came from Louis, a Big Water Lipan; the second term (*díatá seta*) came from Apache John, a Lipan scout at Ft. Griffin in 1884.

8. Opler, *Apache Odyssey*, 56.

9. Opler, *Myths and Legends of the Lipan Apache Indians*, 31.

10. Opler, *Myths and Legends of the Lipan Apache Indians*, 8.

11. Opler, *Myths and Legends of the Lipan Apache Indians*, 8.

12. Ball, *Indeh*, 61–62. Daklugie (Western Apache), interview by Eve Ball.

13. Ball, *Indeh*, 206. Bessie Big Rope (Mescalero), interview by Eve Ball.

14. Opler, *Myths and Legends of the Lipan Apache Indians*, 207.

15. James Mooney, *Comparative Vocabularies: Mescalero Apache and Lipan and Peyote Notes*, 425, MS 425, NAA. For the Lipan term for shaman, see Gatschet, *Lipan Vocabulary Taken at Ft. Griffin, Texas, September–October 1884*, 26.

16. Basso, *Western Apache Raiding and Warfare*, 310n.

17. Opler, *Myths and Legends of the Lipan Apache Indians*, 201–2.

18. Ball, *Indeh*, 206.

19. Haley, *Apaches*, 78.

20. Haley, *Apaches*, 78. Daklugie, son of Juh, also states that Geronimo's prowess was primarily through his ability to foretell the future (see Ball, *Indeh*, 61). See also Basso, *Western Apache Raiding and Warfare*, 311n.

21. Basso, *Western Apache Raiding and Warfare*, 311n.

22. Hunter, *Herman Lehmann*, 131.

5. The Blackbirds

1. Opler, *Myths and Legends of the Lipan Apache Indians*, 18, 30. The Lipans would often substitute a spotted or variegated color pattern for the white of the north. "Because of the shamanistic tenet of Lipan religious practice and the latitude this permits to individuals in the manipulation of ritual patterns, variant color-directional symbolisms are frequent" (Opler, *Myths and Legends of the Lipan Apache Indians*, 18n).

2. Ball, *Indeh*, 63. See also Opler, *Myths and Legends of the Lipan Apache Indians*, 70n; and Opler, *Apache Odyssey*, 257.

3. Opler, *Myths and Legends of the Lipan Apache Indians*, 70n.

4. Opler, *Myths and Legends of the Lipan Apache Indians*, 69–70. This same story is told, with variations, by Philemon Venego, Lipan, in Ball, *Indeh*, 269–70. Venego's story has the woman held hostage in a cave by the bear; when she is rescued, the rescuers kill the bear. Venego's oral history, however, has a number of factual errors.

5. Basso, *Western Apache Raiding and Warfare*, 318n. See also Farrer, *Living Life's Circle*, 26, 29. The owl is considered a messenger from the dead.

6. Opler, *Myths and Legends of the Lipan Apache Indians*, 38–39.

7. Opler, *Myths and Legends of the Lipan Apache Indians*, 39n.

8. Opler, *Myths and Legends of the Lipan Apache Indians*, 4, 59n. The Jicarillas also had two separate terms distinguishing between the body of the deceased and the spirit. The Jicarillas, with the Lipans, are the only two Apache tribes to make this distinction. In addition, the Mescaleros and Chiricahuas do not use the term *vakoc* or a similar term.

9. Opler, *Myths and Legends of the Lipan Apache Indians*, 4–5. The Jicarillas also had

this concept of the afterworld, but this picture is not found among any other Apache groups.

10. Opler, *Myths and Legends of the Lipan Apache Indians*, 31, 70.

11. Opler, *Apache Odyssey*, 134.

6. Chevato and Dinero Leave the Bandits

1. Rodriguez, "Sequoyah Pilgrimage 2002."

2. Rodriguez, "Sequoyah Pilgrimage 2002."

3. Diary of Juan de Ugalde, entries February 22–26, 1788, AGM, *Provincias Internas*, 2Q207, vol. 494, 321–22, CAH.

4. Opler, *Apache Odyssey*, 25. Opler states that "the peyote cult because established among the Mescalero about 1870 or a little before"—at precisely the time when Chevato and other Lipan survivors of the Zaragosa massacre were taken in by the Mescalero.

5. Stewart, "Origins of the Peyote Religion in the United States," 211–12, and figure 1, "Source Areas of Peyote."

6. Rogers, "CNM Recognition."

7. The Thirty-two Burros

1. Hunter, *Herman Lehmann*, 87–91.

2. Ball, *Indeh*, 60–61.

3. Dobie, *Apache Gold and Yaqui Silver*.

4. *New Encyclopedia Britannia*, 489.

9. The Capture of Herman Lehmann

1. For a detailed discussion of the central Texas children taken captive by Indians in the nineteenth century, see Zesch, *The Captured*. For Frank Buckelew's account of his captivity by the Lipans, see Dennis and Dennis, *Life of F. M. Buckelew, the Indian Captive*. For official correspondence relating to these children, see KAR, *Military Relations and Affairs: Indian Captives, 1870–1934*.

2. James P. Newcomb, Texas Secretary of State, to Gen. E. S. Parker, Commissioner of Indian Affairs, March 25, 1870, KAR, *Military Relations and Affairs: Indian Captives, 1870–1934*, microfilm #KA-42, OHS.

3. Reward poster, February 27, 1870, posted by P. Field, KAR, *Military Relations and Affairs: Indian Captives, 1870–1934*, microfilm #KA-42, OHS. As it turned out, evidence was later found that Mrs. Field was not abducted by Indians, but had fled her husband (see Lt. Schafler to Gen. Augur, Headquarters San Antonio TX, December 16, 1872, KAR, *Military Relations and Affairs: Indian Captives, 1870–1934*, microfilm #KA-42, OHS).

4. Henry M. Smith to Laurie Tatum, Indian Agent, March 19, 1871, KAR, *Military Relations and Affairs: Indian Captives, 1870–1934*, microfilm #KA-42, OHS. See also the Smith brothers' own account of their abduction in Smith and Hunter, *The Boy Captives*.

5. H. M. Smith and his wife to Capt. Sansom, the Texas Ranger leading the search for the boys, March 8, 1871, KAR, *Military Relations and Affairs: Indian Captives, 1870–1934*, microfilm #KA-42, OHS.

6. Brooks, *Captives and Cousins*, 180–81, 186–87.

7. See letter from H. R. Clum, Acting Commissioner, to the Dept. of the Interior, Office of Indian Affairs, June 8, 1871, stating that one of the Smith boys had been traded by the Mescaleros to the Comanche band headed by Mow-way, KAR, *Military Relations and Affairs: Indian Captives, 1870–1934*, microfilm #KA-42, OHS. For Laurie Tatum's record of this fact, see KAR, *Indian Depredations, 1869–1877*, microfilm #KA-6, OHS.

8. *San Antonio Daily Herald*, April 23, 1870. The full name of the semianonymous letter writer was J. G. O'Grady, a forty-year-old storekeeper living near Boerne, Texas. See Bureau of the Census, *U.S. Federal Census for Texas, Kendall County, 1870*, NA.

9. *San Antonio Daily Herald*, April 23, 1870.

10. Basso, *Western Apache Raiding and Warfare*, 16.

11. Basso, *Western Apache Raiding and Warfare*, 16.

12. Basso, *Western Apache Raiding and Warfare*, 18.

13. Kenner, *The Comanchero Frontier*, 165.

14. We know that the Mescalero group under Cadette had joined with at least one Comanche band from about 1869 (see New Mexico District report, September 1871, RACC). We also know that the Muchoque trade was going strong in 1872, when it was reported to New Mexico military officials (see report from Ft. Concho commanding officer to headquarters, June 16, 1872, RACC, *Special Files, Headquarters Department of the Missouri: Rio Grande Disturbances, March 1872–November 1875*, microfilm publication #M1495, roll 11, NA). For evidence that Mescalero were camped in 1872 at Muchoque along with Kwahada Comanche, see Kavanagh, *The Comanches*, 429.

15. Herman Lehmann discusses Mexican traders coming to trade directly with the Indians at Mescalero. Hunter, *Herman Lehmann*, 92.

16. Basso, *Western Apache Raiding and Warfare*, 17.

17. Report of Ft. Concho commanding officer to headquarters, June 16, 1872, RACC. The report states that "eight hundred head of cattle were taken by fifty (reported) Indians from the herd of Doctor Bartley . . . 25 miles west of this post [Ft. Concho]. . . . As the Indians would, before the troops could be put upon the trail, be half-way to Mucha-que." The thieves were believed to be Mescalero Apaches. See also RACC, *Headquarters Records, Ft. Stockton, Texas, 1867–1886*, microfilm publication #M1189, roll 8, NA for numerous reports of Mescalero cattle thefts.

18. Ball, *Indeh*, 213. Solon Sombrero, interview by Eve Ball.

19. Carney Saupitty, phone interview by Nancy McGown Minor, November 10, 2004. Saupitty's father (1883–1963) knew Chevato. Chevato told Mr. Saupitty Sr. the story of the capture of Herman Lehmann, a story that Mr. Saupitty Sr. passed down to his son.

20. *San Antonio Daily Herald*, March 22, 1870.

21. *San Antonio Daily Herald*, March 26, 1870.

22. *San Antonio Daily Herald*, April 19, 1870.

23. *San Antonio Daily Herald*, June 2, 1870.

24. Hunter, *Herman Lehmann*, 2–3.

25. *San Antonio Daily Herald*, May 21, 1870.

26. Hunter, *Herman Lehmann*, 4–6.

27. Hunter, *Herman Lehmann*, 10–12. See also *San Antonio Daily Herald*, June 2, 1870.

28. *The Roads of Texas*, 5.

29. For a thorough discussion of Mackenzie's Texas postings, see Wallace, *Ranald S. Mackenzie on the Texas Frontier*.

30. Hunter, *Herman Lehmann* 12.

10. The Capture of Children

1. Brooks, *Captives and Cousins*, 17.

2. Brooks, *Captives and Cousins*, 70.

3. Brooks, *Captives and Cousins*, 73–74.

4. Kavanagh, *The Comanches*, 63–83.

5. Opler, *Myths and Legends of the Lipan Apache Indians*, 237–46.

6. For further discussion of honor/dishonor as the basis of capture, see Brooks, *Captives and Cousins*, 26–40.

7. Gatschet, *Lipan Vocabulary Taken at Ft. Griffin, Texas, September–October 1884*, 30. Louis was a Lipan informant for Gatschet.

8. Hunter, *Herman Lehmann*, 57, 64.

9. Ball, *Indeh*, 239–42.

10. Smith and Hunter, *The Boy Captives*, 79–80, 126.

11. Mow-way told Tatum that he had bought Clint Smith from "New Mexico Apaches" (i.e., the Mescaleros). See Laurie Tatum, Kiowa and Comanche Agent, to Enoch Hoag, Superintendent of Indian Affairs, May 13 and June 8, 1871, KAR, *Military Relations and Affairs: Indian Captives, 1870–1934*, microfilm #KA-42, OHS; and KAR, *Letters Sent from the Kiowa Agency 1869–1877*, vol. 2, *Letterpress Book*, microfilm #KA-6, OHS. Tatum also requested military assistance in securing Clint Smith from Mow-way's band, if Mow-way did not turn him over as promised. See Laurie Tatum to Col. Grierson and Col. Mackenzie, Ft. Richardson, August 4, 1871, BIA, *Letters Received by the Office of Indian Affairs from the Kiowa Agency*, microfilm publication #M234, roll 376, NA.

12. Smith and Hunter, *The Boy Captives*, 99, 137. See also *Census and Enrollment: Undated and 1869–1883*, KAR.

13. Kavanagh, *The Comanches*, 434.

14. Despatches 101, 103, 109, 110, May 8, 1873, July 20, 1873, and August 28, 1873, U.S. Department of State, *Despatches from the U.S. Consul at Piedras Negras, Mexico, to the U.S. Secretary of State* (vol. 2, 1873–81), microfilm publication #M299, roll 1, NA.

15. Hunter, *Herman Lehmann*, 18–19.

16. Hunter, *Herman Lehmann*, 18–19.

17. Hunter, *Herman Lehmann*, 20–21.

18. Affidavit attached to Tourtellotte to Tatum, May 27, 1871, KAR. A second copy of

the affidavit was re-sent to Tatum by the Gillespie County, Texas, justice of the peace Radeleff on December 3, 1872. See KAR, *Military Relations and Affairs: Indian Captives, 1870–1934*, microfilm #KA-42, OHS.

19. Tourtellotte to Tatum, May 27, 1871, KAR

20. Department of the Interior, Office of Indian Affairs, to Laurie Tatum, Indian Agent, June 25, 1871, KAR, *Military Relations and Affairs: Indian Captives, 1870–1934*, microfilm #KA-42, OHS.

21. Lt. Thomas C. Davis, Headquarters District of New Mexico, Santa Fe, to Assistant Adjutant General, Department of the Missouri, Leavenworth, Kansas, January 15, 1875, RACC, *Letters Received by the Adjutant General: Letters from Ft. Stanton, New Mexico*, microfilm publication #M666, roll 187, NA.

22. Hunter, *Herman Lehmann*, 57–58, 61.

23. Capt. James J. Stewart, temporary commander Ft. Stanton, New Mexico, to Acting Assistant Adjutant General, District of New Mexico, Santa Fe, December 22, 1874, RACC, *Letters Received by the Adjutant General: Letters from Ft. Stanton, New Mexico*, microfilm publication #M666, roll 187, NA.

24. Stewart to Acting Assistant Adjutant General, December 22, 1874, RACC.

25. Stewart to Acting Assistant Adjutant General, December 22, 1874, RACC; Maj. D. R. Clendennin, Post Commander, Ft. Stanton, New Mexico, to Acting Assistant Adjutant General, District of New Mexico, Santa Fe, January 5, 1875, RACC, *Letters Received by the Adjutant General: Letters from Ft. Stanton, New Mexico*, microfilm publication #M666, roll 187, NA.

26. Clendennin to Acting Assistant Adjutant General, January 5, 1875, RACC.

27. Scouting report of Capt. E. G. Fechet, Eighth Cavalry, Ft. Stanton, New Mexico, to Post Adjutant, Ft. Stanton, New Mexico, February 6, 1875, RACC, *Letters Received by the Adjutant General: Letters from Ft. Stanton, New Mexico*, microfilm publication #M666, roll 187, NA.

28. Scouting report of Capt. E. G. Fechet, February 6, 1875, RACC.

29. Scouting Report of Capt. E. G. Fechet, February 6, 1875, RACC.

11. Herman Lehmann Leaves the Apaches and Becomes a Comanche

1. Hunter, *Herman Lehmann*, 124–28.

2. Apache Reservation census rolls, 1885 Mescalero census, *Mescalero Reservation 1885–1914*, BIA.

3. Nye, *Carbine and Lance*, 116–17.

4. Nye, *Carbine and Lance*, 143.

5. Laurie Tatum to Enoch Hoag, Superintendent of Indian Affairs, September 30, 1871, KAR, *Letters Sent from the Kiowa Agency 1869–1877*, vol. 2, *Letterpress Book*, microfilm #KA-6, OHS.

6. Laurie Tatum to Enoch Hoag, Superintendent of Indian Affairs, May 12, 1871, BIA, *Letters Received by the Office of Indian Affairs from the Kiowa Agency*, microfilm pub-

lication #M234, roll 376, NA. See also Enoch Hoag, Superintendent of Indian Affairs, to Laurie Tatum, Comanche and Kiowa Agent, June 8 and June 25, 1871, KAR, *Military Relations and Affairs: Indian Captives, 1870–1934*, microfilm #KA-42, OHS.

7. Hoag to Tatum, June 25, 1871, KAR

8. Hunter, *Herman Lehmann,* 28.

9. William Chebahtah, interview by Nancy McGown Minor, San Antonio TX, July 28, 2004; Saupitty interview, November 10, 2004.

10. Ball, *Indeh,* 211–12. Solon Sombrero, interview by Eve Ball.

11. New Mexico District report, September 1871, RACC.

12. Hunter, *Herman Lehmann,* 192.

13. Smith and Hunter, *The Boy Captives,* 123–24.

14. Table prepared by Laurie Tatum, Indian Agent, "Captives Received from Indians," KAR, *Indian Depredations, 1869–1877,* microfilm #KA-6, OHS.

15. Neeley, *The Last Comanche Chief,* 68–69.

16. Odom, *Quanah Parker and His People,* 73.

17. Odom, *Quanah Parker and His People,* 73–74. When Quanah surrendered at Ft. Sill in 1875, Ta-ho-yea was not with him.

18. Neeley, *The Last Comanche Chief,* 157n.

19. Hagan, *Quanah Parker, Comanche Chief,* 53.

20. Kavanagh, *The Comanches,* 445.

21. Kavanagh, *The Comanches,* 447.

22. Kavanagh, *The Comanches,* 446.

23. Stewart, "Origins of the Peyote Religion in the United States," 220. This description of the peyote ritual is based on the way the ritual was performed, after 1875, by the Comanches and Kiowas. Since Quanah Parker introduced the peyote cult to the Comanches and Chevato played a large part in the cult as practiced by Parker and the Comanches, we can also assume that the peyote ritual, as practiced by the Lipans living among the Mescaleros, was similar.

24. Stewart, "Origins of the Peyote Religion in the United States," 218.

25. Stewart, "Origins of the Peyote Religion in the United States," 218.

26. Davis to Assistant Adjutant General, January 15, 1875, RACC.

27. Stewart to Acting Assistant Adjutant General, December 22, 1874, RACC.

28. Scouting report from Capt. Fechet to Maj. Clendennin, Ft. Stanton, New Mexico, January 27, 1875, RACC, *Letters Received by the Adjutant General: Letters from Ft. Stanton, New Mexico,* microfilm publication #M666, roll 187, NA. See also Sonnichsen, *The Mescalero Apaches,* 171. For evidence that Chevato was a member of Natzili's group, see Apache Reservation census rolls, 1886, *Mescalero Reservation 1885–1914,* BIA.

29. Hagan, *Quanah Parker, Comanche Chief,* 21.

30. Hagan, *Quanah Parker, Comanche Chief,* 22.

31. Neeley, *The Last Comanche Chief,* 151–52. Neeley states that Parker turned over

four Comanches to Company A of the Tenth Cavalry, led by Capt. Nicholas Nolan and Capt. Charles Cooper. This exchange occurred near Cedar Lake in present-day Gaines County, Texas.

32. Affidavit of Quanah Parker, sworn out as part of Herman Lehmann's enrollment into the Comanche tribe, August 26, 1901, KAR, *Kiowa Agency Census and Enrollment: 1893–1901*, microfilm #KA-4, OHS.

33. Affidavit of Herman Lehmann, April 15, 1901, KAR, *Letters Sent from the Kiowa Agency*, April 2 to June 28, 1901, and May 10 to July 26, 1901, vol. 2, *Letterpress Book*, microfilm #KA-6, OHS.

34. Chevato to Parker, January 3, 1889, BIA.

12. Geronimo

1. Basso, *Western Apache Raiding and Warfare*, 21.

2. Basso, *Western Apache Raiding and Warfare*, 21.

3. Basso, *Western Apache Raiding and Warfare*, 22.

4. Basso, *Western Apache Raiding and Warfare*, 22. See also Ball, *Indeh*, 37–38, for an explanation of the containment policy given in an interview by Eve Ball with Daklugie.

5. Basso, *Western Apache Raiding and Warfare*, 23.

6. Sonnichsen, *The Mescalero Apaches*, 190–92.

7. Tiller, *The Jicarilla Apache Tribe*, 77, 89–90.

8. Sonnichsen, *The Mescalero Apaches*, 171.

9. The 1886 Mescalero census is broken down by tribe (Mescalero and Jicarilla) as well as by groups within each tribe. The total number of all Indians living on the Mescalero Reservation in 1886 was 1,202. Of that number, 417 were Mescaleros (this number included 5 Comanches; 5 "half-breeds," which comprised the family of the Mexican captive Juan Carillo; and 20 Lipans) and 785 Jicarillas (this number included 2 Navajos and 1 Ute). The Mescalero chiefs were Natzili and San Juan, while the Jicarilla chief was San Pablo. See, Apache Reservation census rolls, 1886 census, *Mescalero Reservation 1885–1914*, BIA.

10. Pruit, *Santana*, 234–35, 238.

11. E. M. Marble report, BIA, *Report to the Commissioner of Indian Affairs for 1880 from the Mescalero Reservation*, 44, 129, record group 75, NA.

12. Sonnichsen, *The Mescalero Apaches*, 192.

13. Apache Reservation census rolls, 1886 census, *Mescalero Reservation 1885–1914*, BIA.

14. Sonnichsen, *The Mescalero Apaches*, 199–201.

15. S. A. Russell report, BIA, *Report to the Commissioner of Indian Affairs for 1880 from the Mescalero Reservation*, 44, 130, record group 75, NA.

16. Fort Stanton, New Mexico, returns for September 30, 1880, and October 31, 1880, RACC, *Returns from U.S. Military Posts, Ft. Stanton, New Mexico*, microfilm publication #M617, roll 1218, NA.

17. RACC, *Letters Received by the Adjutant General: Report on the Starvation of the Mescalero Due to Congress' Neglect in Funding*, microfilm publication #M689, roll 101, NA.

18. Basso, *Western Apache Raiding and Warfare*, 103–4. This excerpt is taken from Grenville Goodwin's interview with John Rope, a White Mountain Apache.

19. *Record of Enlistments for the 20th Regiment of Infantry, U.S. Army, 1878–1914: Indian Scouts*, RACC.

20. Fort Stanton, New Mexico, return for October 31, 1883, RACC, *Returns from U.S. Military Posts, Ft. Stanton, New Mexico*, microfilm publication #M617, roll 1218, NA. See also *Record of Enlistments for the 20th Regiment of Infantry, U.S. Army, 1878–1914: Indian Scouts*, RACC for the names and enlistment dates of the additional 1883 South Fork scouts.

21. Fort Stanton, New Mexico, return for April 30, 1883, RACC, *Returns from U.S. Military Posts, Ft. Stanton, New Mexico*, microfilm publication #M617, roll 1218, NA.

22. R. C. Drum, Adjutant General, to Lt. Thomas W. Symons, Corps of Engineers, September 22, 1883, RACC, *Letters Received by Headquarters, District of New Mexico*, microfilm publication #M1088, roll 52, NA.

23. For an account of Ranald S. Mackenzie's postings, see Wallace, *Ranald S. Mackenzie on the Texas Frontier*.

24. Lt. Thomas W. Symons to R. C. Drum, Adjutant General, October 8, 1883, RACC, *Letters Received by Headquarters, District of New Mexico*, microfilm publication #M1088, roll 52, NA.

25. Haley, *Apaches*, 361.

26. Haley, *Apaches*, 368.

27. Symons to Drum, October 8, 1883, RACC.

28. Basso, *Western Apache Raiding and Warfare*, 94, 148–72. See Goodwin's interview with John Rope, a scout for Crook's expedition into Mexico, 1883.

29. Symons to Drum, October 8, 1883, RACC.

30. Fort Stanton, New Mexico, return for September 30, 1885, RACC, *Returns from U.S. Military Posts, Ft. Stanton, New Mexico*, microfilm publication #M617, roll 1218, NA.

31. *Record of Enlistments for the 20th Regiment of Infantry, U.S. Army, 1878–1914: Indian Scouts*, RACC.

32. Inspector Gardner's report, October 13, 1886, BIA, *Mescalero Reservation Inspection Reports*, microfilm publication #M1070, roll 25, NA.

33. *Record of Enlistments for the 20th Regiment of Infantry, U.S. Army, 1878–1914: Indian Scouts*, RACC

34. Ball, *Indeh*, 262–63. The son of Alabama Charlie Smith and Cumpah, Charlie Smith Jr. was the informant "Chris" used by Opler in *Apache Odyssey*.

35. Ball, *Indeh*, 273–74.

13. The Murder Trial

1. Saupitty interview, November 10, 2004. Carney Saupitty, a Comanche who was told the story of Dinero's arrest and trial at Mescalero by his father, who knew Che-

vato, believes that Dinero might have been jailed after his trial at the Yuma, Arizona, federal penitentiary. This fact, however, does not square with any of the evidence that does exist.

2. Bureau of the Census, *U.S. Federal Census for Oklahoma, Comanche County*, 1910, NA. See also, Apache Reservation census rolls, 1886 Mescalero census, *Mescalero Reservation 1885–1914*, BIA. Chevato's son, Harry Heath, stated in his 1910 census return that his mother was born in Mexico. The Mescalero census for 1886 specified she was a Lipan but only lists her as "wife." Her name was not preserved in the oral history per the Apache taboo against speaking the name of a deceased person.

3. Apache Reservation census rolls, Mescalero census returns for the years 1885–90, *Mescalero Reservation 1885–1914*, BIA.

4. Chevato to Parker, January 3, 1889, BIA.

5. Inspector Ward's report, July 22, 1884, BIA, *Mescalero Reservation Inspection Reports*, microfilm publication #M1070, roll 25, NA.

6. Tiller, *The Jicarilla Apache Tribe*, 78.

7. Tiller, *The Jicarilla Apache Tribe*, 80–81.

8. Tiller, *The Jicarilla Apache Tribe*, 90.

9. Tiller, *The Jicarilla Apache Tribe*, 90.

10. Tiller, *The Jicarilla Apache Tribe*, 98.

11. Inspector Pearson's report, December 26, 1885, BIA, *Mescalero Reservation Inspection Reports*, microfilm publication #M1070, roll 25, NA.

12. Inspector Gardner's report, October 13, 1886, BIA.

13. Inspector Gardner's report, October 13, 1886, BIA.

14. Inspector Gardner's report, October 13, 1886, BIA.

15. Inspector Gardner's report, October 13, 1886, BIA.

16. Tiller, *The Jicarilla Apache Tribe*, 94–95.

17. Tiller, *The Jicarilla Apache Tribe*, 93–95.

18. Pruit, *Santana*, 243. Pruit edited a manuscript written by Almer B. Blazer, son of the first physician at Mescalero as well as owner of the first mill at Mescalero. The manuscript contains reminiscences of early Mescalero leaders as told by Dr. Blazer to his son, as well as Almer Blazer's memories of life on the Mescalero Reservation in the 1880s.

19. Pruit, *Santana*, 246.

20. Pruit, *Santana*, 246–47.

21. Apache Reservation census rolls, 1885–90 census returns, *Mescalero Reservation 1885–1914*, BIA.

22. Apache Reservation census rolls, 1885–90 census returns, *Mescalero Reservation 1885–1914*, BIA. Dinero's wife had been married previous to her marriage to Dinero. She had two children from that previous marriage: a daughter named Chalita Chiquita (Little Chalita) and a son named Ec-o-da.

23. Mescalero Agent W. H. Llewellyn to Kiowa Agent Maj. Lee Hall, October 27, 1885, KAR, *Census and Enrollment: Census 1883–1890*, microfilm #KA-2, OHS.

24. W. Belt, Acting Commissioner of Indian Affairs, to W. D. Myers, Kiowa Agent, June 5, 1889, KAR, *Census and Enrollment: Census 1883–1890*, microfilm #KA-2, OHS.

26. Hagan, *United States–Comanche Relations*, 150–52.

27. Neeley, *The Last Comanche Chief*, 191–92.

28. Telegram from Maj. Gen. O. O. Howard, San Francisco, to Adjutant General, Washington DC, August 12, 1887, relaying information from General Miles, RACC, *Letters Received by the Adjutant General: Report of Escapes from the Mescalero Reservation*, microfilm publication #M689, roll 548, NA.

29. Fort Stanton, New Mexico, return for August 8, 1887, RACC, *Returns from U.S. Military Posts, Ft. Stanton, New Mexico*, microfilm publication #M617, roll 1218, NA.

30. Escapes from the Mescalero Reservation, file 3517 AGO 1887, RACC, *Letters Received by the Adjutant General: Report of Escapes from the Mescalero Reservation*, microfilm publication #M689, roll 548, NA.

31. Chevato to Quanah Parker, October 26, 1888, attached to a letter from W. D. Myers, Kiowa Agent, to the Commissioner of Indian Affairs, April 20, 1889, BIA, *Letters Received by the Department of the Interior, 1881–1907*, record group 75, 11319-1889, NA. It is interesting to speculate whether Chevato wrote the letter or whether someone else wrote the letter for him. All available evidence shows that Chevato could not write; a 1901 document was signed by him with an *X*. However, he was multilingual, speaking Spanish, English, Apache, and Comanche.

32. Chevato to Parker, January 3, 1889, BIA.

33. Chevato to Parker, January 3, 1889, BIA.

34. Attached letter from Chevato to Quanah Parker, March 17, 1889, BIA, *Letters Received by the Department of the Interior, 1881–1907*, record group 75, 11319-1889, NA.

35. Myers to Commissioner of Indian Affairs, April 20, 1889, BIA.

36. Attached letter from Comanche John (Roan Horse) to Quanah Parker (no month) 17, 1888, BIA, *Letters Received by the Department of the Interior, 1881–1907*, record group 75, 11319-1889, NA. From the text of the letter, it seems it was written in October.

37. Belt to Myers, June 5, 1889, KAR.

38. 1889 inspection report, BIA, *Mescalero Reservation Inspection Reports*, microfilm publication #M1070, roll 25, NA.

39. The confusion over identification of the woman with whom Dinero allegedly had the affair stems from the chaotic situation on the Mescalero Reservation from 1890 to 1894. During this period, the agency saw one agent removed and two other agents who each served only two years in the job. In each census from these years, many persons are not named, ticket numbers do not correspond to the same families from year to year, and names of person are changed from year to year. However, from the best evidence available at Mescalero, Dinero allegedly had the affair with Guerdo, wife of Charles Wyeth. Wyeth is listed in the census returns from 1885 to 1891, but not thereafter, reflecting his death in 1891. Guerdo (Agatha Wyeth) is listed on census returns from 1887 to 1893 and then disappears. Her mother, who was called Sally Wyeth on

several census returns, is listed simply as "Guerdo" in 1894, assuming her daughter's name. The ages of mother and daughter reflect what occurred, however. The daughter, Guerdo, would have been eighteen in 1894. The woman listed as Guerdo in 1894 is given the age of thirty-five (an age that would be correct if it were referring to the mother, Sally Wyeth). Data from the census rolls at the Kiowa Agency in Oklahoma give Dinero's female companion the name Ad-do-che-nah (reflecting the Agatha name by which she was known at Mescalero) and the age of seventeen in the 1892–93 census returns. See Apache Reservation census rolls, 1885–94 census returns, *Mescalero Reservation 1885–1914*, BIA. See also 1892–93 census returns, *Kiowa Agency Census and Enrollment: 1890–1894*, KAR.

40. 1889–94 inspection reports, BIA, *Mescalero Reservation Inspection Reports*, microfilm publication #M1070, roll 25, NA.

41. Sonnichsen, *The Mescalero Apaches*, 240.

42. Sonnichsen, *The Mescalero Apaches*, 240.

43. Opler, *Myths and Legends of the Lipan Apache Indians*, 230.

44. 1891 census returns, *Kiowa Agency Census 1890–1894*, KAR. Comanche tribal records indicate that both Chevato and Dinero were in Oklahoma by 1890, but this is not borne out by census data, both Comanche and Mescalero. Dinero was in Oklahoma by 1891 and Chevato by late 1892 or January 1893.

45. 1892–93 census returns, *Kiowa Agency Census 1890–1894*, KAR. The Mescalero census returns for the pertinent years (1891–92) show Dinero listed in both 1891 and 1892, but things were so chaotic at Mescalero that this might just be evidence of the disorganized state of affairs, rather than Dinero's actual presence at Mescalero. The 1892 Mescalero census shows his wife, Chalita, had brought her daughter from a previous marriage to live with her, and the 1893 Mescalero census shows Chalita as a widow. Agatha Wyeth also disappears from the Mescalero census after 1893. See Apache Reservation census rolls, 1891–93 census returns, *Mescalero Reservation 1885–1914*, BIA.

14. The Bodyguards

1. Hagan, *Quanah Parker, Comanche Chief*, 74.

2. Commissioner of Indian Affairs to Capt. Hugh Brown, Kiowa Agent, September 21, 1893, 34072-1893, KAR, *Kiowa Agency Census and Enrollment: Undated and 1869–1883*, microfilm #KA-1, OHS.

3. Commissioner of Indian Affairs to Brown, September 21, 1893, KAR.

4. Apache Reservation Census Rolls, 1885–90 census returns, *Mescalero Reservation 1885–1914*, BIA.

5. 1892–93 census returns, *Kiowa Agency Census 1890–1894*, KAR.

6. Levi Burnett, Mescalero Agent, to Commissioner of Indian Affairs, September 4, 1893, 34072-1893, KAR, *Kiowa Agency Census and Enrollment: Undated and 1869–1883*, microfilm #KA-1, OHS.

7. Burnett to Commissioner of Indian Affairs, September 4, 1893, KAR.

8. Memo from D. M. Browning, Commissioner of Indian Affairs, to Capt. Baldwin, Kiowa Agent, June 8, 1896, authority to enroll as Comanches given to Carrie Heath, Corine Heath, Tah-ne-we-kin (Mrs. Sanavoy), and Pe-si-ya (Corine Heath was the daughter of Carrie Heath), 20979-96, KAR, *Kiowa Agency Census and Enrollment: Undated and 1869–1883*, microfilm #KA-1, OHS.

9. Commissioner of Indian Affairs to Maury Nichols, Kiowa Agent, September 29, 1894, 37352-1894, KAR, *Kiowa Agency Census and Enrollment: Undated and 1869–1883*, microfilm #KA-1, OHS.

10. Commissioner of Indian Affairs to Nichols, September 29, 1894, KAR.

11. Apache Reservation census rolls, 1890–94 census returns, *Mescalero Reservation 1885–1914*, BIA.

12. Apache Reservation Census Rolls, 1890–94 census returns, *Mescalero Reservation 1885–1914*, BIA.

13. Memo from Browning to Baldwin, June 8, 1896, KAR.

14. 1895–1904 Comanche census returns, *Kiowa Agency Census 1893–1901*, KAR; and *Kiowa Agency Census 1902–1922*, KAR.

15. Opler, *Myths and Legends of the Lipan Apache Indians*, 214n.

16. Apache Reservation census rolls, 1890–1907 census returns, *Mescalero Reservation 1885–1914*, BIA. See also 1900–1907 census returns, *Kiowa Agency Census 1893–1901*, KAR; and *Kiowa Agency Census 1901–1922*, KAR. Harry Heath died February 14, 1929, of pulmonary TB on the Comanche Reservation, Comanche County, Oklahoma. His daughter, Maggie Heath, married Elmer Parker, grandson of Quanah Parker. All three are buried in the new Post Oak Mission Cemetery, Indiahoma, Oklahoma. Paul Heath, also known as Paul Chebahtah, died May 1, 1918, on the Comanche Reservation, Comanche County, Oklahoma. He is buried in the New Post Oak Cemetery, Indiahoma, Oklahoma. See Bowen, *Kiowa, Comanche, Apache, Ft. Sill Apache, Wichita, Caddo and Delaware Indians*, 106. See also Post Oak Mennonite Brethren Church, *Post Oak Mission Centennial 1895–1995*; and Mills and Mullenax, *Relocated Cemeteries in Oklahoma and Parts of Texas, Kansas, and Arkansas*.

17. Jordan and Holm, *Indian Leaders*, 171.

18. Neeley, *The Last Comanche Chief*, 206–7. The law authorizing the Jerome Commission was the Dawes Act.

19. Neeley, *The Last Comanche Chief*, 207.

20. Neeley, *The Last Comanche Chief*, 208.

21. Neeley, *The Last Comanche Chief*, 213.

22. Address by Quanah Parker to the Oklahoma Senate at Guthrie, Oklahoma, undated but probably delivered around 1900, KAR, *Indian History, Culture and Acculturation: Peyote/Mescal Use*, microfilm #KA-50, OHS.

15. Pi-he

1. Kavanagh, *The Comanches*, 485.

2. Kavanagh, *The Comanches*, 485

3. The source for Pi-he's relationship to Quanah Parker and Peta Nocona is the oral history of the Chebahtah family, passed down from Pi-he to her son, Thomas David Chebahtah, and thus to her grandson, William Chebahtah.

4. J. M. Haworth, Kiowa Agent, to Commissioner of Indian Affairs, June 14, 1875, BIA, *Letters Received by the Office of Indian Affairs from the Kiowa Agency*, microfilm publication #M234, roll 376, NA. The actual date of surrender was June 3, 1875, as reported in a telegram sent by Haworth to the commissioner. The number of Kwahadas coming into Ft. Sill totaled 407 men, women, and children and about 2,000 horses. For information as to Quanah Parker being a part of Isatai's band, see Kavanagh, *The Comanches*, 450.

5. 1879–80 census returns, *Kiowa Agency Census and Enrollment: Undated and 1869–1883*, KAR. It must be noted that the 1879 census returns are only a partial list of the entire Comanche tribe; the Penetekas were not included.

6. Wallace and Hoebel, *The Comanches*, 139.

7. Wallace and Hoebel, *The Comanches*, 139.

8. 1895–1910 census returns, *Kiowa Agency Census 1893–1902*, KAR; and *Kiowa Agency Census 1902–1922*, KAR.

16. Quanah Parker and Wild Horse

1. Neeley, *The Last Comanche Chief*, 2–8.

2. Kavanagh, *The Comanches*, 231–34.

3. Kavanagh, *The Comanches*, 234.

4. Kavanagh, *The Comanches*, 234–35.

5. Kavanagh, *The Comanches*, 235.

6. Kavanagh, *The Comanches*, 241.

7. Kavanagh, *The Comanches*, 242–43.

8. Neeley, *The Last Comanche Chief*, 4. Neeley cites no sources for the numbers of Comanches who attacked Parker's Fort, merely stating that there are numerous estimates. The Rachel Plummer narrative would seem to indicate that there were great numbers of Indians, more than the usual ten to twenty in a raiding party.

9. Kavanagh, *The Comanches*, 242–43.

10. Neeley, *The Last Comanche Chief*, 9.

11. Neeley, *The Last Comanche Chief*, 11–12.

12. Neeley, *The Last Comanche Chief*, 11–12.

13. Brooks, *Captives and Cousins*, 187.

14. Hunter, *The Bloody Trail in Texas*, 14–27. Hunter took Virginia Webster's narrative from her account published in the *San Antonio Express* on April 27, 1913.

15. Hunter, *The Bloody Trail in Texas*, 19–20.

16. Wallace and Hoebel, *The Comanches*, 123.

17. Hunter, *The Bloody Trail in Texas*, 21.

18. Hunter, *The Bloody Trail in Texas*, 23.

19. Kavanagh, *The Comanches*, 263.

20. Hunter, *The Bloody Trail in Texas*, 26. Virginia Webster's mother "was never herself again after her sufferings, hardships and bereavements, and she died July 29, 1845." Her brother was placed in school at Galveston by Sam Houston, who saw that the young boy was afraid to go aboard the vessel that was to take his mother and sister back to Virginia after their release from Comanche captivity. The brother later enlisted in the U.S. Army during the Mexican War and died at the battle of Monterrey. Virginia stayed with extended family members in Virginia until 1849, when she returned to Texas with her uncle. She married M. G. Strickland in 1853 and moved to Burnet County, Texas, "to the place where my father was going to build his fort." Strickland died in 1865, and Virginia remarried to Charles Munro Simmons. After Simmons's death in 1889, she moved with her children (three sons and a daughter) to Oregon and then to California, where she wrote her reminiscences about the Comanche attack on the Webster party. She ended by stating, "In looking back over my past life, full of sorrow and grief, I wonder how I could have endured it all and live to be as old as I am. . . . I alone am left. I am now 76 years old, am able to do my housework and have written this story with my own hand."

21. Neeley, *The Last Comanche Chief*, 12. U.S. representatives Butler and Lewis met with Cynthia Ann in 1846 at a Comanche camp on the upper Canadian River. They offered trade goods in the amount of $400–$500 to redeem her, but she ran and hid in order to avoid those who would ransom her.

22. Brooks, *Captives and Cousins*, 367.

23. Brooks, *Captives and Cousins*, 366.

24. Brooks, *Captives and Cousins*, 196.

25. Neeley, *The Last Comanche Chief*, 32.

26. Neeley, *The Last Comanche Chief*, 32.

27. Neeley, *The Last Comanche Chief*, 42–51.

28. Neeley, *The Last Comanche Chief*, 53.

29. Opler, *Myths and Legends of the Lipan Apache Indians*, 236–37. See the story "The Two Comanche with Supernatural Power," where two Comanches brag about their power but are bested by a Lipan who concludes, "You Comanche fellows have no power from anywhere, not the least bit."

30. Maj. Gen. George Getty, Headquarters New Mexico, to Adj. Gen. McKeever, Ft. Hays, Kansas, March 13, 1869, RACC, *Letters Sent; Ninth Military District, New Mexico, 1849–1890*, vol. 13, July–September 1868–September 1870, NA.

31. Getty to McKeever, March 13, 1869, RACC.

32. Getty to McKeever, March 13, 1869, RACC.

33. Adj. Gen. E. D. Townsend to L. D. Cox, Secretary of the Interior, July 3, 1869, BIA, *Letters Received by the Office of Indian Affairs from the Kiowa Agency*, microfilm publication #M234, roll 376, NA.

34. Telegram from Kiowa Agent Haworth to Ft. Sill, April 19, 1875, BIA, *Letters Received by the Office of Indian Affairs from the Kiowa Agency*, microfilm publication

#M234, roll 376, NA. See also Haworth to Commissioner of Indian Affairs, April 20, 1875, BIA, *Letters Received by the Office of Indian Affairs from the Kiowa Agency*, microfilm publication #M234, roll 376, NA.

35. Wallace and Hoebel, *The Comanches*, 210–11.

36. "Miscellaneous Papers about Wild Horse," 66.

37. Wallace and Hoebel, *The Comanches*, 242–43.

38. Brooks, *Captives and Cousins*, 178.

39. Wallace and Hoebel, *The Comanches*, 141.

40. Neeley, *The Last Comanche Chief*, 222–23.

41. Apache Reservation census rolls, 1885–1900 census returns, *Mescalero Reservation 1885–1914*, BIA.

17. Warriors

1. Horace Jones, U.S. Interpreter, to Laurie Tatum, Kiowa Agent, December 6, 1870, BIA, *Letters Received by the Office of Indian Affairs from the Kiowa Agency*, microfilm publication #M234, roll 376, NA.

2. Wallace and Hoebel, *The Comanches*, 245.

3. Opler, *Myths and Legends of the Lipan Apache Indians*, 252–56.

4. Opler, *Myths and Legends of the Lipan Apache Indians*, 256–59, 244–46.

5. Opler, *Myths and Legends of the Lipan Apache Indians*, 259.

6. Opler, *Myths and Legends of the Lipan Apache Indians*, 48–49.

7. Opler, *Myths and Legends of the Lipan Apache Indians*, 48–49.

18. The Lost Sister

1. Opler, *Myths and Legends of the Lipan Apache Indians*, 230.

2. Chevato to Parker, October 26, 1888, BIA.

3. Chevato to Parker January 3, 1889, BIA.

4. Opler, *Myths and Legends of the Lipan Apache Indians*, 272.

5. Bureau of the Census, *U.S. Federal Census for Texas, Presidio County, 1880*, Precinct 1, Ft. Davis, NA.

20. The Peyote Singer

1. Stewart, "Origins of the Peyote Religion in the United States," 212–13.

2. Stewart, "Origins of the Peyote Religion in the United States," 218–19.

3. Mooney, *Comparative Vocabularies*. The Mooney informant for his information was a Mescalero named Nayoka, or Andy Miller, with the interview conducted on November 25, 1897. Nayoka's information regarding the No Water band of Lipan indicates that they came to southern New Mexico at a late date, moving north out of Coahuila.

4. Opler, *Myths and Legends of the Lipan Apache Indians*, 2.

5. Stewart, "Origins of the Peyote Religion in the United States," 215.

6. Gerhard, *The North Frontier of New Spain*, 332.

7. Stewart, "Origins of the Peyote Religion in the United States," 211–12.

8. Diary of Juan de Ugalde, entries February 22–26, 1788, AGR.

9. Stewart, "Origins of the Peyote Religion in the United States," 215.

10. Salinas, *Indians of the Rio Grande Delta*, 132–33.

11. Dinero's quote was taken from the *American Indian YMCA Bulletin*, November 1918; Stewart, "Origins of the Peyote Religion in the United States," 218.

12. Butterworth, "Earliest Methodist Missionary Work in the Comanche-Kiowa Area," 73–74.

13. Opler, *Apache Odyssey*, 25.

14. Opler, *Apache Odyssey*, 27.

15. James A. Carroll, Mescalero Agent, to Quanah Parker, Comanche chief, July 13, 1908, KAR, *Indian History, 1870–1914*, microfilm #KA-48, OHS. After the killings, many of the Lipans clamored to leave Mescalero for Oklahoma, and Agent Carroll wrote to Quanah Parker requesting that Parker "talk strong to them" to get them to stay in New Mexico.

16. Address by Quanah Parker to the Oklahoma Senate, KAR

17. Stewart, "Origins of the Peyote Religion in the United States," 213.

18. Stewart, "Origins of the Peyote Religion in the United States," 213.

19. Kavanagh, *The Comanches*, 509n15.

20. Opler, *Myths and Legends of the Lipan Apache Indians*, 236.

21. Saupitty interview, November 10, 2004.

21. The Community on the Creek

1. Jordan and Holm, *Indian Leaders*, 173.

2. 1900 census returns, Comanche and Kiowa Reservation enumerations, *U.S. Federal Census for Oklahoma, Comanche County*, Bureau of the Census.

3. Southwestern Oklahoma Genealogy Society, *Comanche County History*, 47.

4. Southwestern Oklahoma Genealogy Society, *Comanche County History*, 47.

5. Carroll to Parker, July 13, 1908, KAR.

6. Carroll to Parker, July 13, 1908, KAR.

7. Southwestern Oklahoma Genealogy Society, *Comanche County History*, 47.

8. Southwestern Oklahoma Genealogy Society, *Comanche County History*, 47.

9. Southwestern Oklahoma Genealogy Society, *Comanche County History*, 47.

10. Southwestern Oklahoma Genealogy Society, *Comanche County History*, 48.

22. The Death of Chevato

1. KAR, *Comanche Vital Statistics*, Genealogy Library microfilm #0576911, Church of Jesus Christ of Latter Day Saints, Salt Lake City UT. See also 1920 census returns, *U.S. Federal Census for Oklahoma, Comanche County*, Bureau of the Census.

2. Post Oak Mennonite Brethren Church, *Post Oak Mission Centennial 1895–1995*. See also Mills and Mullenax, *Relocated Cemeteries in Oklahoma and Parts of Arizona, Kansas, and Texas*.

3. Perry and Focke, *A New Look at Nine Years among the Indians 1870–1875*, 284–85.

Bibliography

Archival Sources

Archivo General de Mexico, Center for American History, University of Texas at Austin.

Kiowa Agency Records, Church of Jesus Christ of Latter Day Saints, Salt Lake City UT.

Kiowa Agency Records, Oklahoma Historical Society, Oklahoma City.

National Anthropological Archives, Smithsonian Institution, Washington DC.

National Archives, Washington DC.

    Bureau of Indian Affairs

    Bureau of the Census

    Records of the U.S. Army Continental Commands, 1821–1910

    U.S. Department of State

Romero, Daniel Castro Jr. *The Castro Family History of the Lipan Apache Band of Texas.* Sophienburg Archives, New Braunfels TX.

Published Sources

Ball, Eve. *Indeh: An Apache Odyssey.* Norman: University of Oklahoma Press, 1988.

Basso, Keith H., ed. *Western Apache Raiding and Warfare (from the notes of Grenville Goodwin).* Tucson: University of Arizona Press, 1971.

Berlandier, Jean Louis. "The Indians of Texas in 1830." In *Voyage au Mexique 1826–1834,* edited by John C. Ewers. Washington DC: Smithsonian Institution Press, 1969.

Betty, Gerald. *Comanche Society Before the Reservation.* College Station: Texas A&M Press, 2002.

Bowen, Jeff. *Kiowa, Comanche, Apache, Ft. Sill Apache, Wichita, Caddo and Delaware Indians: Birth and Death Rolls 1924–1932.* Signal Mountain TN: Mountain Press, 1996.

Brooks, James S. *Captives and Cousins: Slavery, Kinship and Community in the Southwest Borderlands.* Chapel Hill: University of North Carolina Press, 2002.

Butterworth, Rev. A. E. "Earliest Methodist Missionary Work in the Comanche-Kiowa Area." *Chronicles of Comanche County* 5, no. 2 (Autumn 1959).

Cobos, Rubén. *Dictionary of New Mexico and Southern Colorado Spanish.* Santa Fe: Museum of New Mexico Press, 1993.

Dennis, T. S., and Mrs. T. S. Dennis. *Life of F. M. Buckelew, the Indian Captive.* Kerrville TX: Herring Printing House, 1925.

Dobie, J. Frank. *Apache Gold and Yaqui Silver.* Boston: Little, Brown, 1939.

Dunn, William Edward. "Missionary Activities among the Eastern Apaches Previous to the Founding of the San Saba Mission." *Southwestern Historical Quarterly* 15, no. 3 (January 1912): 19333–95.

Farrer, Claire R. *Living Life's Circle: Mescalero Apache Cosmovision*. Albuquerque: University of New Mexico Press, 1991.

Gerhard, Peter. *The North Frontier of New Spain*. Norman: University of Oklahoma Press, 1920.

Gill, Mary McVey, and Brenda Wegmann. *Streetwise Spanish Dictionary/Thesaurus*. Chicago: McGraw Hill, 2001.

Hagan, William T. *Quanah Parker, Comanche Chief*. Norman: University of Oklahoma Press, 1993.

———. *United States–Comanche Relations: The Reservation Years*. Norman: University of Oklahoma Press, 1990.

Haley, James L. *Apaches: A History and Culture Portrait*. New York: Doubleday, 1981.

Hoxie, Frederick E., ed. *Encyclopedia of North American Indians*. New York: Houghton Mifflin, 1996.

Hunter, J. Marvin, ed. *The Bloody Trail in Texas: Sketches and Narratives of Indian Raids and Atrocities on Our Frontier*. Bandera TX: privately printed, 1931.

———. *Herman Lehmann: Nine Years among the Indians 1870–1879*. Albuquerque: University of New Mexico Press, 2001.

John, Elizabeth A. H. *Storms Brewed in Other Men's Worlds: The Confrontation of Indians, Spanish, and French in the Southwest, 1540–1795*. Lincoln: University of Nebraska Press, 1981.

Jordan, H. Glenn, and Thomas M. Holm, eds. *Indian Leaders: Oklahoma's First Statesmen*. Norman: Oklahoma Historical Society, 1979.

Kavanagh, Thomas W. *The Comanches: A History 1706–1875*. Lincoln: University of Nebraska Press, 1996.

Kenner, Charles L. *The Comanchero Frontier: A History of New Mexican–Plains Indian Relations*. Norman: University of Oklahoma Press, 1994.

LaTorre, Felipe A., and Delores L. LaTorre. *The Mexican Kickapoo Indians*. Austin: University of Texas Press, 1976.

Mills, Madeline S., and Helen R. Mullenax. *Relocated Cemeteries in Oklahoma and Parts of Arizona, Kansas, and Texas*. Tulsa OK: privately printed, n.d.

"Miscellaneous Papers about Wild Horse." *Chronicles of Comanche County* 5, no. 2 (Autumn 1959).

Neeley, Bill. *The Last Comanche Chief: The Life and Times of Quanah Parker*. New York: John Wiley and Sons, 1995.

New Encyclopedia Brittania. Vol. 2. Chicago: Encyclopedia Brittania, 1992.

Nye, Col. W. S. *Carbine and Lance: The Story of Old Ft. Sill*. Norman: University of Oklahoma Press, 1969.

Odom, Winston, ed. *Quanah Parker and His People, by Bill Neeley*. Slaton TX: Brazos Press, 1986.

Opler, Morris E. *Apache Odyssey: A Journey between Two Worlds*. Lincoln: University of Nebraska Press, 2002.

———. *Myths and Legends of the Lipan Apache Indians*. Memoirs of the American Folk-Lore Society 36. New York: J. J. Augustine, 1940.

Perry, Garland, and Kitti Focke. *A New Look at Nine Years among the Indians 1870–1875*. San Antonio TX: Lebco Graphics, 1985.

Post Oak Mennonite Brethren Church. *Post Oak Mission Centennial 1895–1995*. Indiahoma OK: Post Oak Mennonite Brethren Church, 1995.

Pruit, A. R., ed. *Santana: War Chief of the Mescalero Apache*. Taos NM: Dog Soldier Press, 1999.

The Roads of Texas. Fredericksburg TX: Shearer, 1995.

Rodriguez, Epigmenio. "Sequoyah Pilgrimage 2002." Cherokee Nation of Mexico. http://www.cherokeediscovery.com.

Rogers, Charles L. "A History of the Cherokee Nation of Mexico." Cherokee Nation of Mexico. http://www.cherokeediscovery.com.

———. "CNM Recognition." Cherokee Nation of Mexico. http://www.cherokeediscovery.com.

Ruiz, Jose Francisco. *Report on the Indian Tribes of Texas in 1828*. Western Americana Series 5. New Haven CT: Yale University Library, 1972.

Salinas, Martin. *Indians of the Rio Grande Delta*. Austin: University of Texas Press, 1990.

Schilz, Thomas F. *Lipan Apaches in Texas*. El Paso: University of Texas, 1987.

Smith, Clinton L., and J. Marvin Hunter. *The Boy Captives*. San Angelo TX: Anchor, 1994.

Sonnichsen, C. L. *The Mescalero Apaches*. Norman: University of Oklahoma Press, 1973.

Southwestern Oklahoma Genealogy Society. *Comanche County History*. Anadarko OK: Southwestern Oklahoma Genealogy Society, 1985.

State of Coahuila, Mexico. "History of Coahuila after 1865." http://www.coahuila.gob.mx.

Stewart, Omer C. "Origins of the Peyote Religion in the United States." *Plains Anthropologist* 19, no. 65 (August 1974): 211–23.

Tiller, Veronica E. Velarde. *The Jicarilla Apache Tribe: A History*. Lincoln: University of Nebraska Press, 1992.

Wallace, Ernest. *Ranald S. Mackenzie on the Texas Frontier*. College Station: Texas A&M Press, 1993.

Wallace, Ernest, and E. Adamson Hoebel. *The Comanches: Lords of the South Plains*. Norman: University of Oklahoma Press, 1986.

Zesch, Scott. *The Captured*. New York: St. Martin's Press, 2004.

Index